DERELICT MERSEYSIDE

JAMES LACEY AND DAVID GOOCH

AMBERLEY

First published 2025

Amberley Publishing, The Hill, Stroud
Gloucestershire GL5 4EP

www.amberley-books.com

British Library Cataloguing in Publication Data.
A catalogue record for this book is available from the British Library.

ISBN 978 1 3981 1980 2 (print)
ISBN 978 1 3981 1981 9 (ebook)

Typesetting by SJmagic DESIGN SERVICES, India.
Printed in Great Britain.

Appointed GPSR EU Representative: Easy Access System Europe Oü, 16879218
Address: Mustamäe tee 50, 10621, Tallinn, Estonia
Contact Details: gpsr.requests@easproject.com, +358 40 500 3575

INTRODUCTION

The county of Merseyside was created on 1 April 1974 with areas previously part of Lancashire and Cheshire forming the new county. Liverpool, however, had already been long established way back in 1207. Originally the name comes from the old English words *lifer* meaning muddy water and *pol* meaning pool. Up until the seventeenth century, things were slow going for Liverpool in terms of population and trade growth, probably due to the proximity of the nearby city of Chester. Chester – ever since the time of the Romans – was the main city in the area and the River Dee was used as the main port on the Irish Sea. However, the River Dee was silting up and becoming increasingly more difficult to use. Consequently, maritime trade shifted to Liverpool via the River Mersey. Because of this shift, the amount of trade increased in Liverpool's favour.

In the eighteenth century the city progressed further, and yet as trade increased rapidly this wasn't sufficient. The city established four more docks, partly due to the increasing trade from Manchester because Liverpool was its closest port. It had turned massive profits through trades such tobacco, sugar refining, shipbuilding, rope making and slaves that helped the town grow rapidly. It became the third busiest port in the country behind London and Bristol.

At the start of the nineteenth century, large volumes of trade passed through the port, and this was reflected in the buildings in the town. In 1830, Liverpool and Manchester became the first places to have an intercity rail link which in turn led to a population boom in the 1840s with the introduction of the Irish migrants arriving in their hundreds of thousands escaping the Great Famine. During the nineteenth century, the Customs House in the town was the biggest contributor to the British Exchequer as Liverpool was wealthier than London.

Liverpool was attracting immigrants from all over Europe, which is the reason for the many different ethnic groups and religious buildings in the city. During the Second World War, the Luftwaffe made eighty bombing raids on the city, killing 2,500 people and causing extensive damage to homes in the metropolitan area. The council used this opportunity to get rid of the inner-city slum houses and created overspill towns such as Kirby and Skelmersdale.

Like other major cities in the UK, Liverpool's decline started in the middle of the twentieth century.

For Liverpool this involved a reduction in the amount of trade and commerce taking place from ships all over the world carrying goods to the port. The advent of the 1970s saw a massive decline in manufacturing, resulting in the unemployment of 17 per cent, which in turn led to large parts of the old docks becoming obsolete due to the use of containers to transport goods instead of ships.

The centre of Liverpool became a ghost town with swathes of the population having moved away to seek job opportunities elsewhere. Factories closed for good, leaving behind buildings which over the years have fallen into a state of disrepair.

Liverpool – like the rest of the country – saw places of leisure and entertainment close. With the advent of home VHS and later DVD, it looked like the reign of cinemas in Britain was coming to an end. Yet, with the advent of multiplex cinemas in the 1990s, cinema attendances started to climb once more. However, the smaller independent cinemas and theatres all suffered, unable to compete with these newer and more modern places of entertainment. Many remain, yet in a parlous state as they have been left to decay over the previous decades since closing for good.

Plans for regeneration and investment happened slowly from the 1980s. One of the first moves was to reopen the docks and use them for tourism via restaurants and shops. A major landmark in this early regeneration is the Tate Liverpool which opened in the mid-1980s and attracted prestigious arts and cultural events.

In the 1990s, Liverpool enjoyed growth rates higher than the national average and focussed on regeneration, which is still happening today. What was once a derelict building without use has now become a fancy spa hotel, upmarket apartment, or the site for a new football stadium for one of the city's two big clubs. Although many of the buildings in this book remain empty and without purpose – or have been demolished – there have been some success stories such as Lister Drive Library, the Tobacco Warehouse and the Southport Grand to name a few that have been redeveloped for other uses fit for the twenty-first century.

In this book a selection of the abandoned buildings around Liverpool and the wider Merseyside area have been photographed. Some have been redeveloped yet some remain in their dormant state. Inside the crumbling exteriors is an opportunity to witness a hidden world.

What happens when the machines are turned off for the last time in the factories, or cinemas have screened their last film and church congregations have listened to their final sermon? The building has come to the end of its natural life as intended when it was built as new shiny buildings spring up around them, resigning these old and tired buildings to redundancy, devoid of meaningful use in a modern world; they stand as mere relics of a bygone age. Dormant artefacts remain inside the decaying building, covered in dust and giving an insight into its former use.

Once a building has served its purpose it is at the mercy of the elements and decay sets in. The aesthetics change as wallpaper peels off damp walls and paint cracks, allowing the colours to transform into something more interesting. A once carefully designed interior becomes a scene of organic chaos as nature makes its way in, bringing a sense of the outdoors into an otherwise inside space.

Entering through the broken door of an abandoned building is like stepping back into the past, as it is presented now, fused with the present. In essence, the building has become photogenic.

Sources

https://localhistories.org/a-history-of-liverpool/

https://en.wikipedia.org/wiki/Liverpool

https://www.culturefighter.eu/structural-support-and-government-policies/local-authorities/liverpools-decline-and-regeneration

https://www.wired.co.uk/article/cinema-industry-uk-collapse

WELLINGTON ROOMS

The Wellington Rooms is a Grade II listed neoclassical building in the heart of Liverpool. Designed by Edmund Aikin and erected by subscription, it was built in 1815–16. Its first function after opening was the Ladies Charity ball held on 31 December 1816, which was attended by 850 of the most respectable and fashionable people. The initial purpose of the Wellington Rooms was as a place to hold balls and other types of entertainment. In the nineteenth century the club became a key part of the Liverpool social scene. In February 1965, it became known as the Liverpool Irish Centre and eventually closed for good in 1997.

The building was placed on the national Heritage at Risk Register in 1999, with urgent work being carried out in 2018 to make the building watertight.

Liverpool City Council owns the freehold of the site and has overall responsibility for this listed building. Since the Merseyside Building Preservation Trust (MBPT) hosted a consultation event in March 2018, nothing has moved forward in terms of the building's renovation. (Images James Lacey)

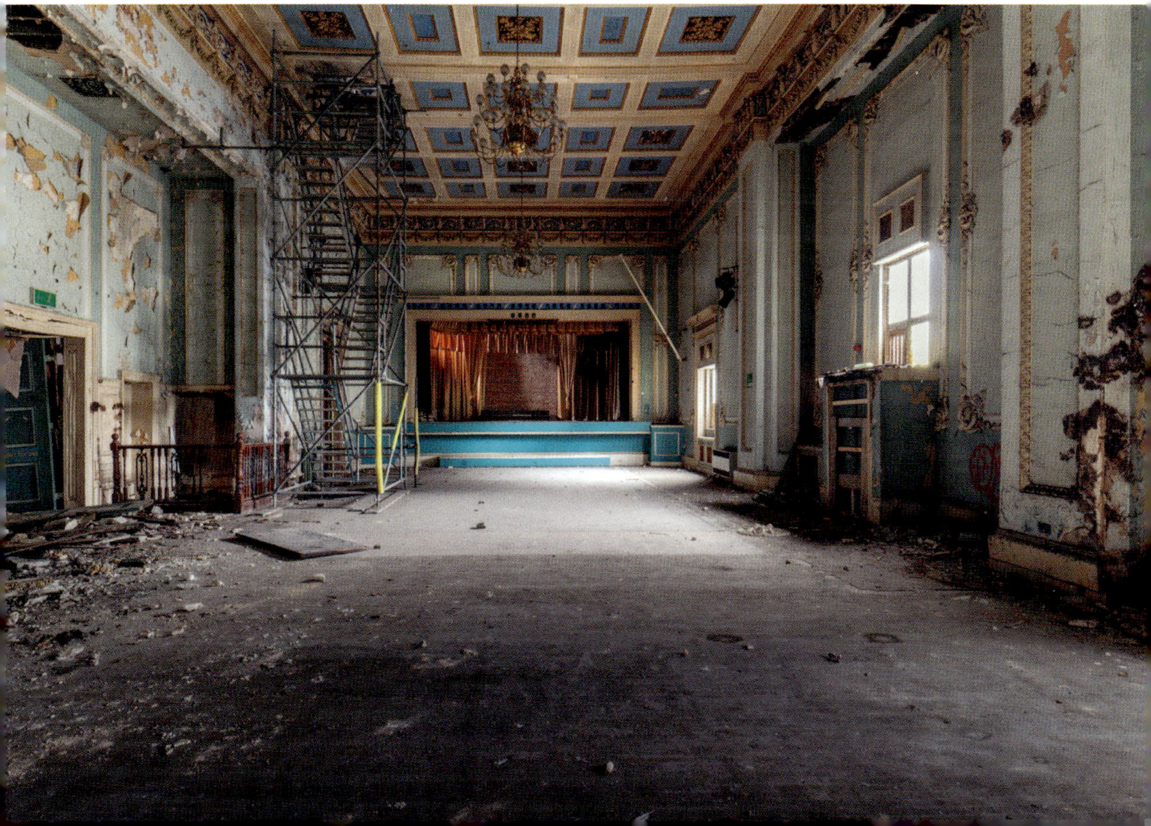

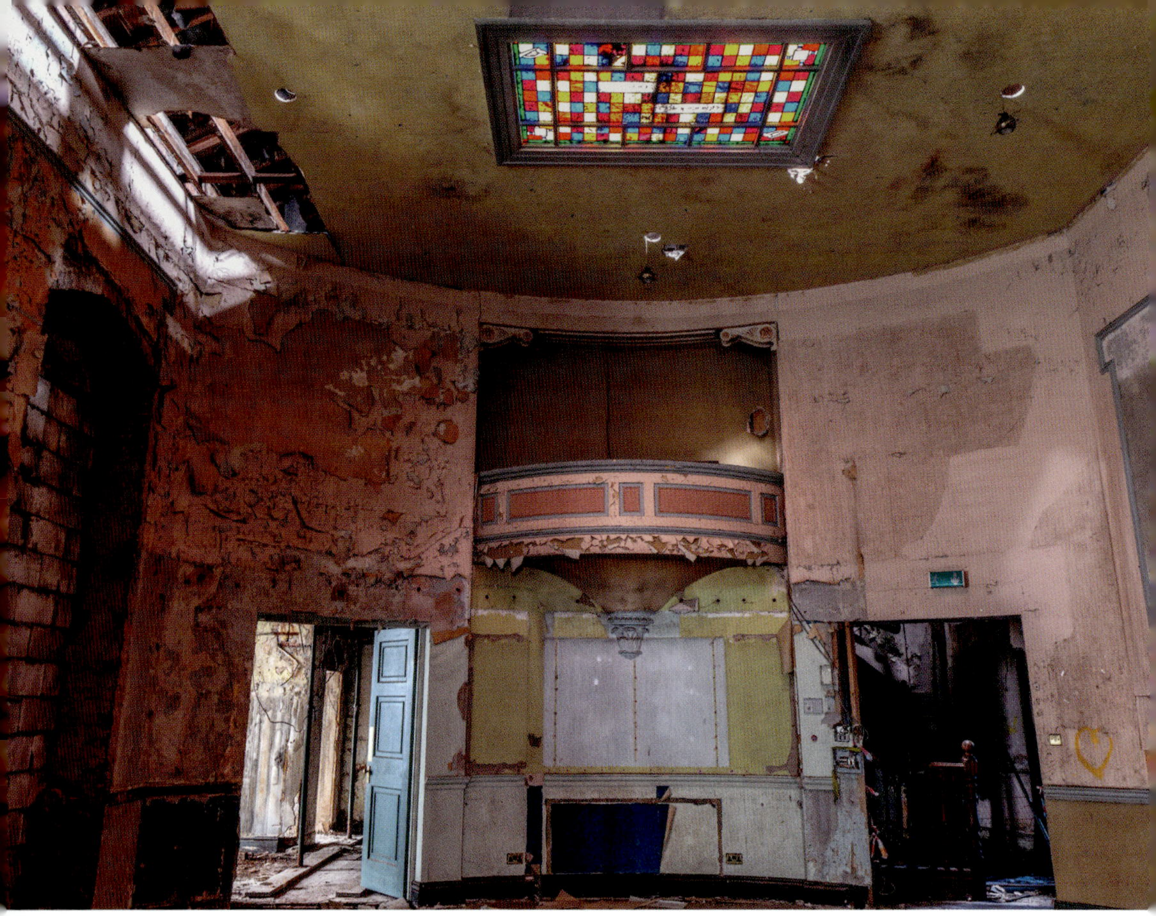

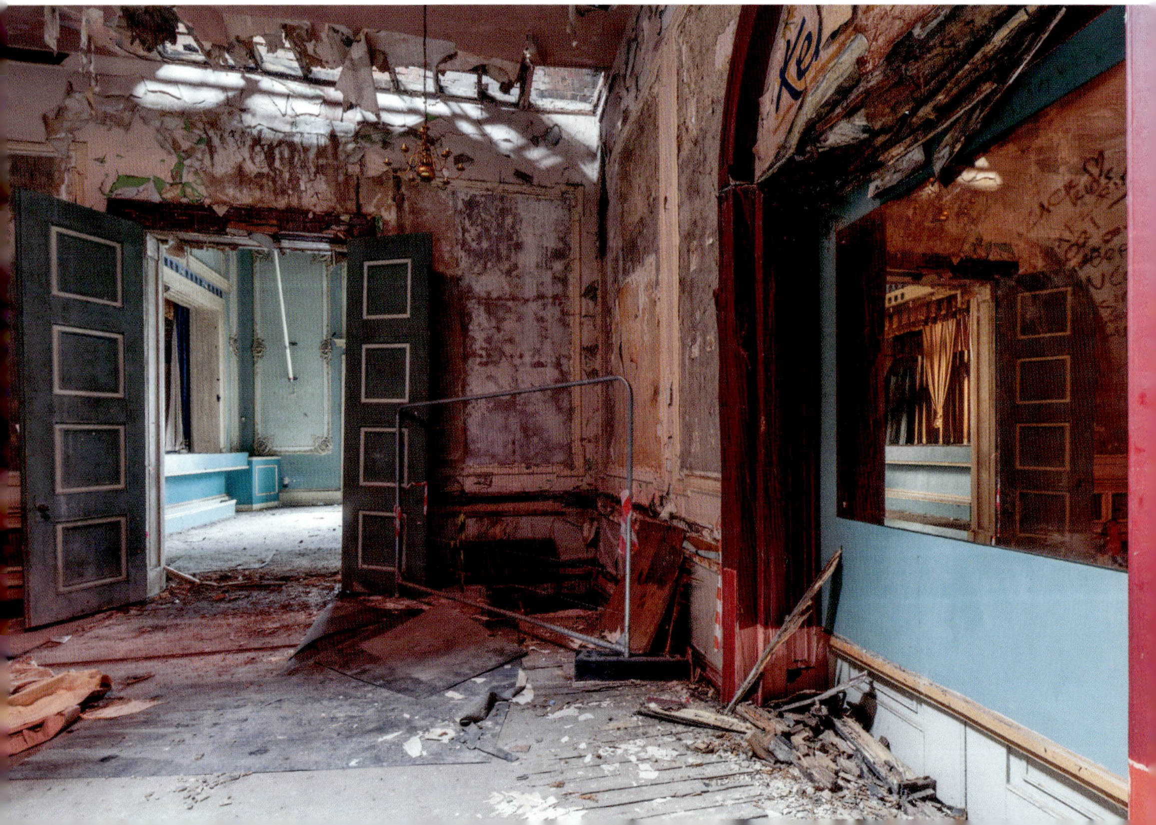

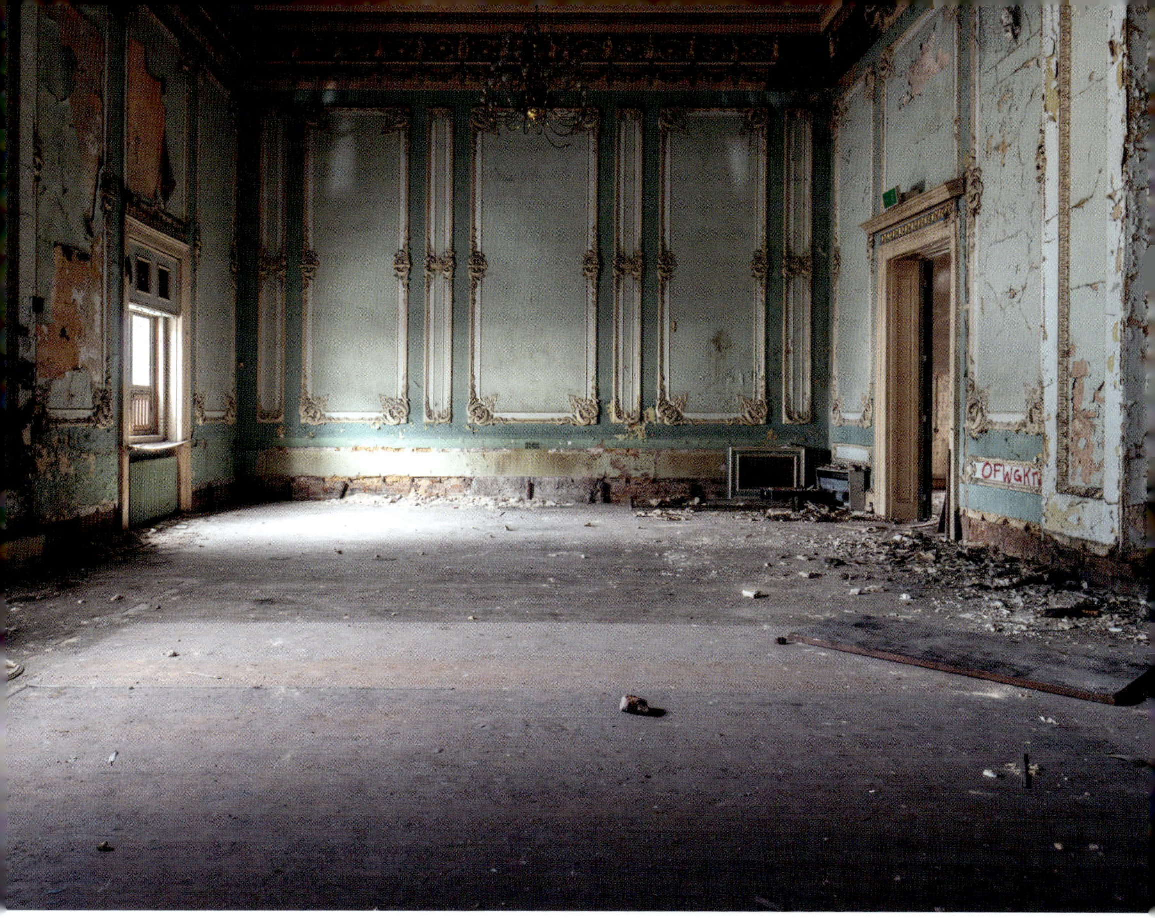

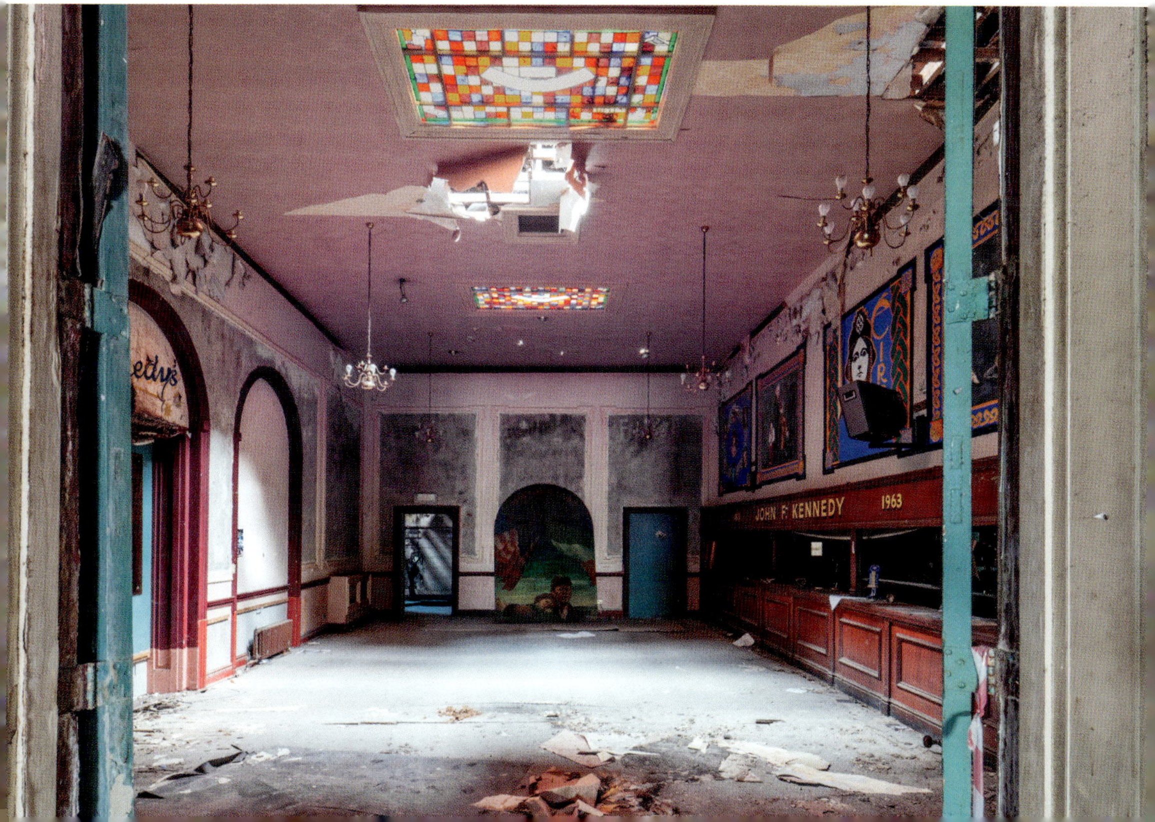
JOHN F. KENNEDY
1963

GAUMONT CINEMA, DINGLE

The Gaumont cinema was opened on 27 March 1937, showing *My Man Godfrey*. The cinema was built on the site of the old Dingle Picturedrome and occupies an imposing corner on Park Lane and Dingle Lane. The building was used as a cinema until 1966 and then became a bingo hall until 1998, when it finally closed. It was briefly used again after being bought in the mid-2000s for rock bands to practice until it finally closed in 2013. Now the site just houses a phone mast and an electronic advertising board. (Images David Gooch)

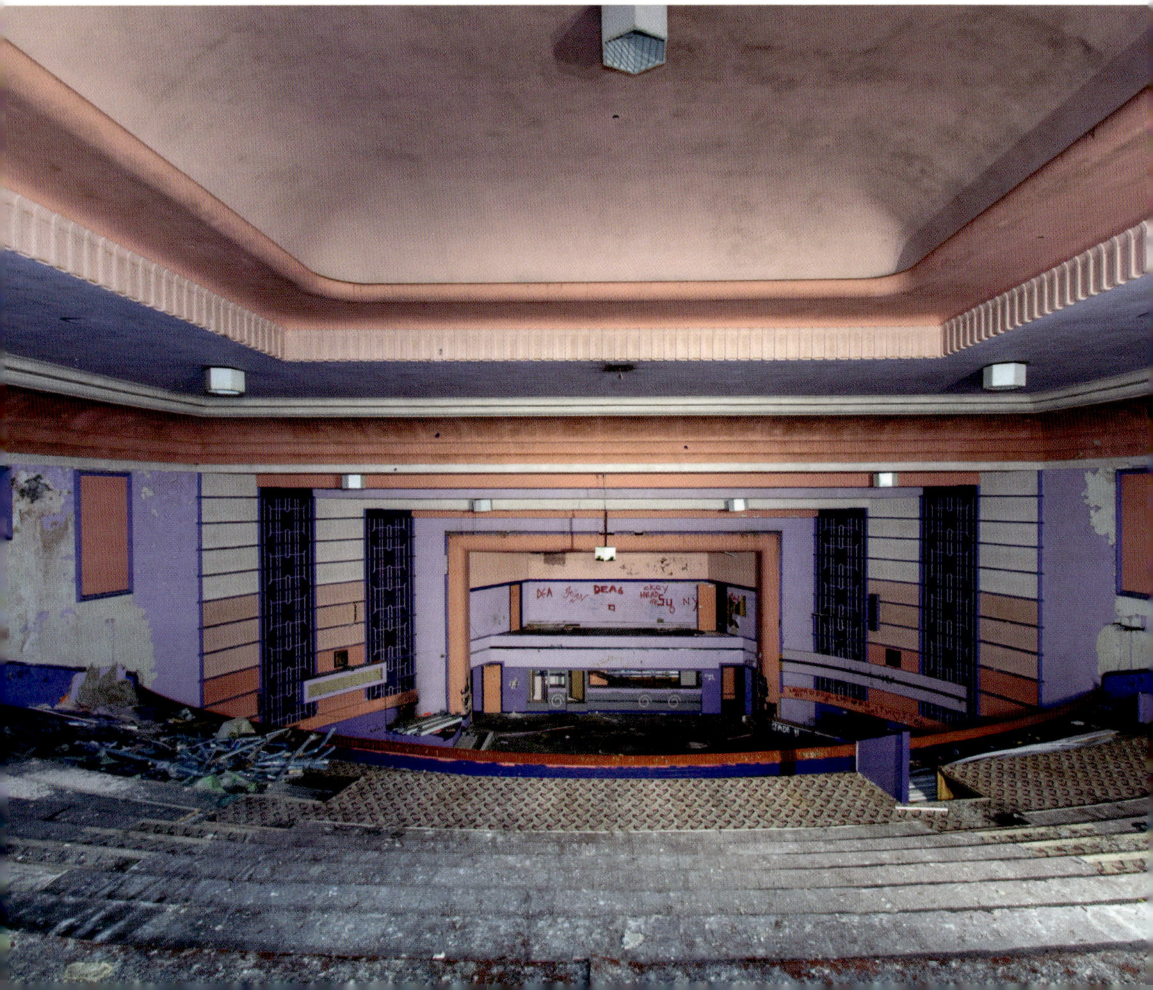

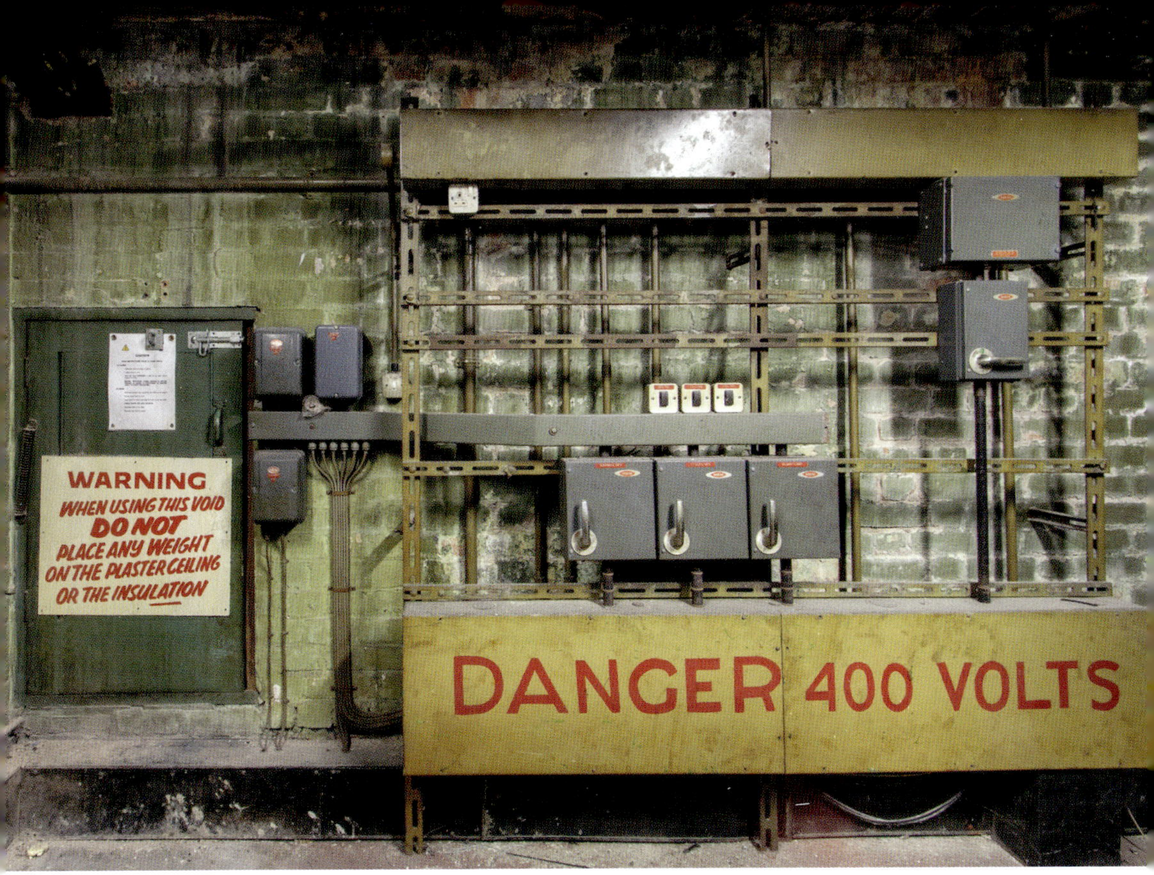
WARNING
WHEN USING THIS VOID
DO NOT
PLACE ANY WEIGHT
ON THE PLASTER CEILING
OR THE INSULATION
DANGER 400 VOLTS

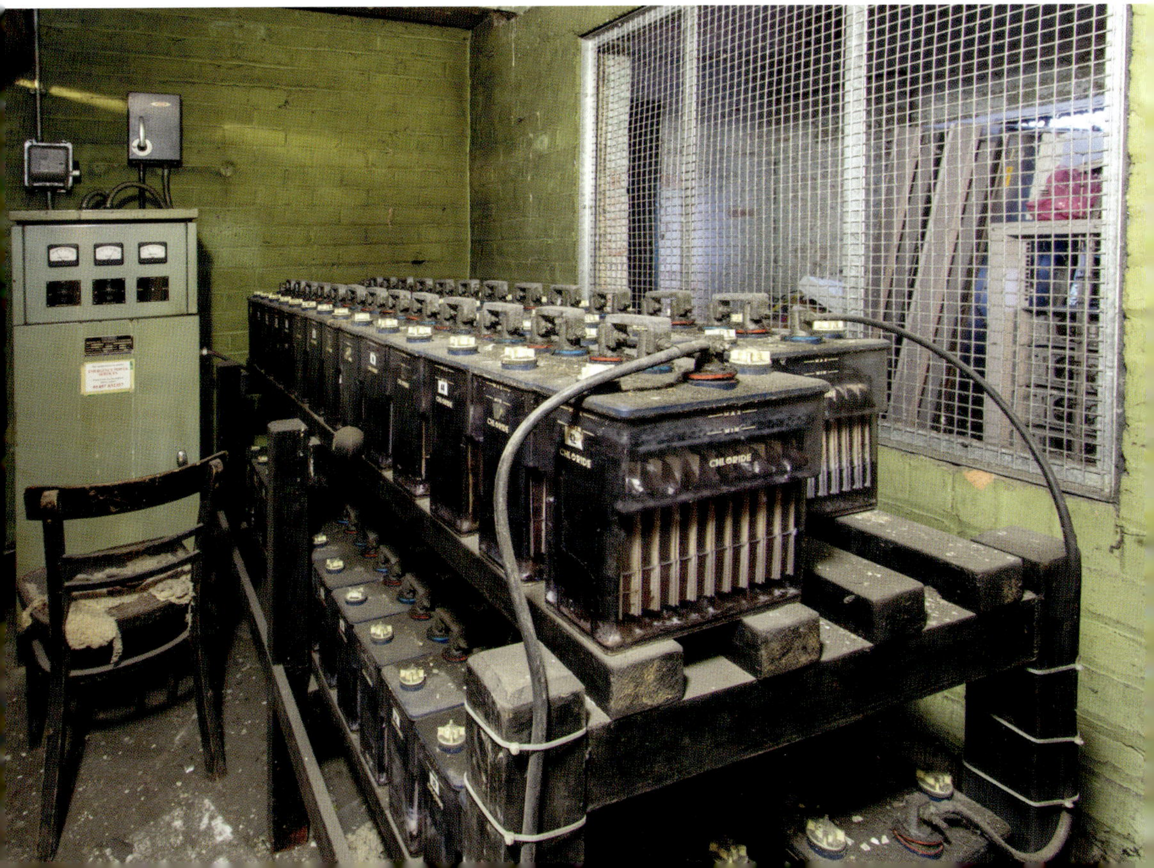
CHLORIDE

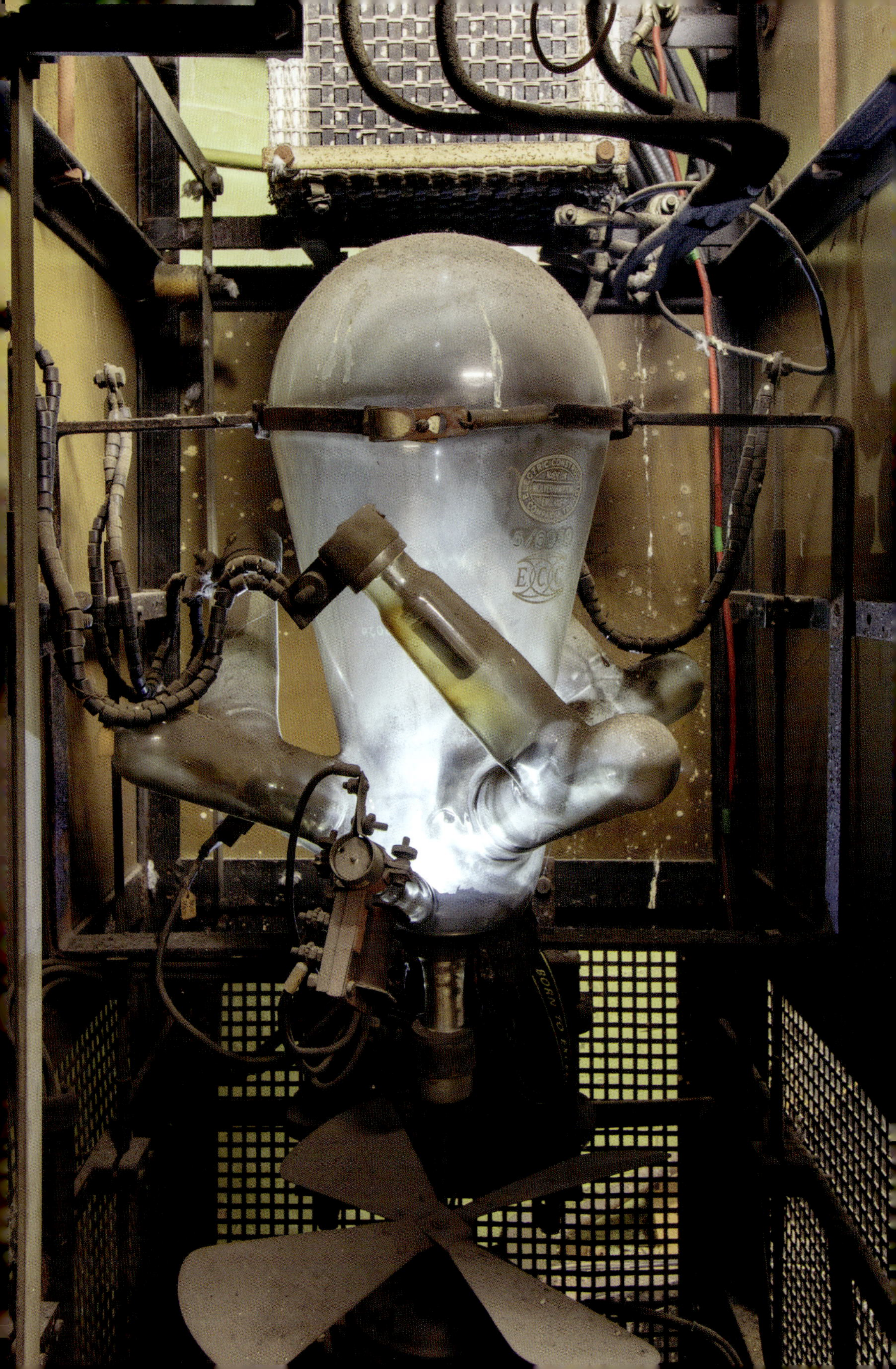
ECC

EVERTON LIBRARY

Constructed in 1896 under the design of Liverpool architect Thomas Shelmerdine, Everton Library was built to an anomalous triangle plan to fit in with the Victorian street layout already in place. The library features a striking octagonal turret, a Jacobean Arts and Crafts exterior as well as an imposing glass barrel-vaulted ceiling and grand mezzanine floor. It was one of the first public libraries in Liverpool – also used as a Technical Institute for dockers – and eventually closed as a public library in 1998. It was then used for community events for four years before closing for good in 2002.

It has remained abandoned ever since, and has significantly deteriorated as result of rain damage and neglect over the years.

It was given listed status in July 1966 and in September 2019 was named on the Victorian Society's list of the top ten most endangered buildings in England and Wales. Previous schemes to restore the building in 2014 and 2016 failed to reach the restoration phase. In 2021, a new transformational project was initiated with the aim of turning the building into a multi-purpose technical institute providing a public space as well as creating employment and making a contribution to the regional economy. (Images James Lacey)

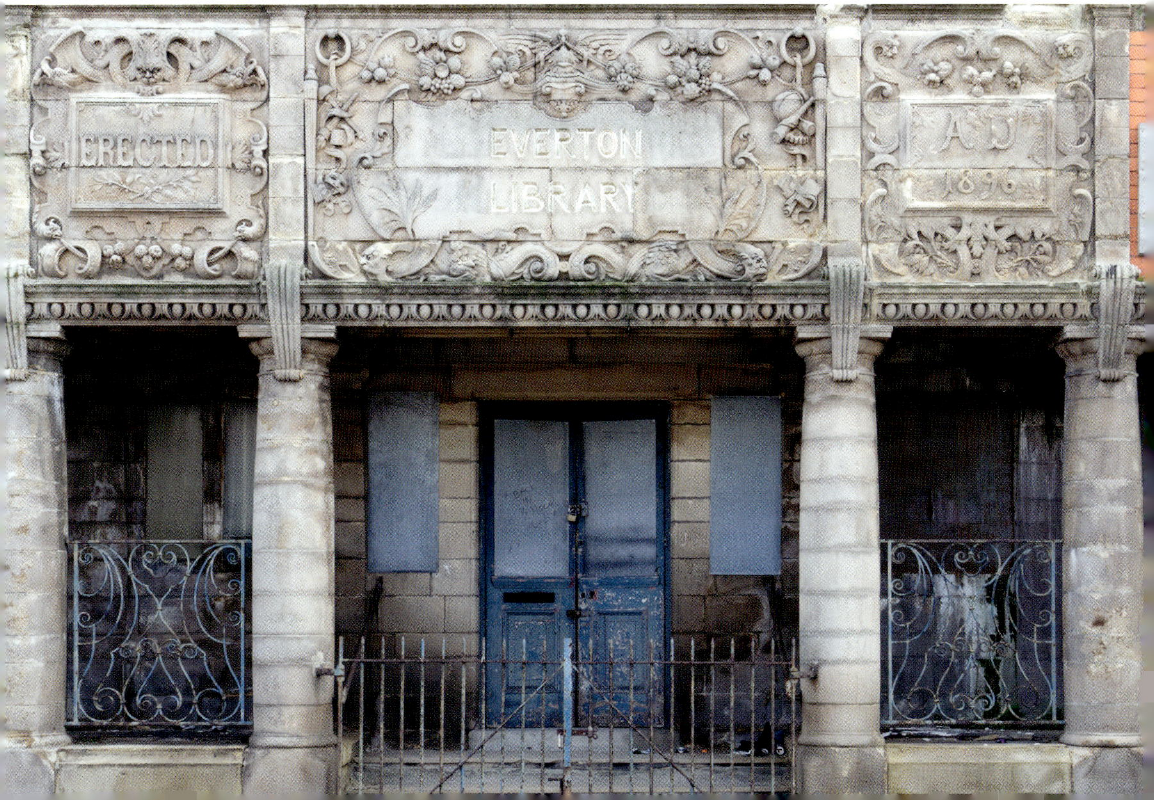

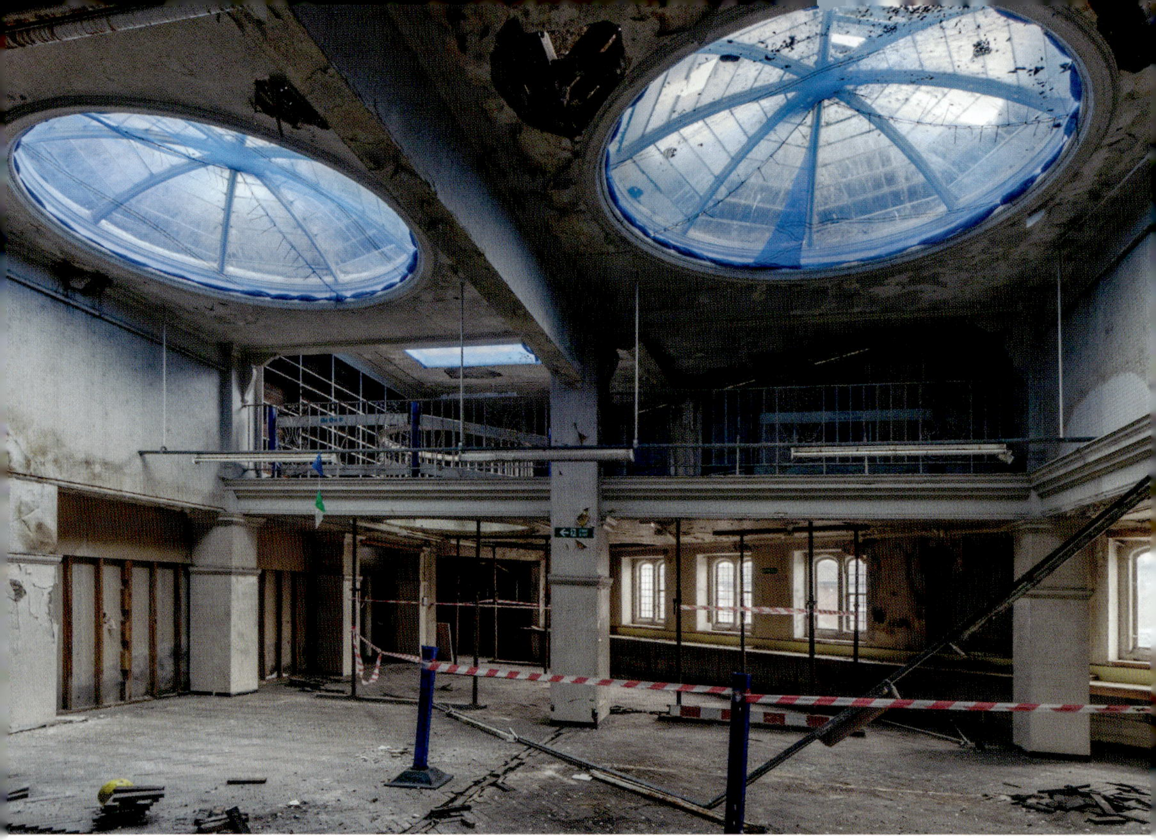

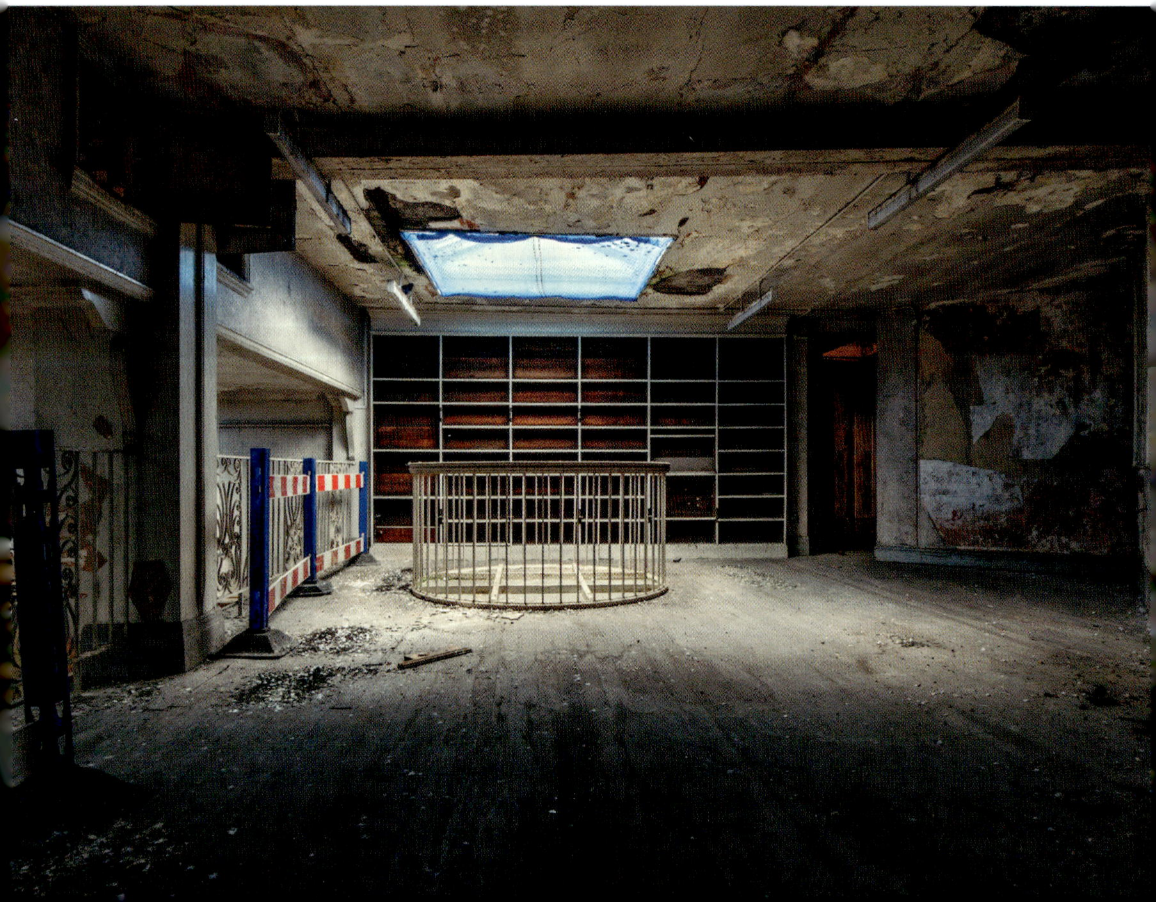

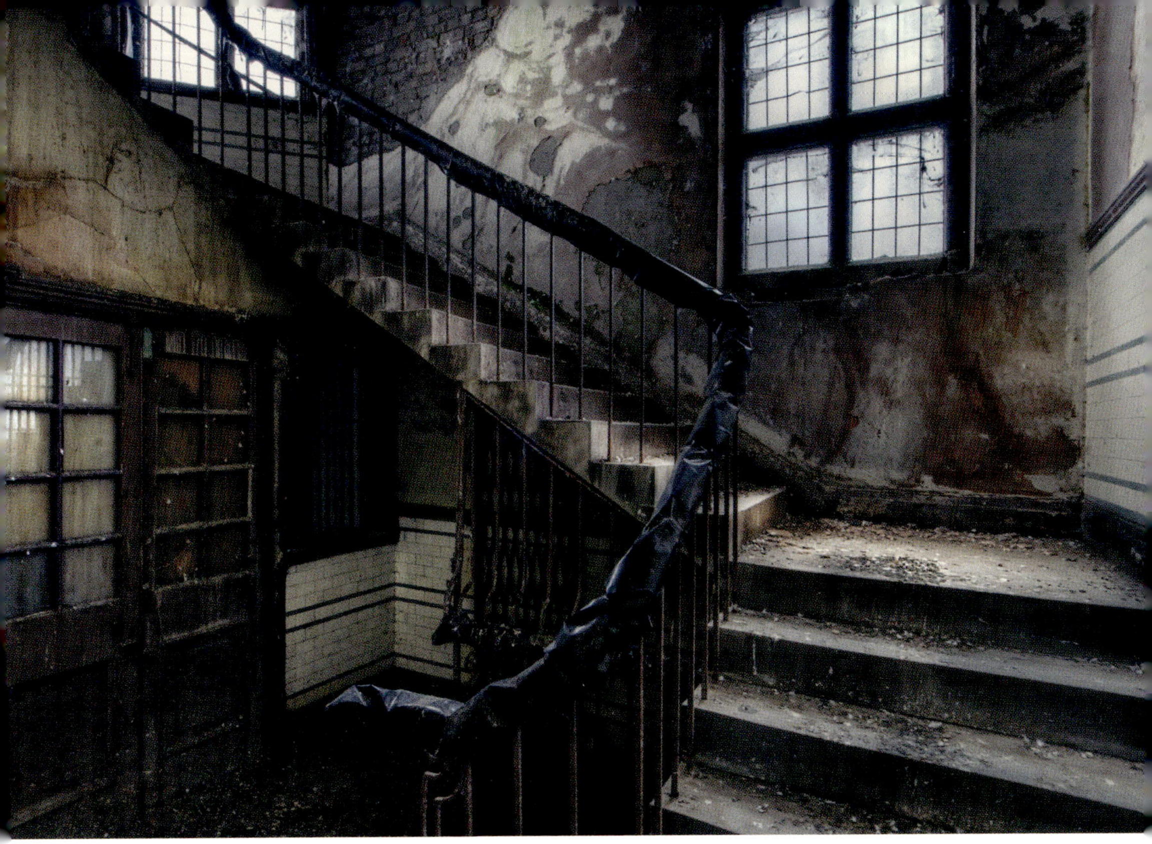

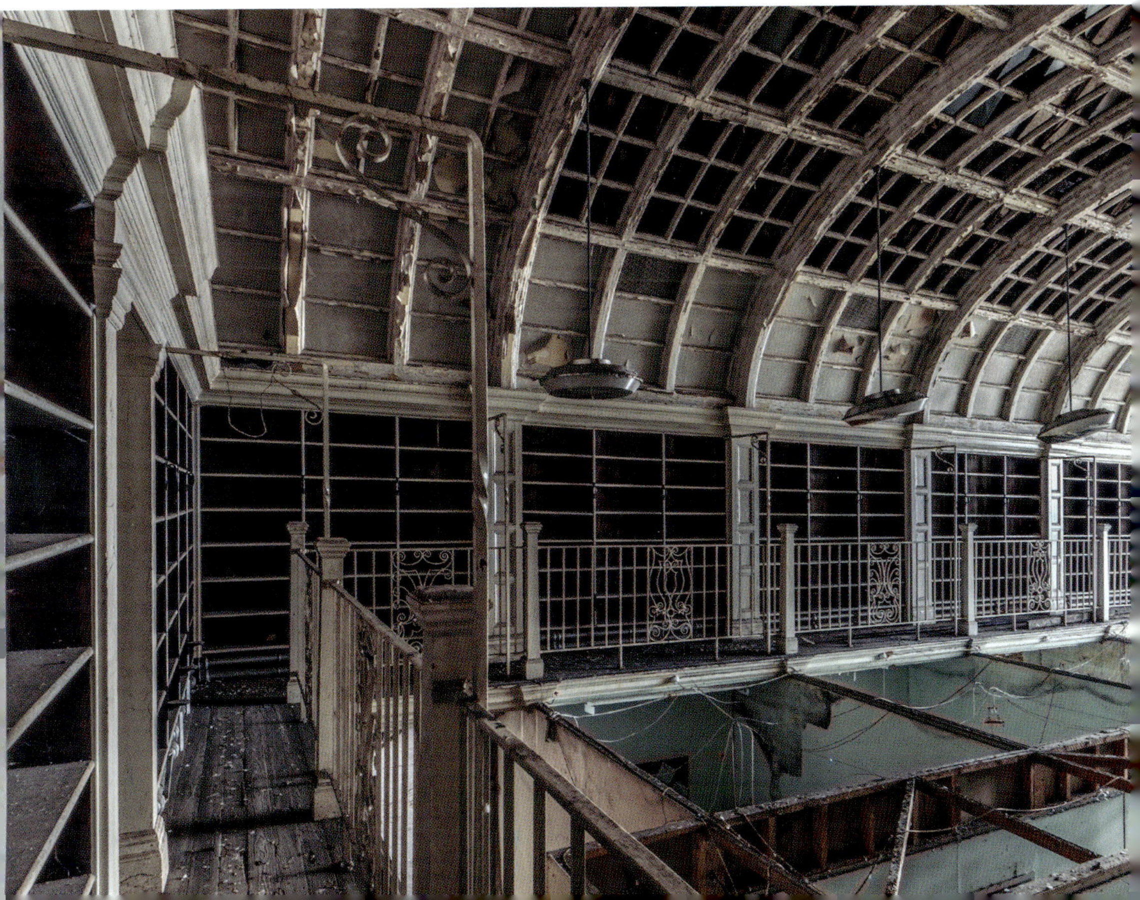

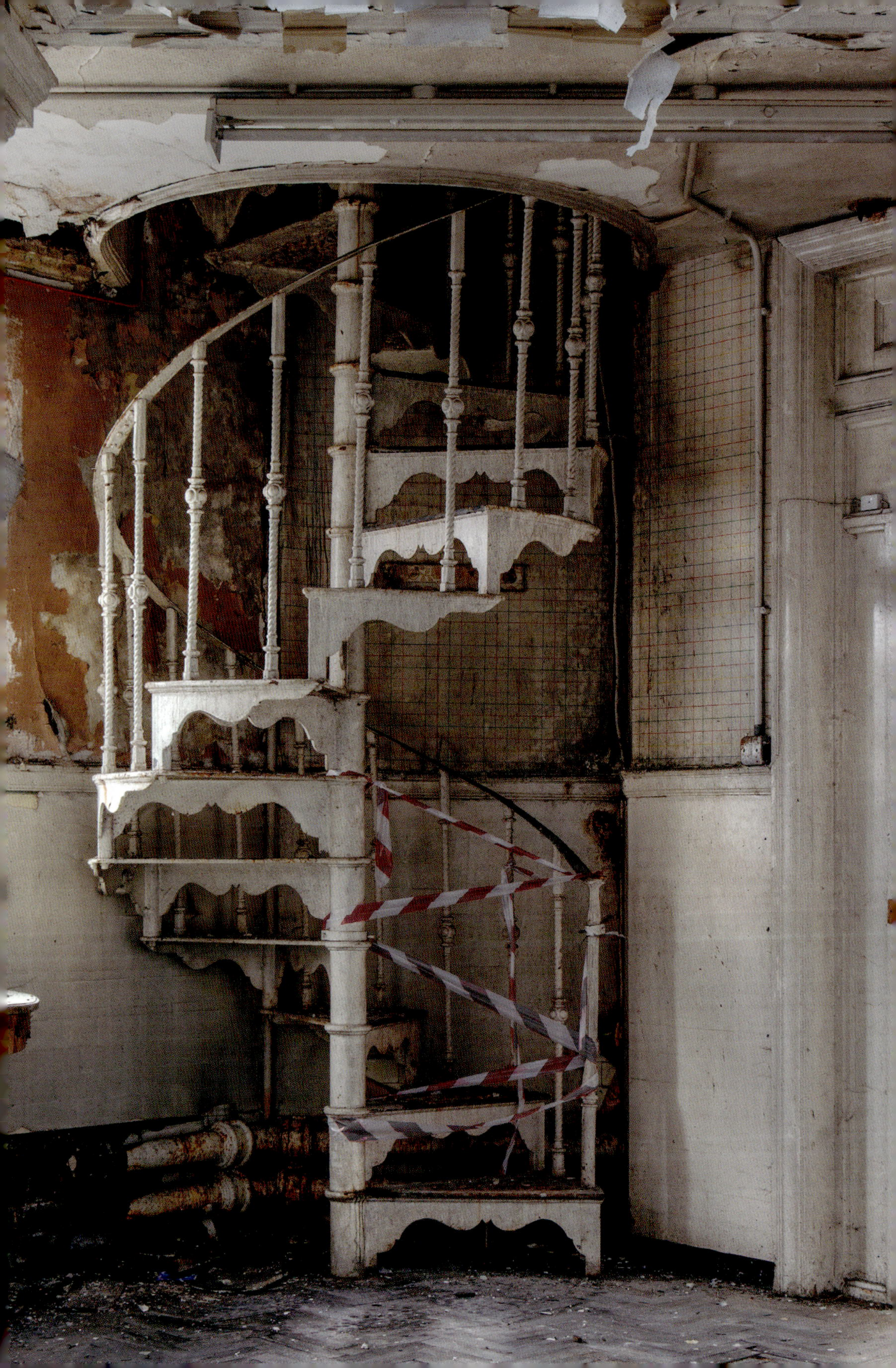

NEWSHAM PARK HOSPITAL

Newsham Park Hospital opened in 1874 as the Liverpool Seamen's Orphanage Institution. The idea and money for the orphanage came from a group of shipowners who were concerned about how to provide help to families of deceased men of Merseyside. The orphanage was closed in 1949 following a decline in parents placing children into care after social service schemes expanded.

The building was opened in 1954 as a hospital with its own psychiatric department. In 1992 Newsham Park took the inmates from Rainhill Lunatic Asylum after its closure. Newsham Park has been empty since 1995. (Images David Gooch)

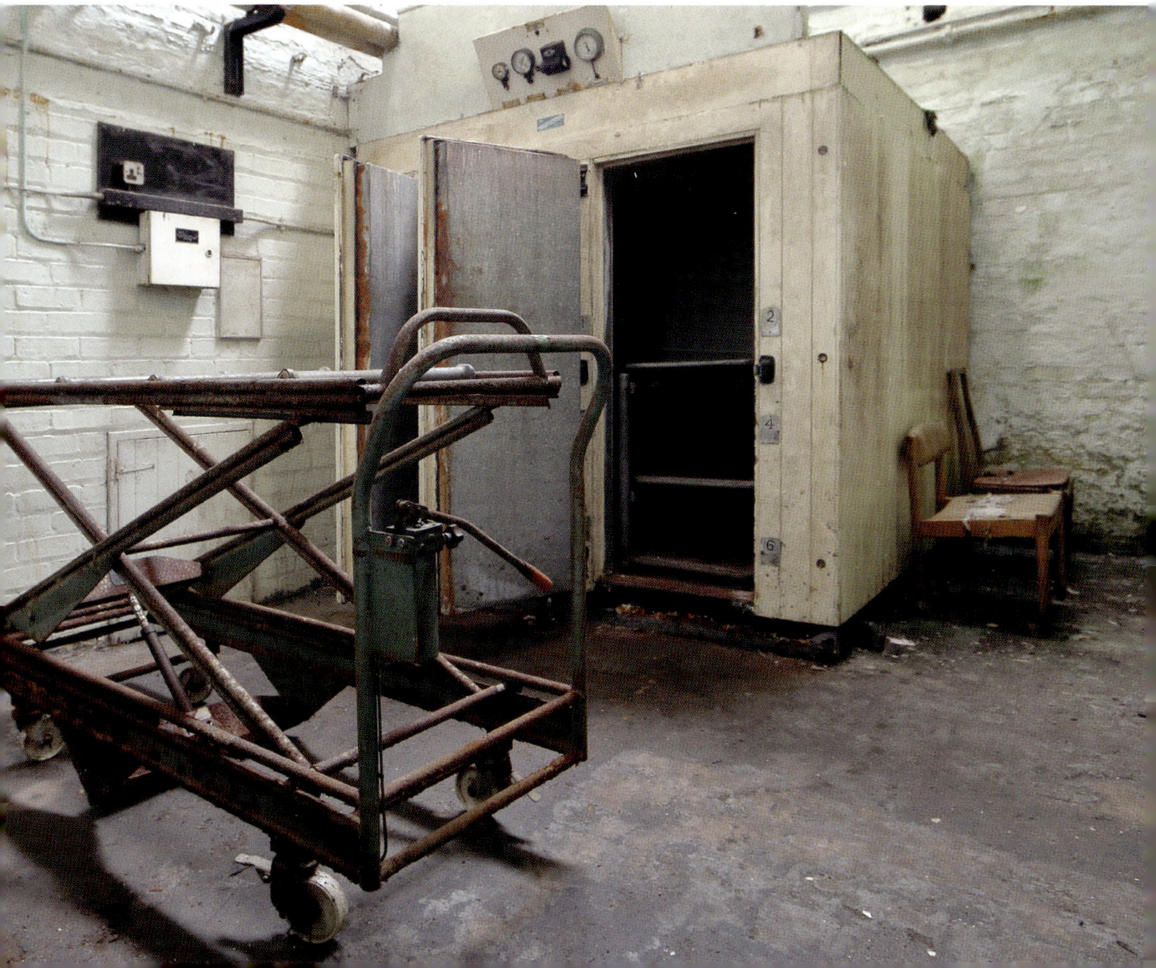

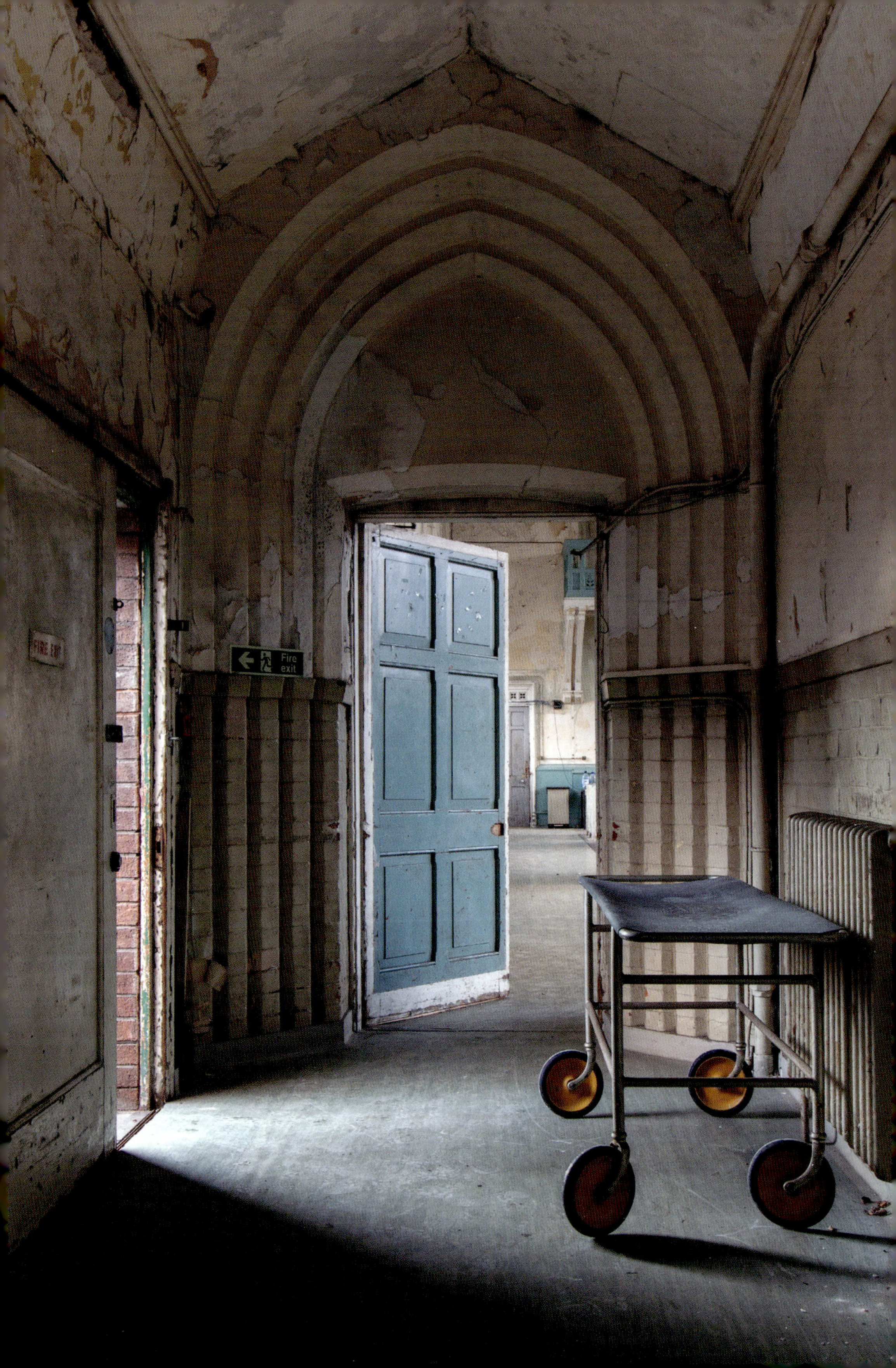
Fire
exit

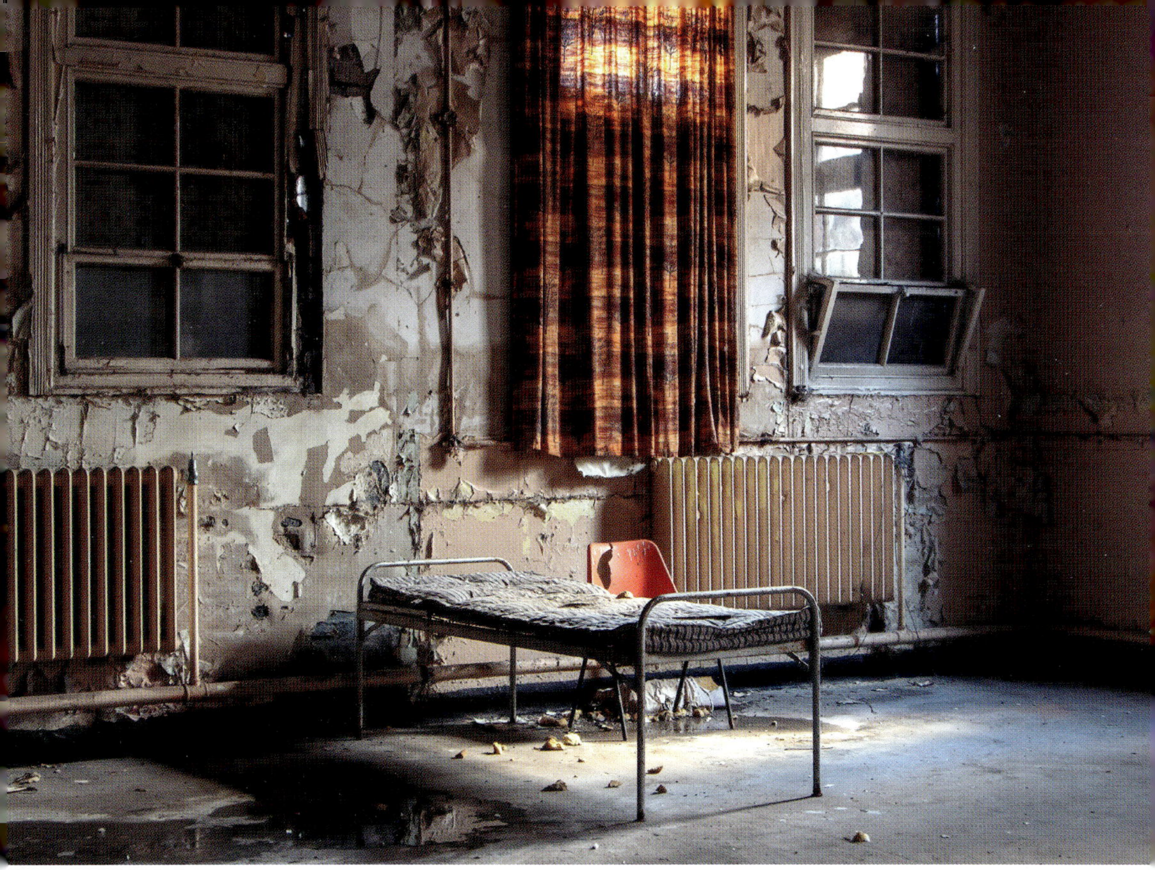

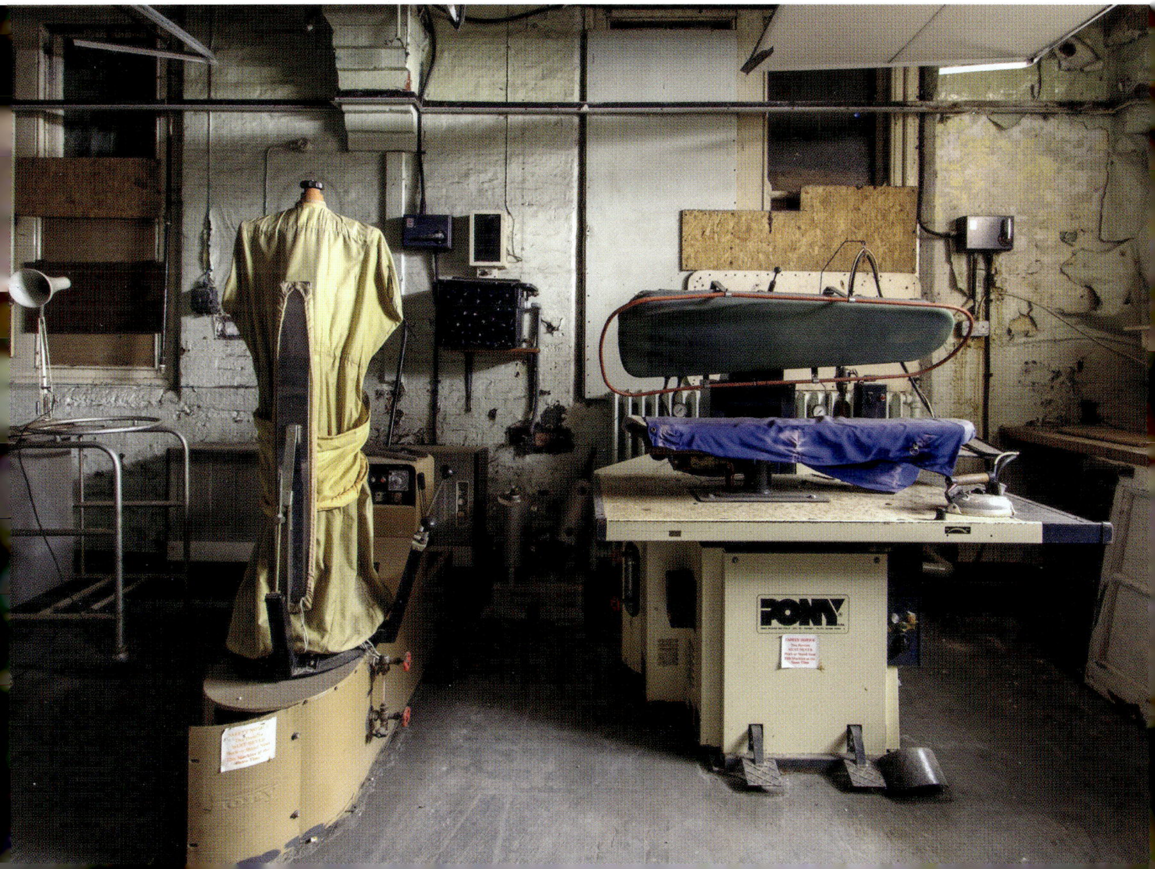
PONY

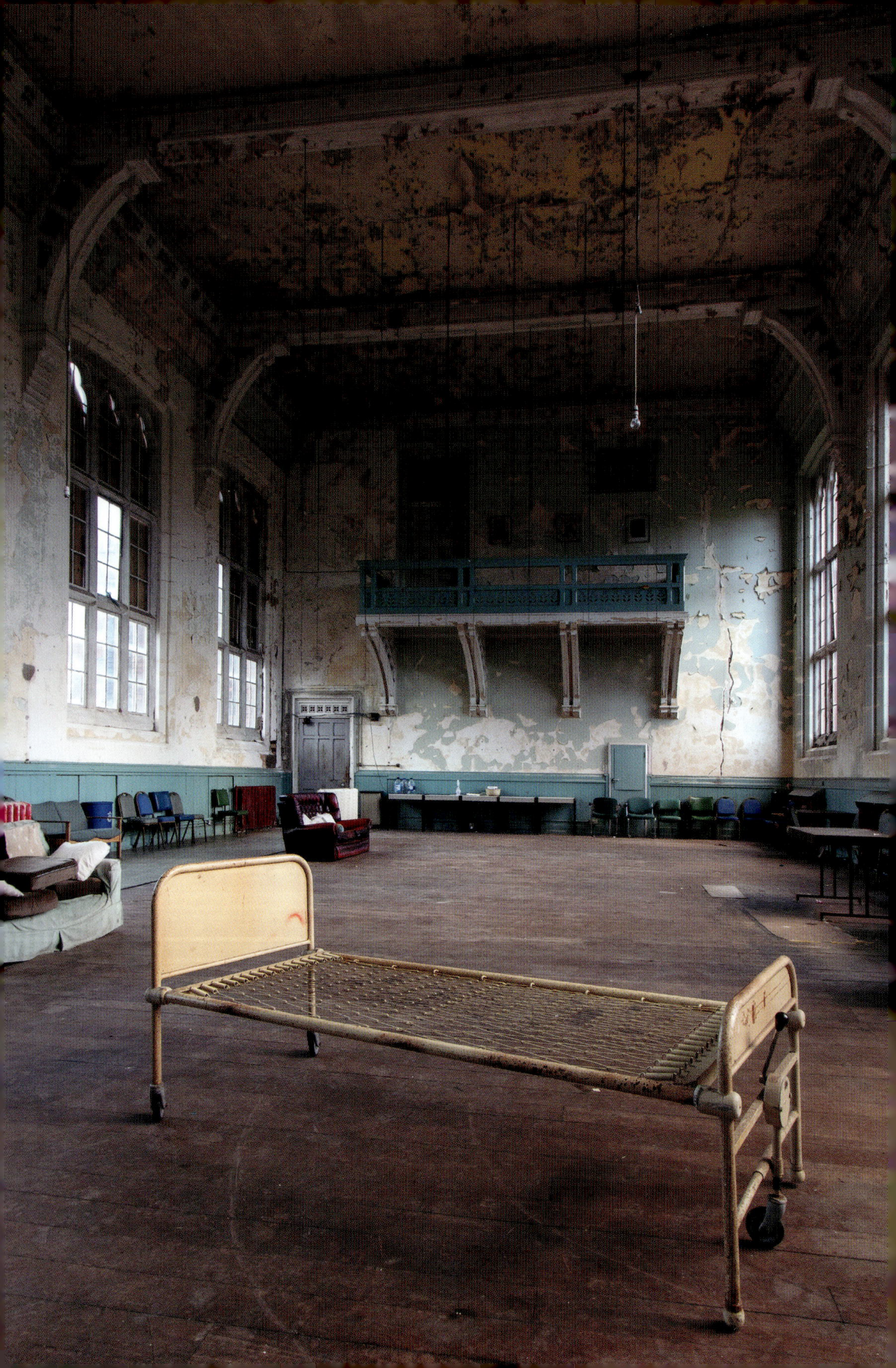

GREENBANK SYNAGOGUE

The former synagogue on Greenbank Drive has been at risk since 2010 and was a focus of the *Liverpool Echo*'s 'Stop the Rot' campaign. Over the years, some emergency work has been carried out to keep the building in a minimum state of good repair while a suitable occupier could be found.

Built in 1936 to a Swedish-influenced art deco style, this historic building was once at the centre of Liverpool's Jewish community and in use by the congregation until 2008. Architecturally, it has been described as the most important twentieth-century synagogue from the interwar period. It attained Grade II listed status in 2008. (Images James Lacey)

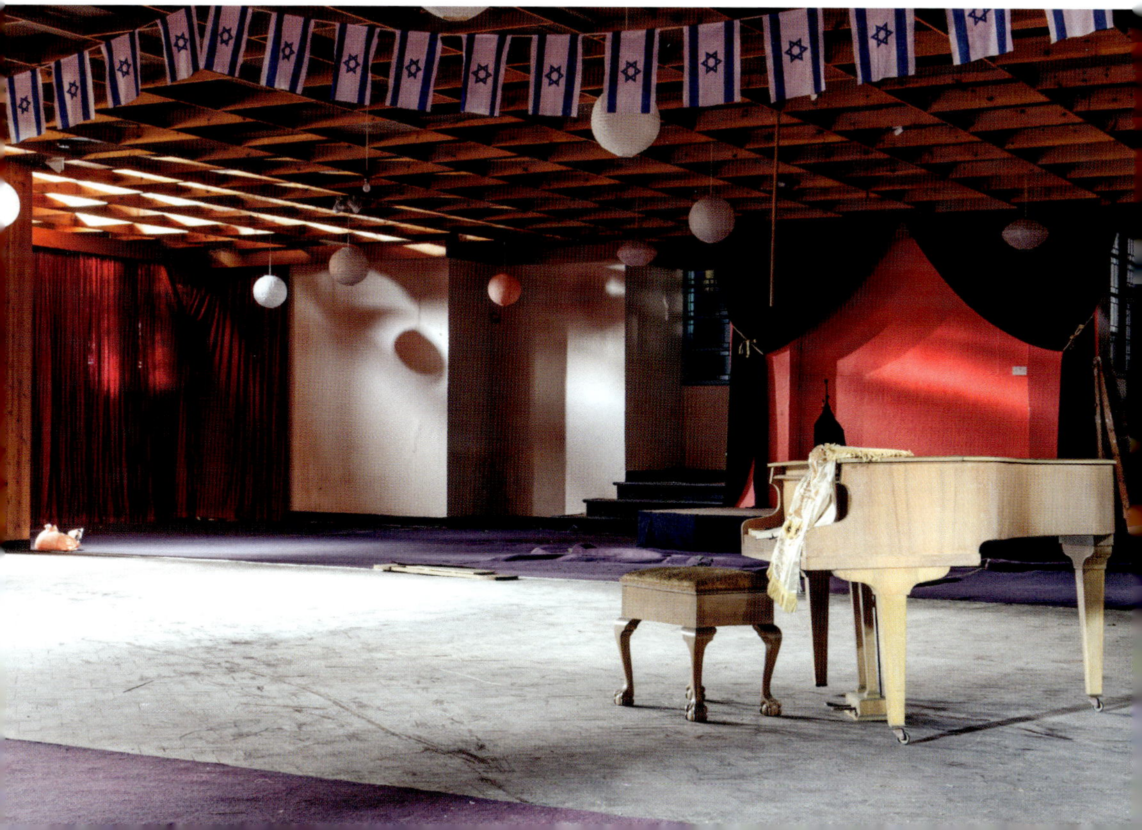

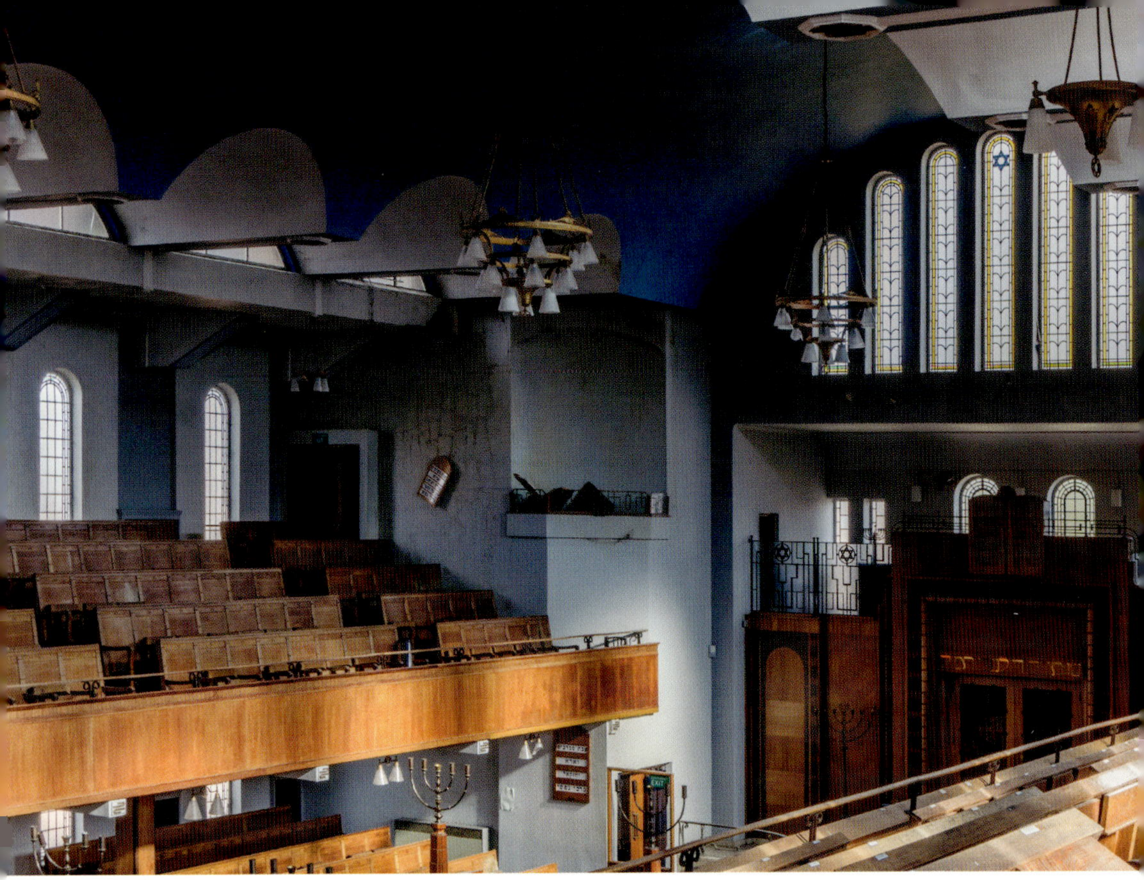
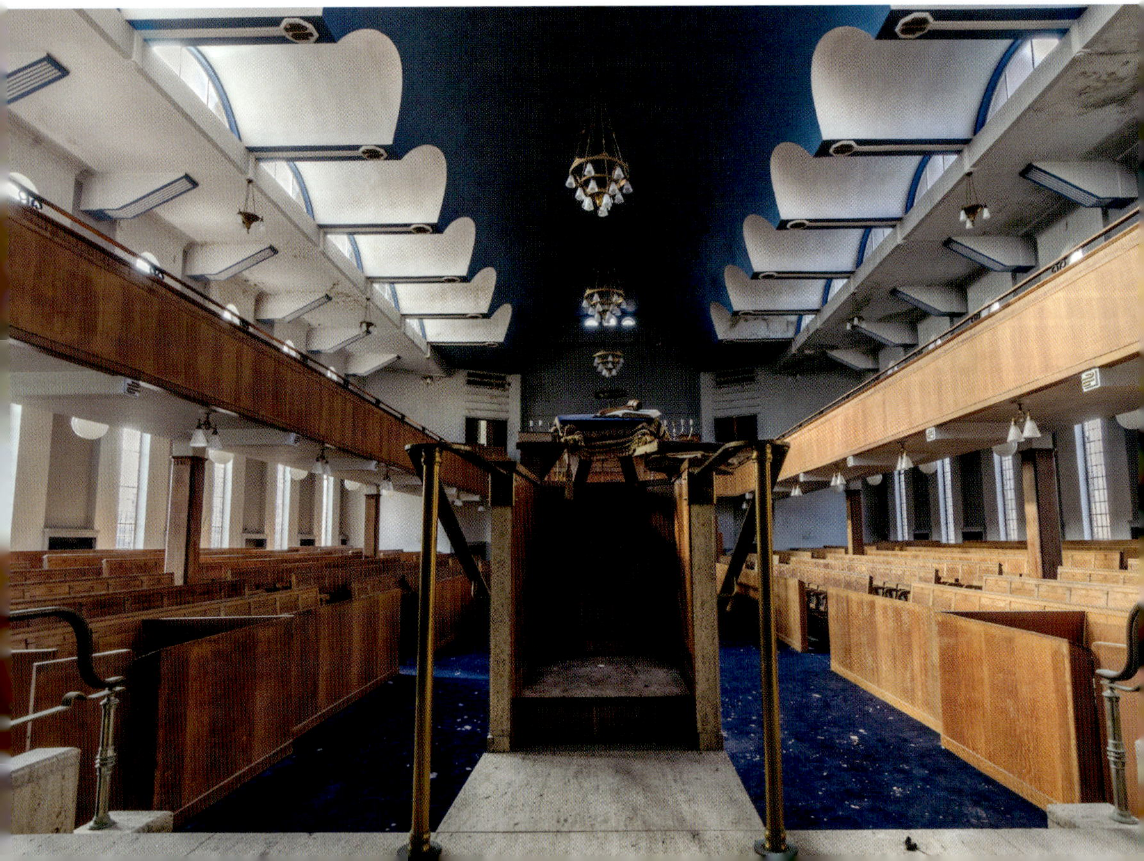

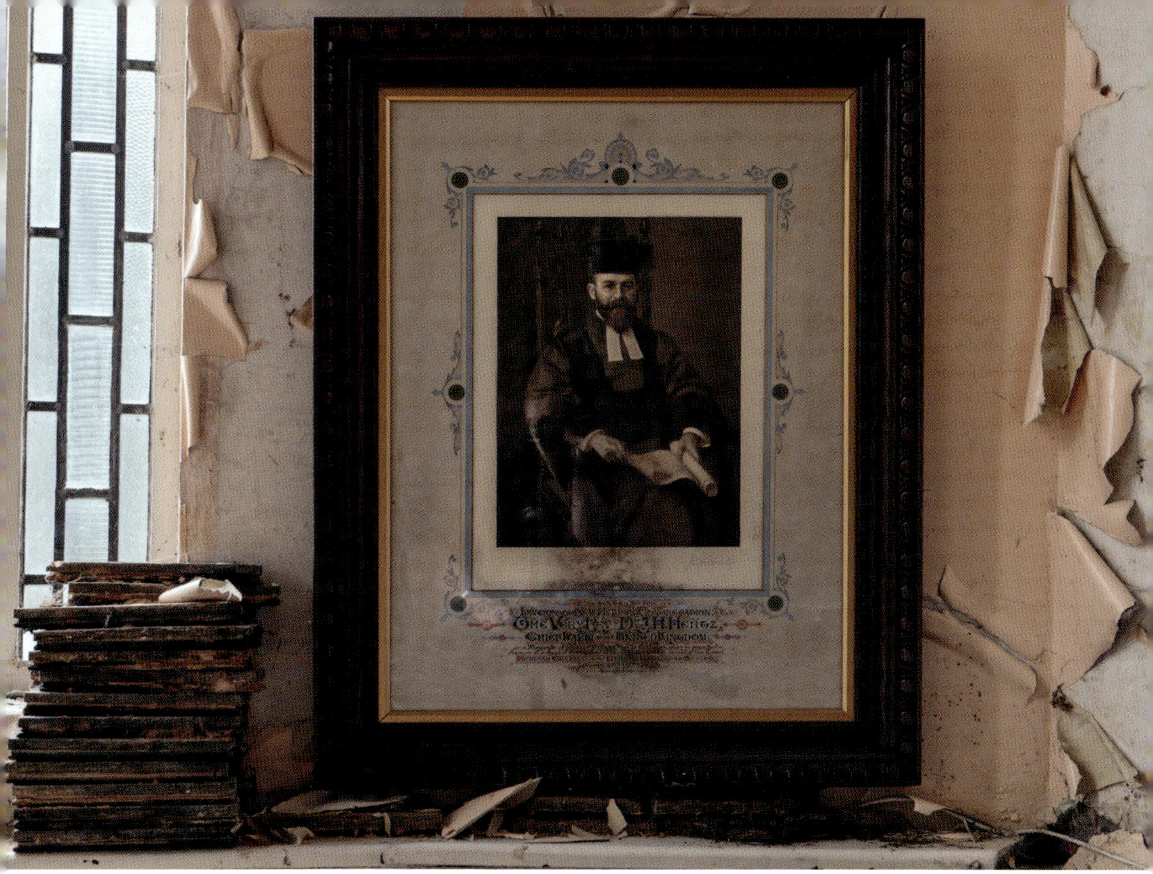

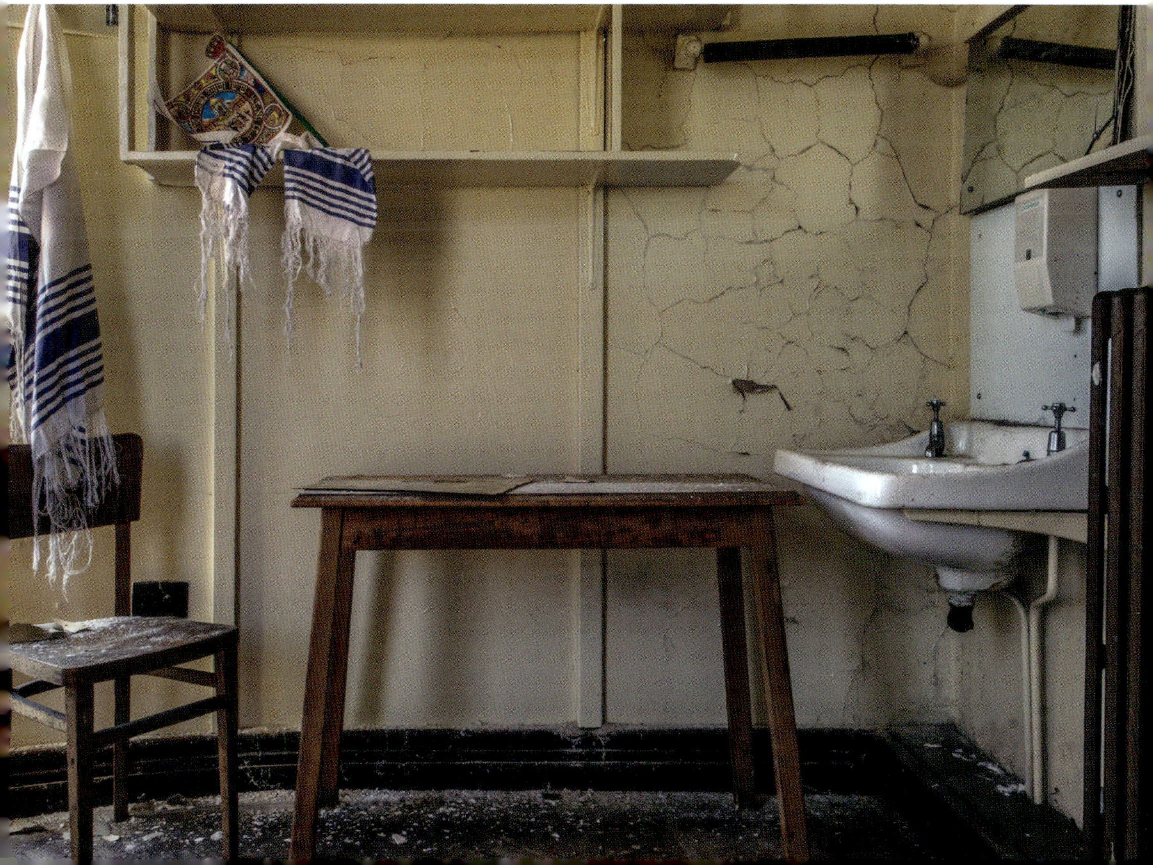

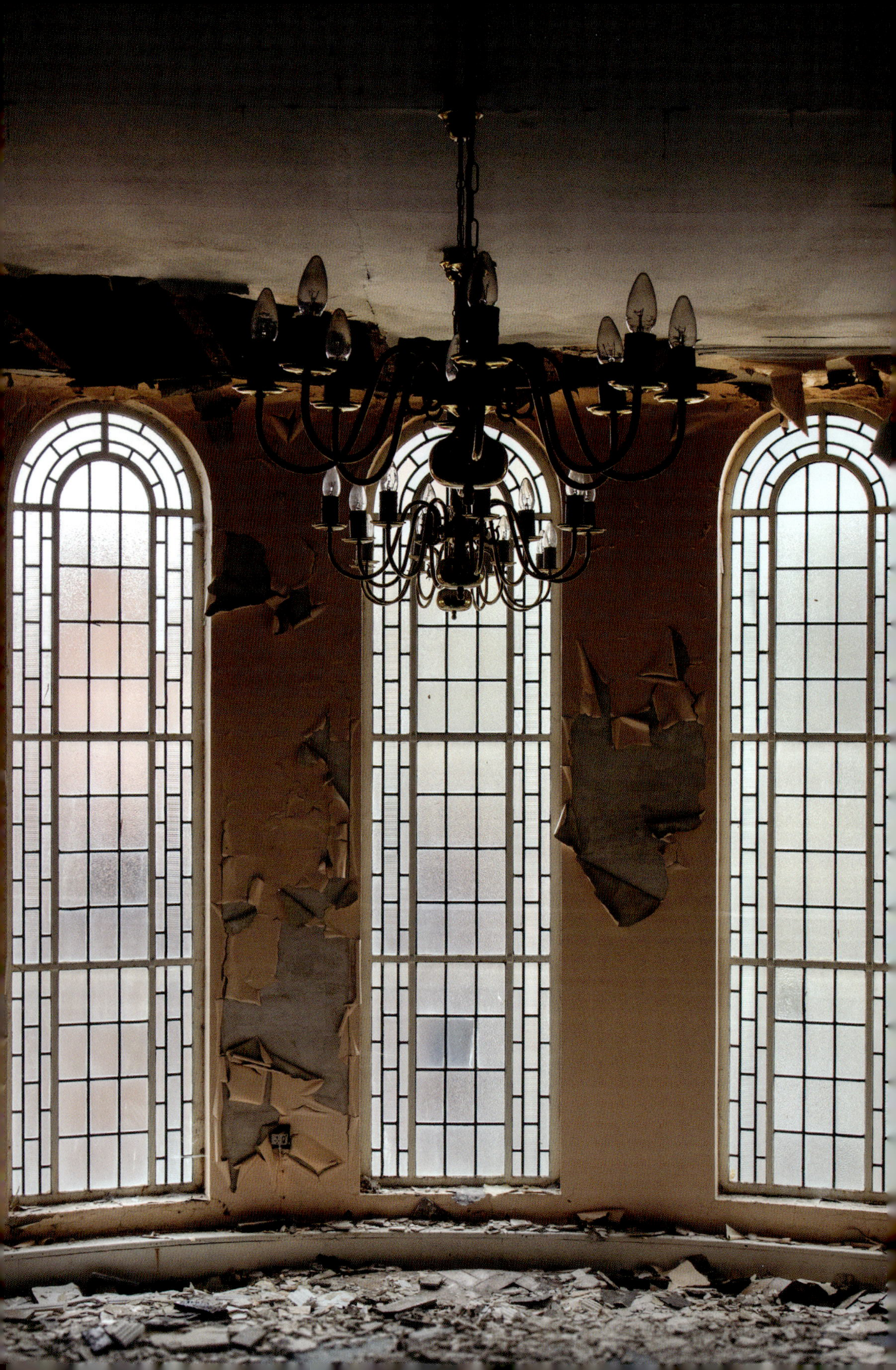

UNITED METHODIST FREE CHURCH, WAVERTREE

The United Methodist Free Church was founded 1903 and it was in use until 2004. It was built to serve the Methodist community of the burgeoning streets of terraced housing being built in Wavertree. The design of the building was by a local Liverpool architect Thomas H. W. Walker in an Edwardian Italianate Baroque style. It was successfully Grade II listed by SAVE Britain's Heritage in 2016 after plans were proposed to demolish the site to make way for student accommodation. (Images David Gooch)

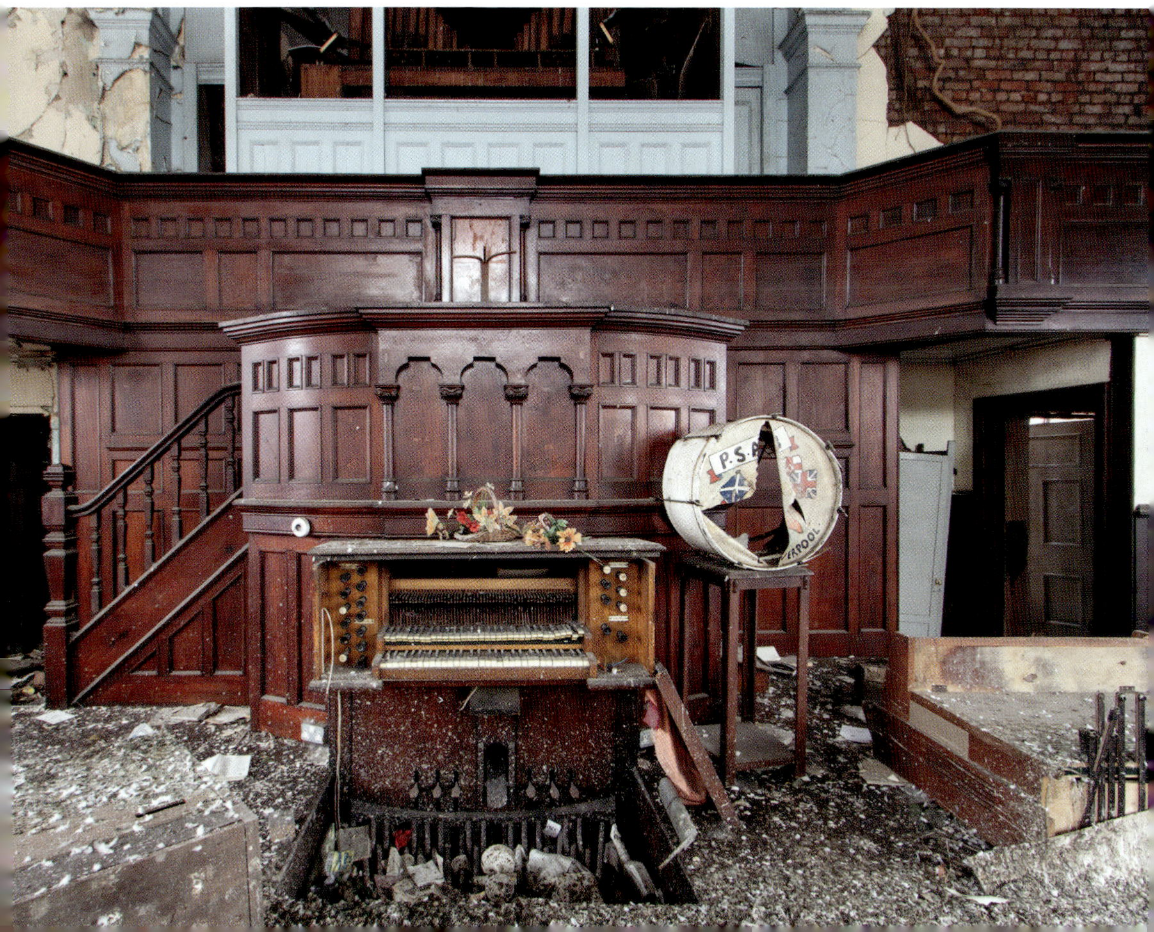

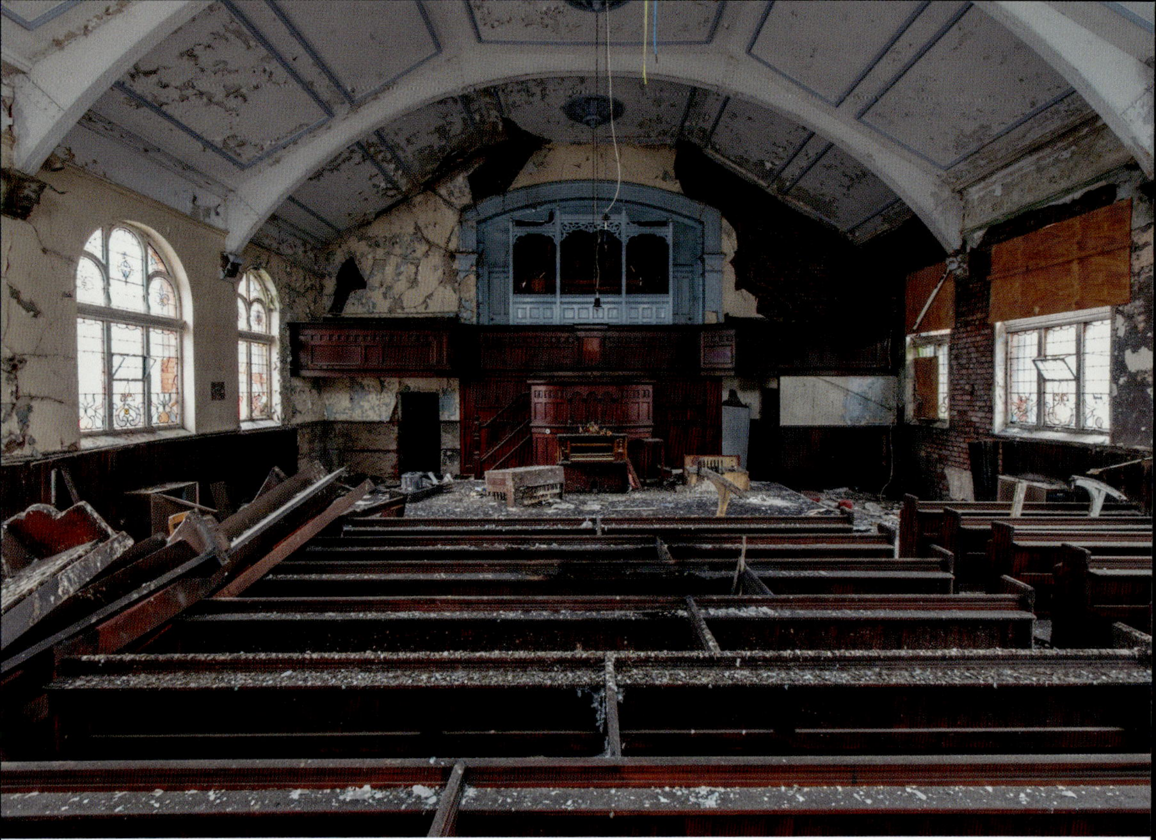

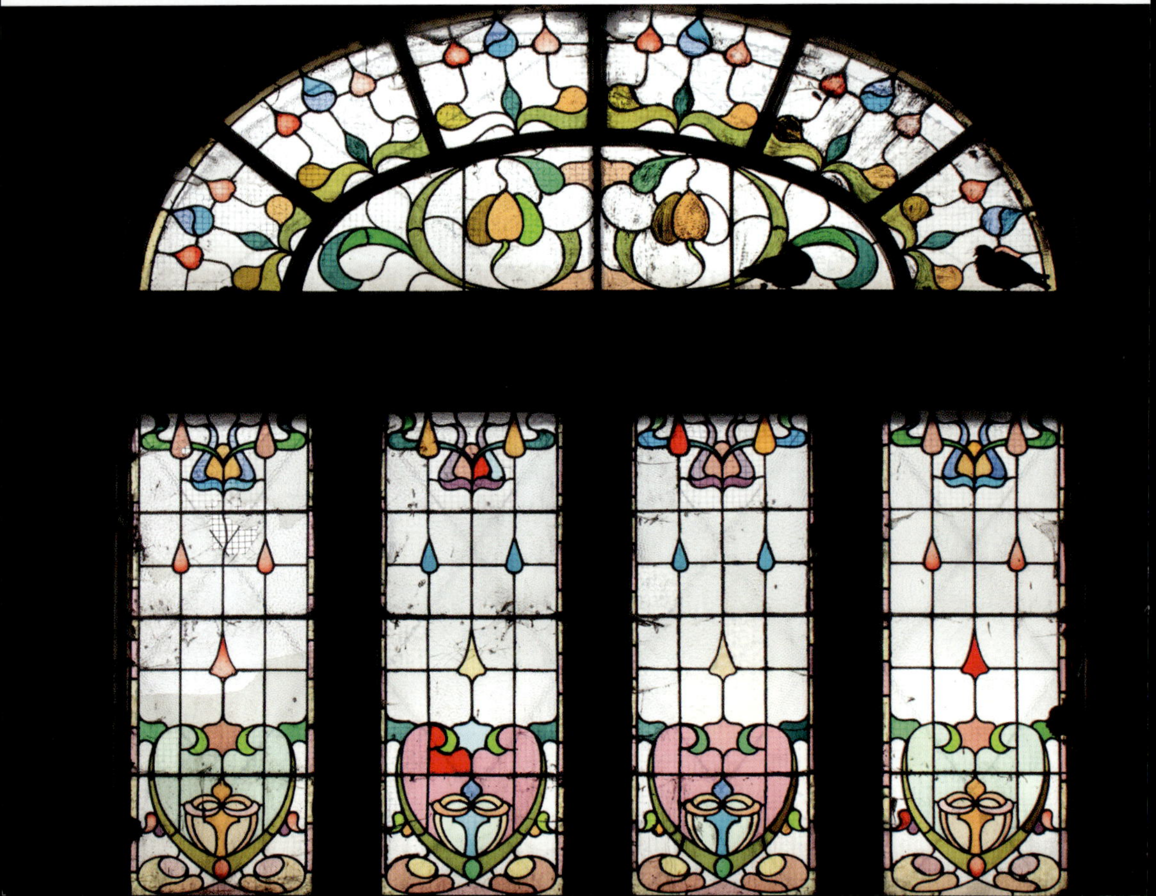

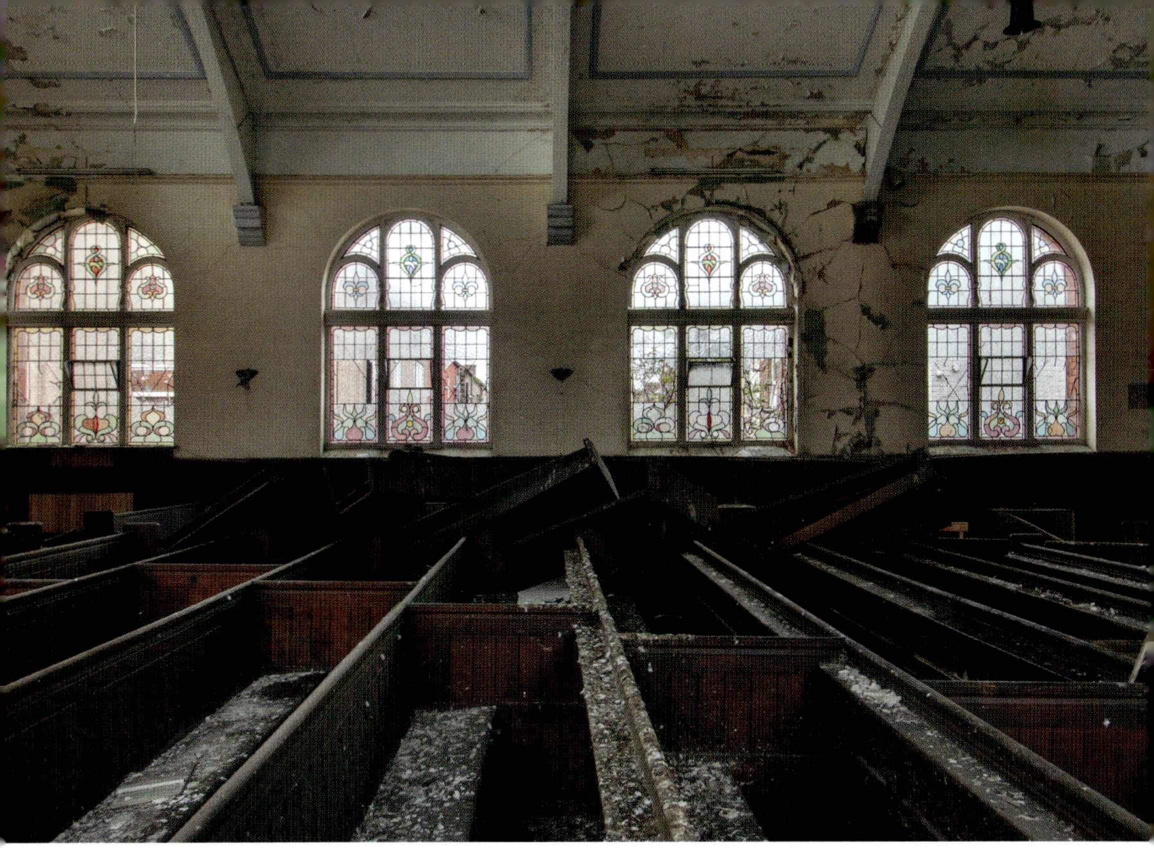

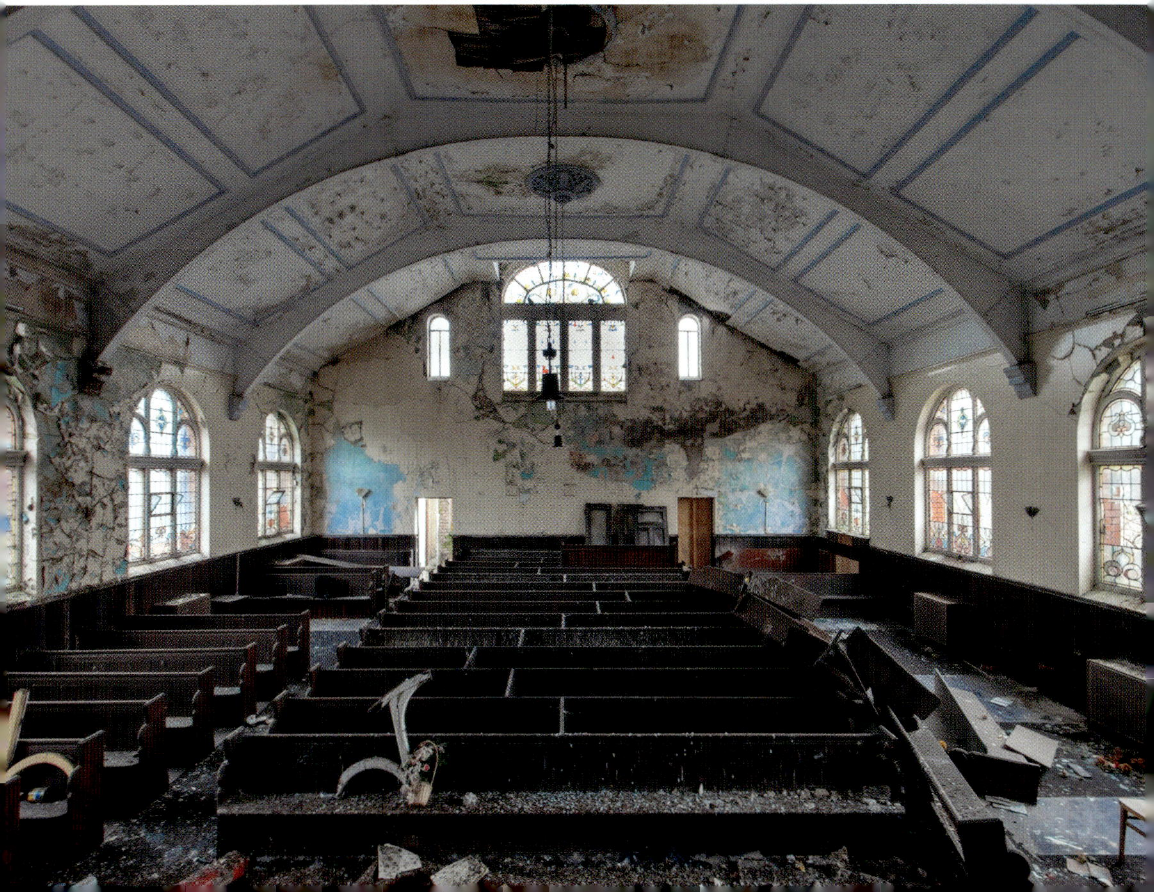

FRUIT EXCHANGE

This Grade II listed building was constructed in 1888 as a railway goods depot for the London and Northwestern Railway to serve the nearby Exchange station. In 1923 the building was converted into a fruit exchange by James B. Hutchins, opening on 14 January 1924. It was the heart of the trading activity in Liverpool at the time and dealt with most fruit imports coming into the city. Hundreds of traders would fill the auction halls and bid for fruit which had arrived via Liverpool docks from all around the world.

Warehouses in the Mathew Street area were used to store the fruit sold at the exchange. Twelve months later the exchange was extended, with the formal opening on 5 January 1925.

Plans are now in place to turn the building into a ninety-two-bedroom hotel, complete with a bar and restaurant. (Images James Lacey)

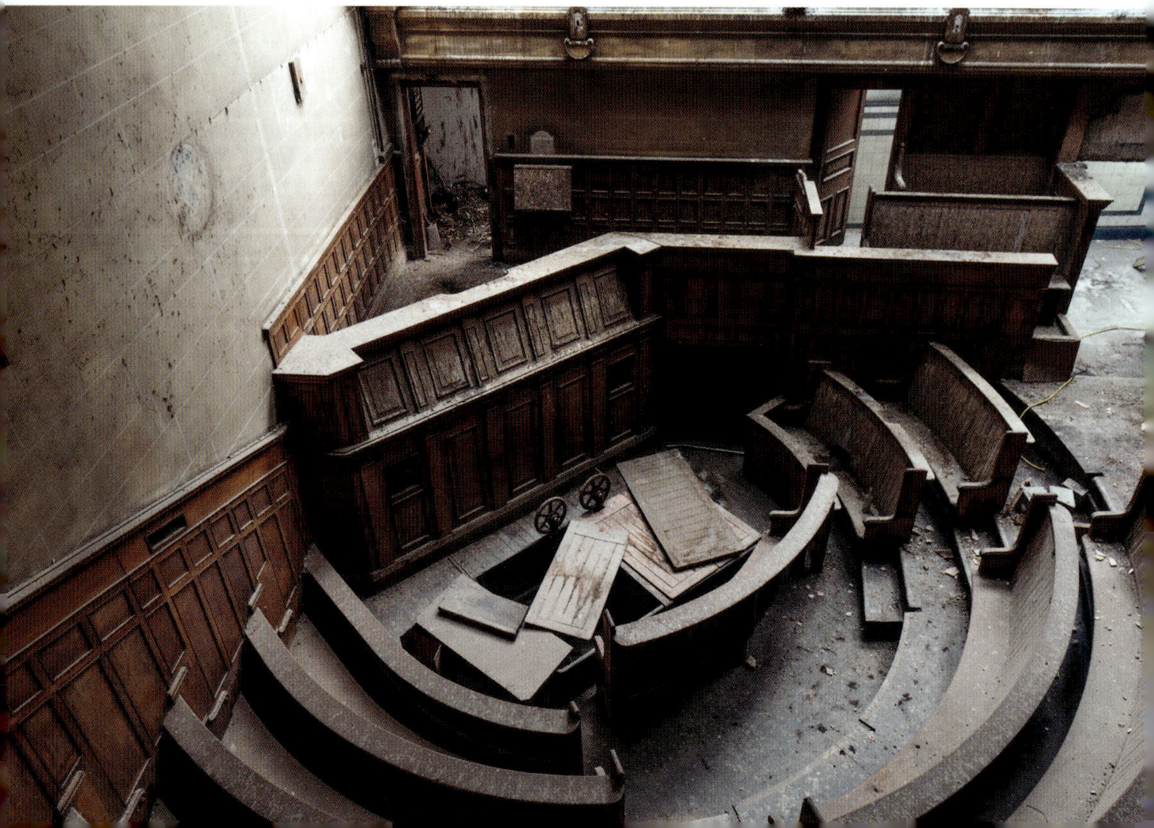

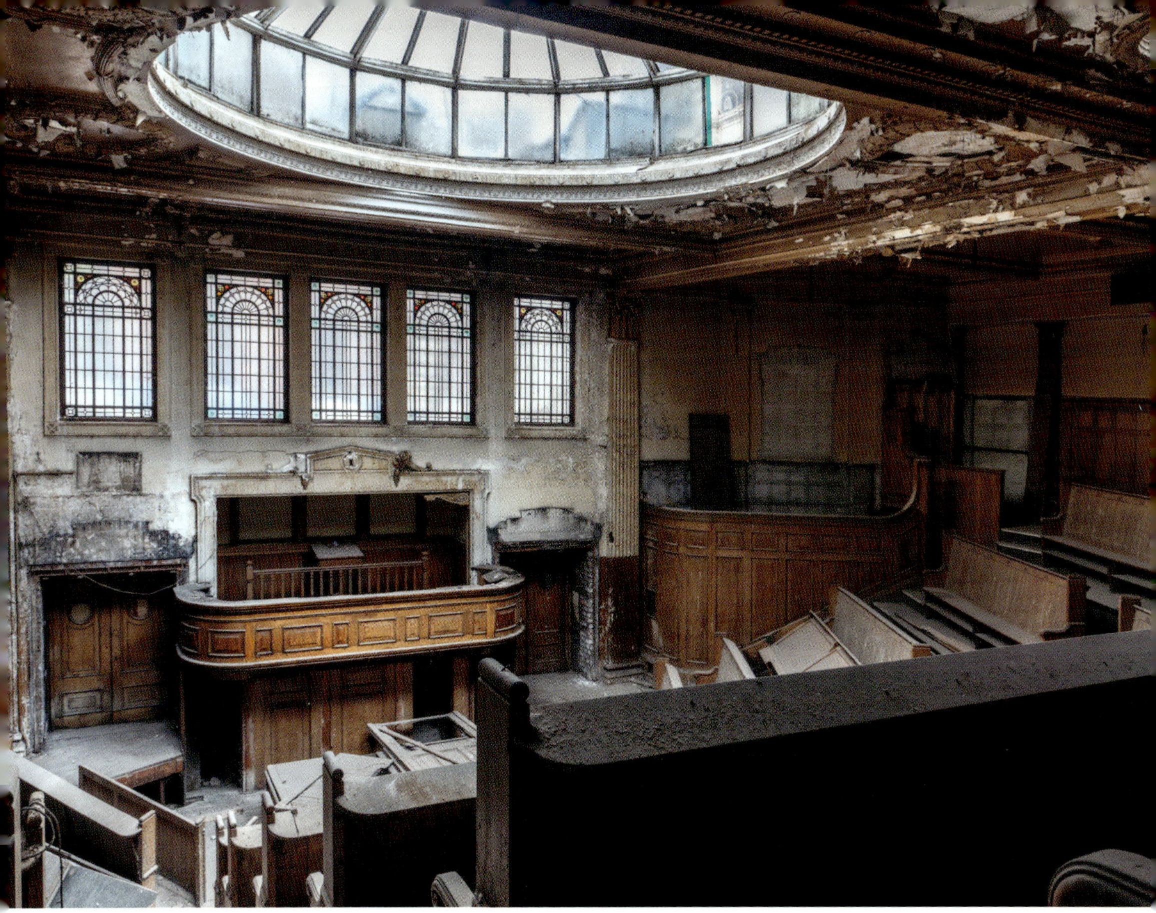

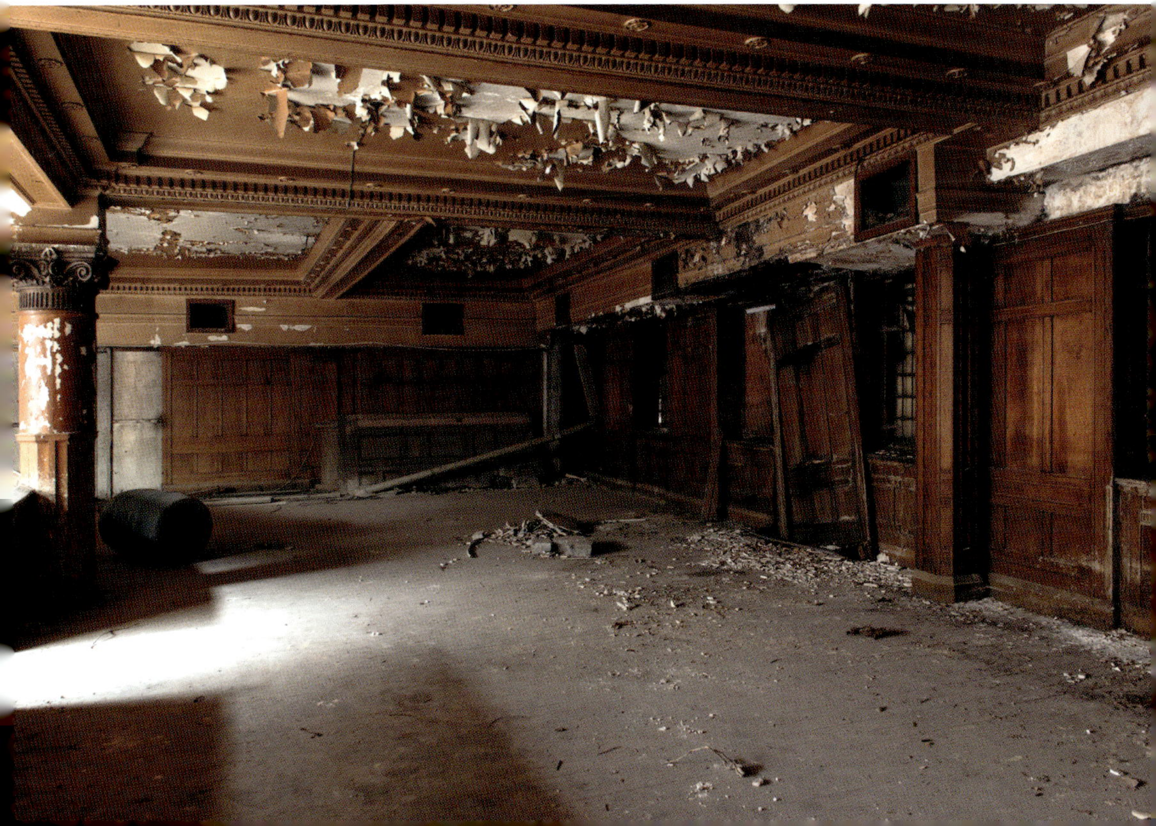

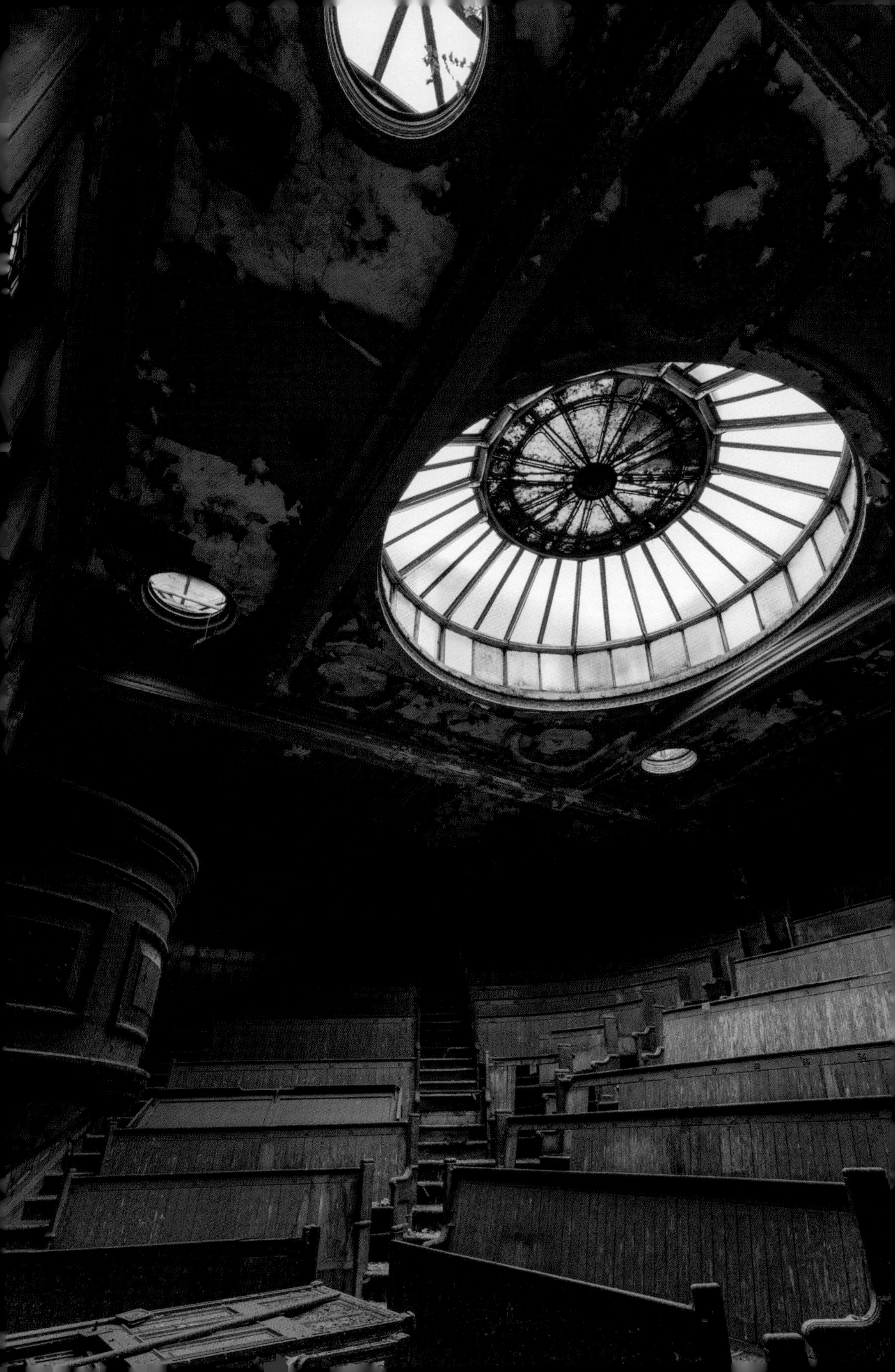

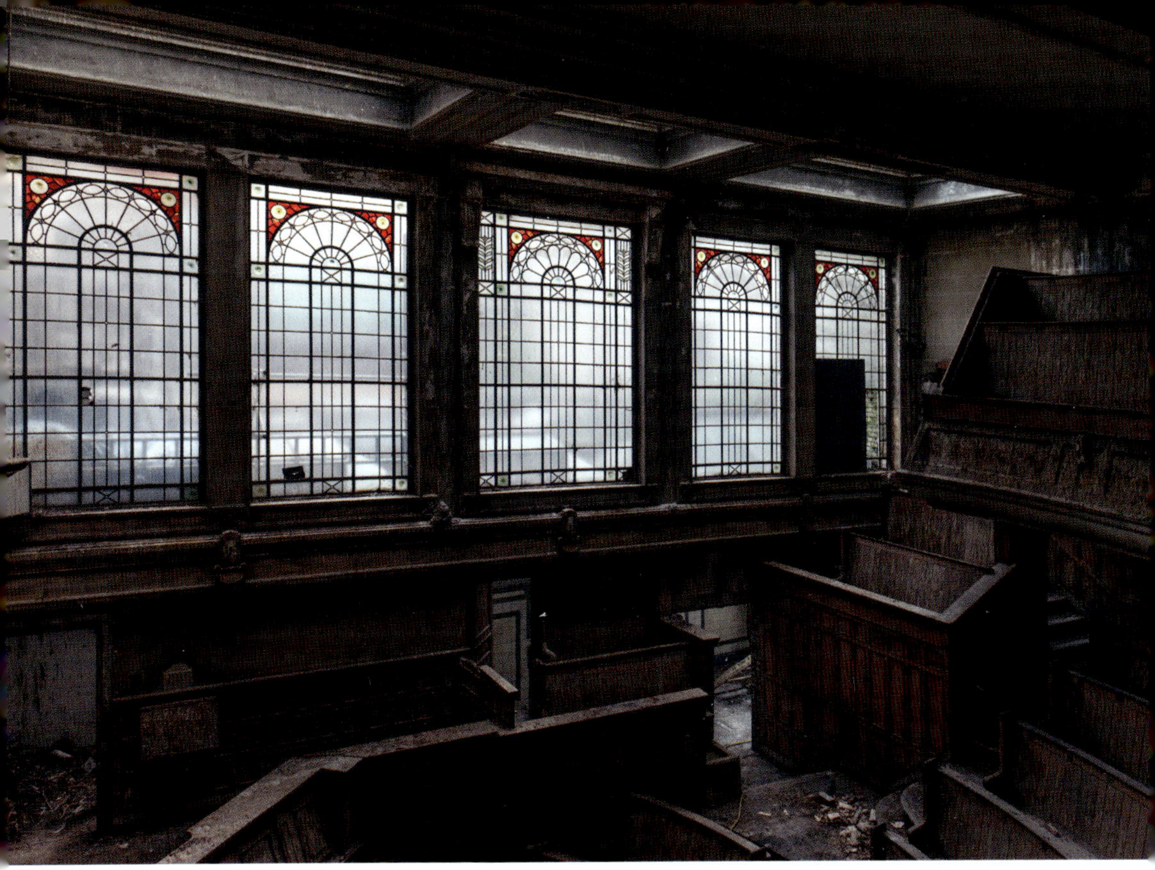

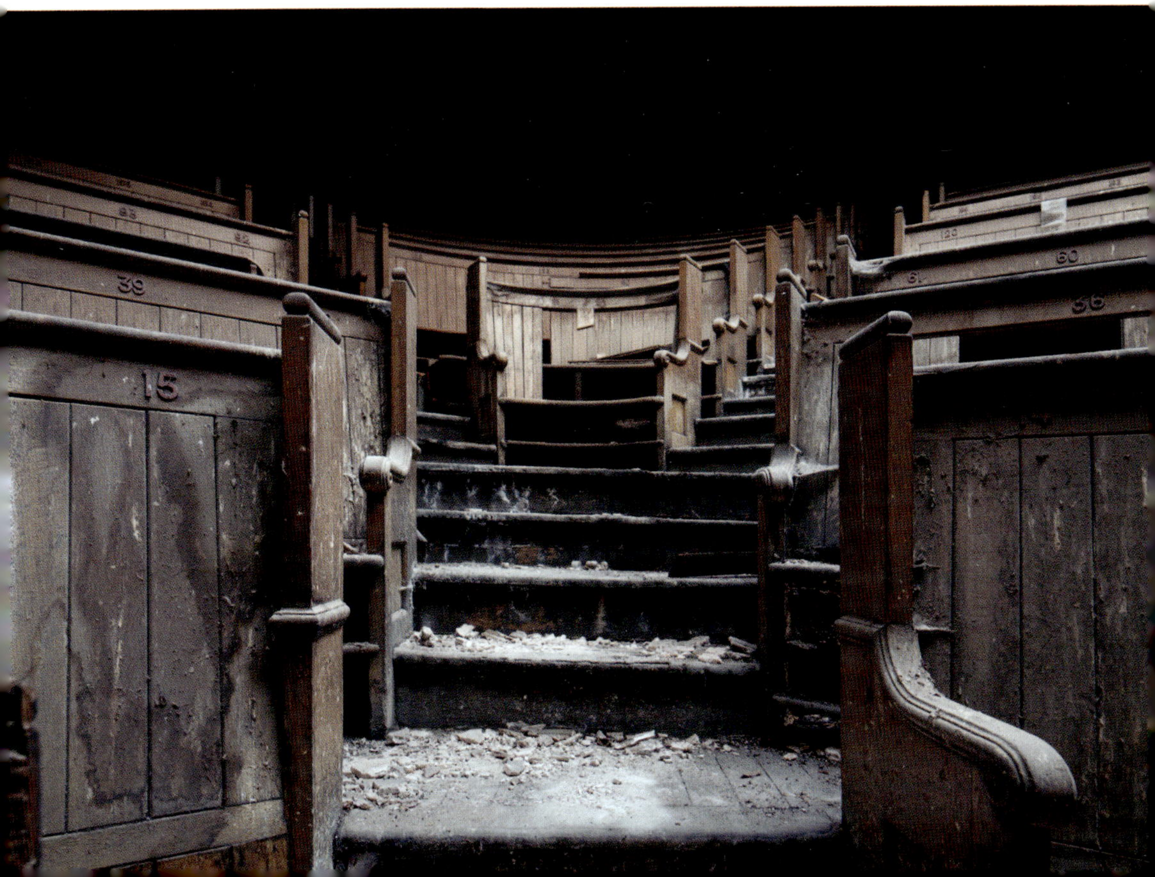
39
15
60
56

CRODA CHEMICALS

Originally, Croda Chemicals was owned by the Prince's Patent Candle Company. Back in 1853 palm oil was brought into Liverpool and the oil needed to be processed at a site nearer the city instead of being transported to London by boat. The company built what is now Bromborough Pool village and opened the factory in Bromborough in 1855 with eighty-four staff, and ended up employing 2,300 staff. The site closed in 2009, costing 115 people their jobs.

The site has now been demolished to make way for a housing estate. (Images David Gooch)

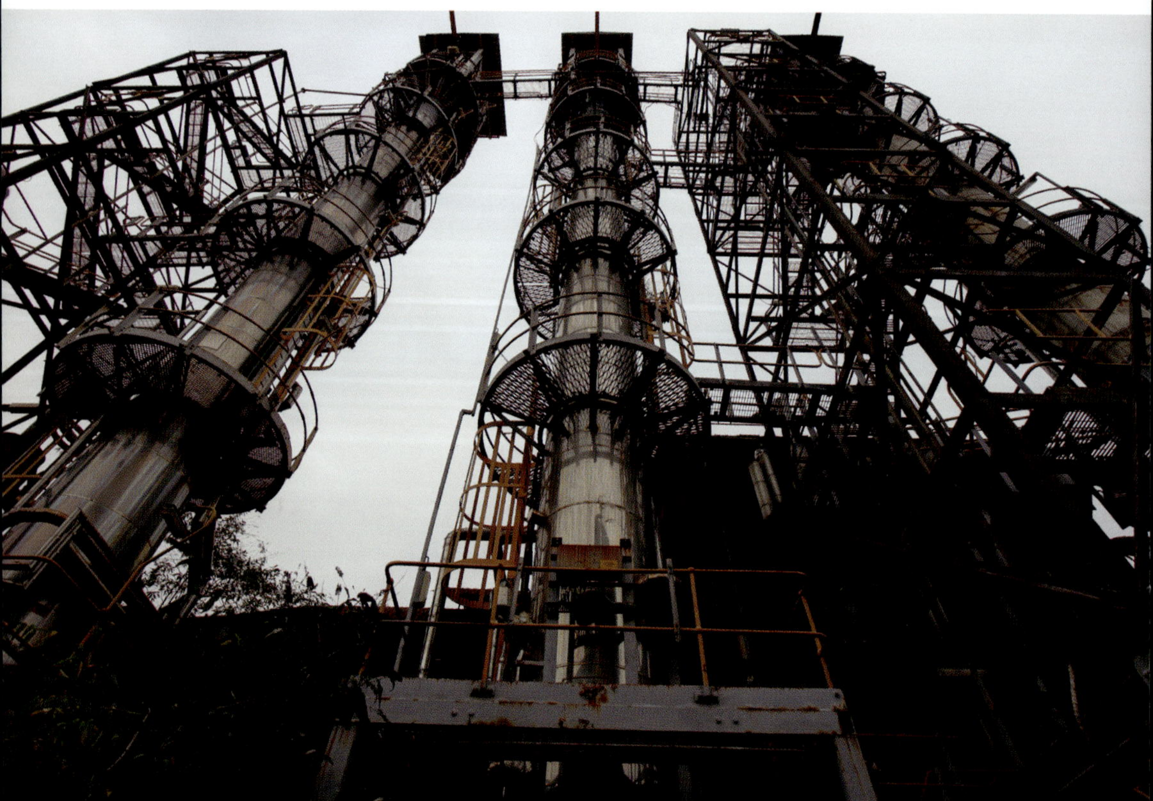

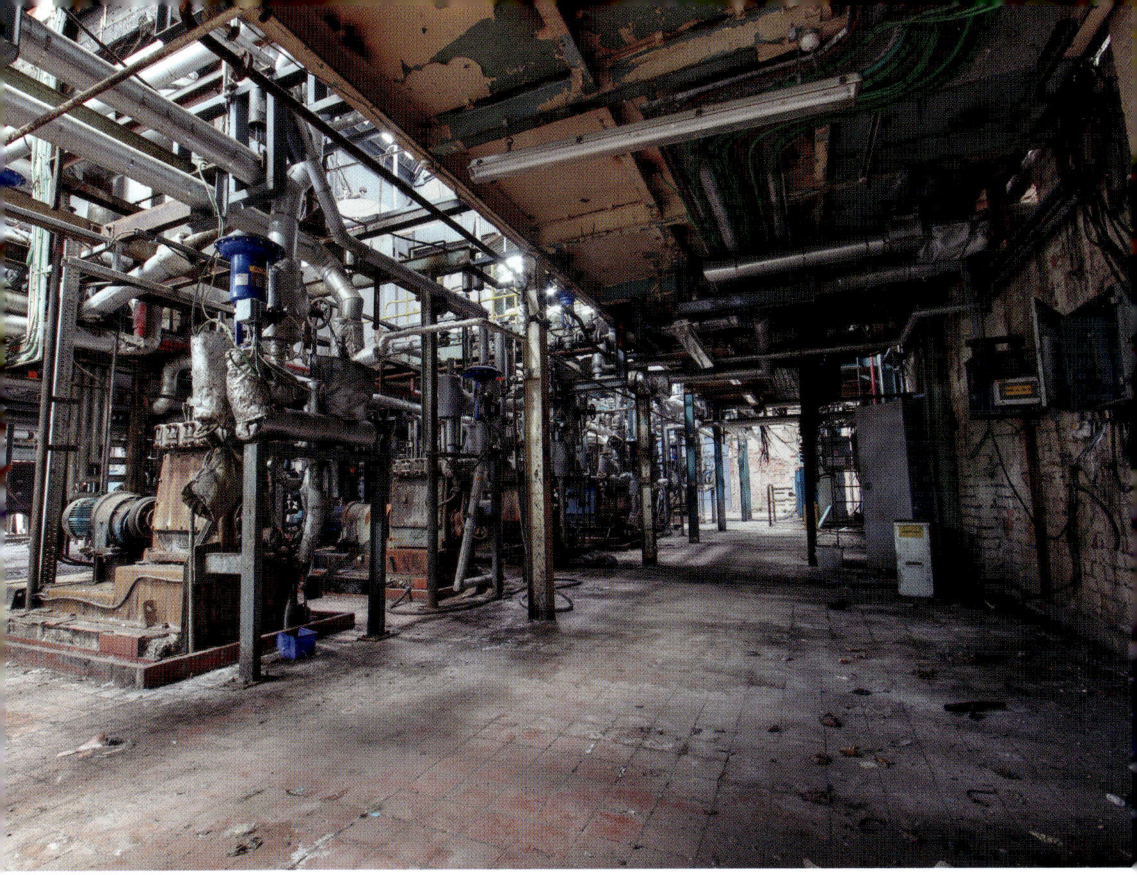

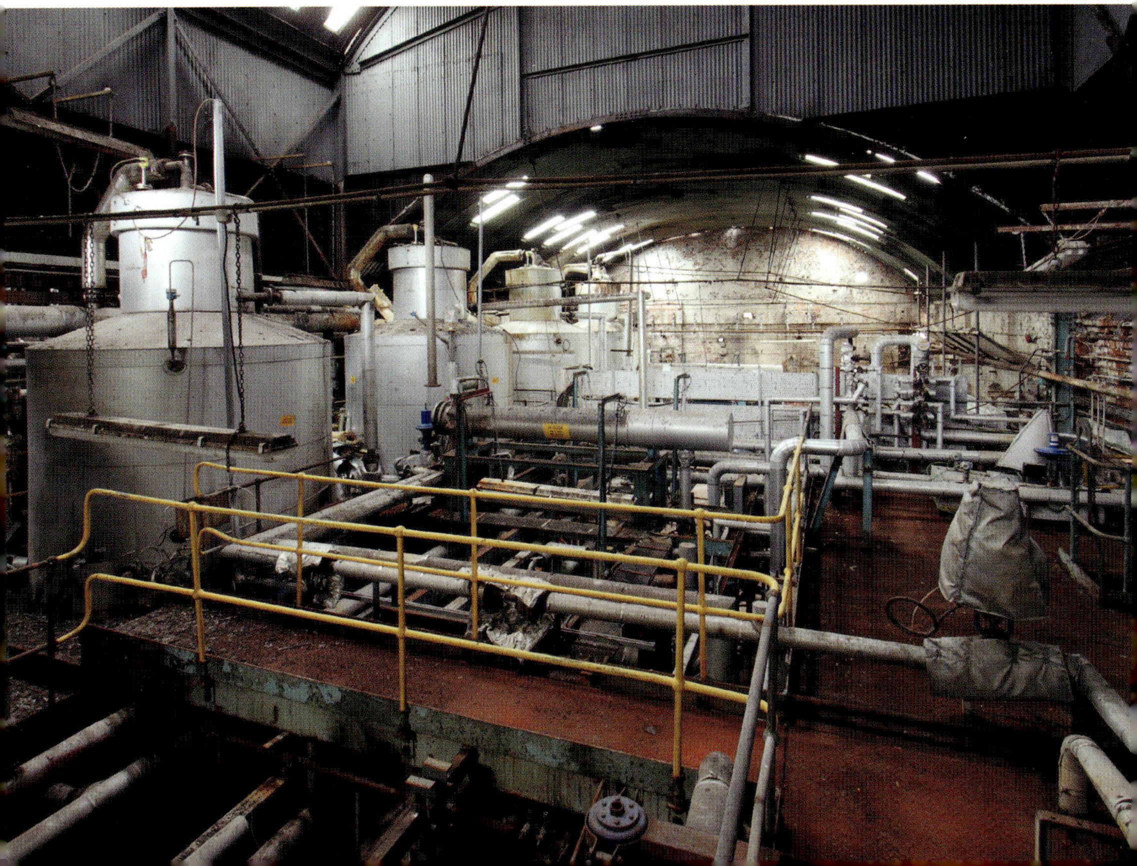

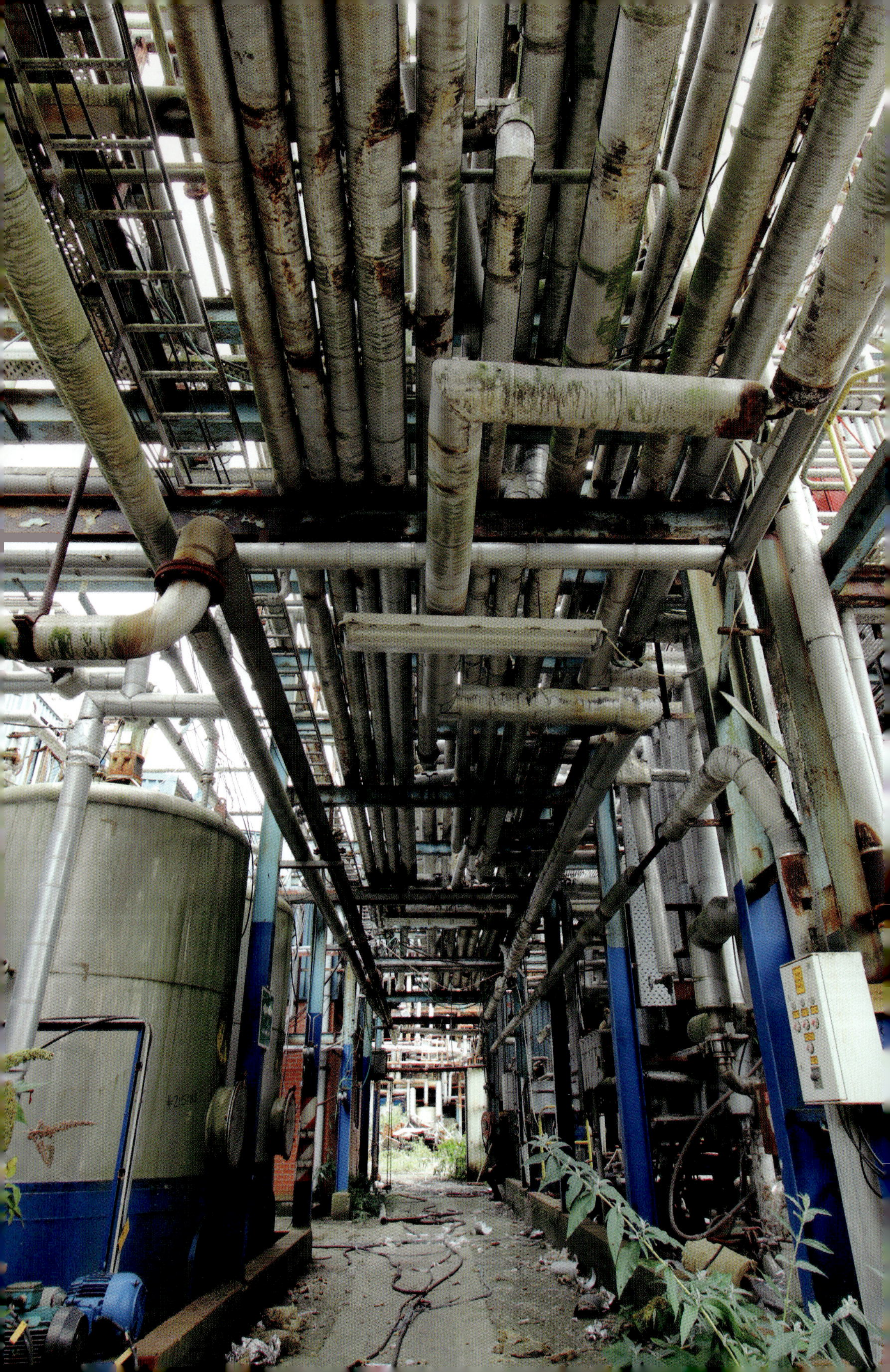

LIVERPOOL UNIVERSITY ZOOLOGY DEPARTMENT

This building is currently undergoing renovation after closing for students in 2008. It was originally founded as a college in 1881 and gained its Royal Charter in 1903 which allowed it to award degrees to the students. The building is also known as one of the original six red-brick civic universities.

In its early days, the building hosted the departments of zoology and botany and in later years engineering, geology, archaeology, biology, and the classics. In the 1980s, additional buildings were added and were home to several different departments. These were further expanded by the addition of an annex in the mid-1980s. Before its closure, the building hosted the Egyptology, biology and engineering departments. (Images James Lacey)

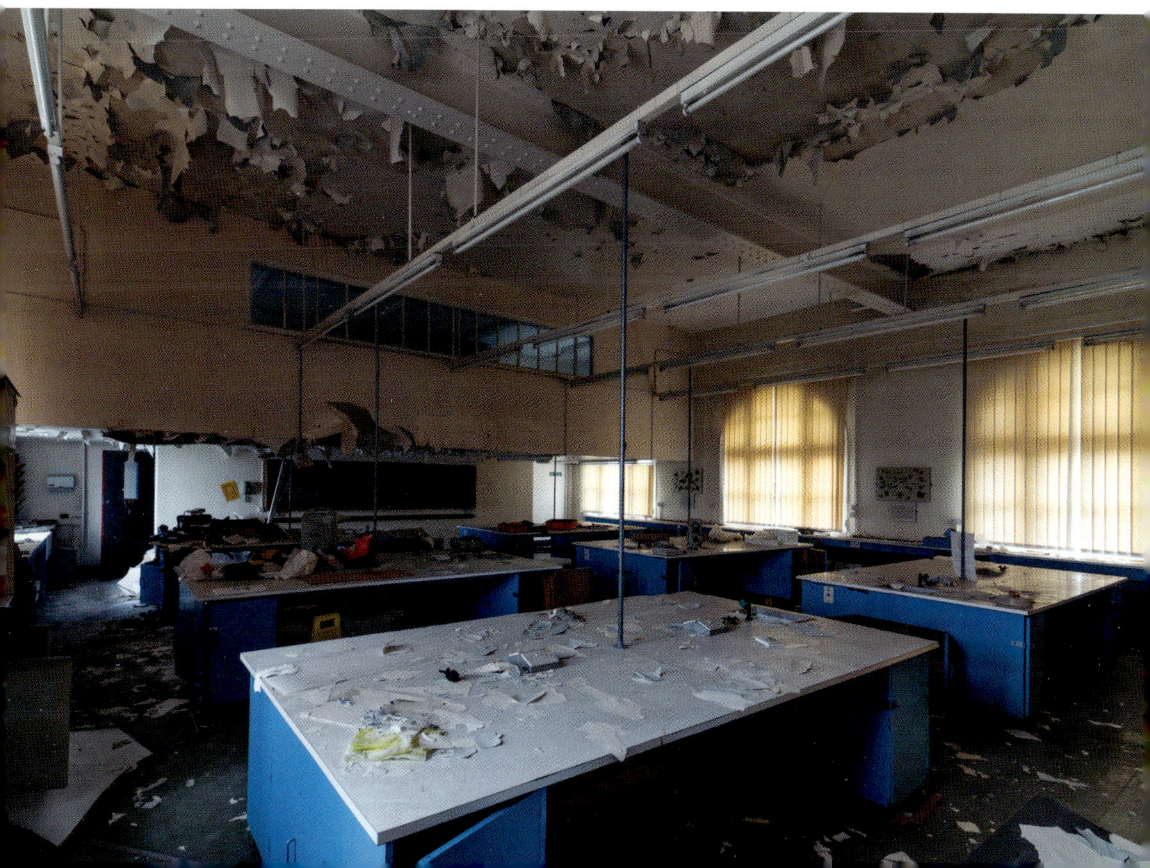

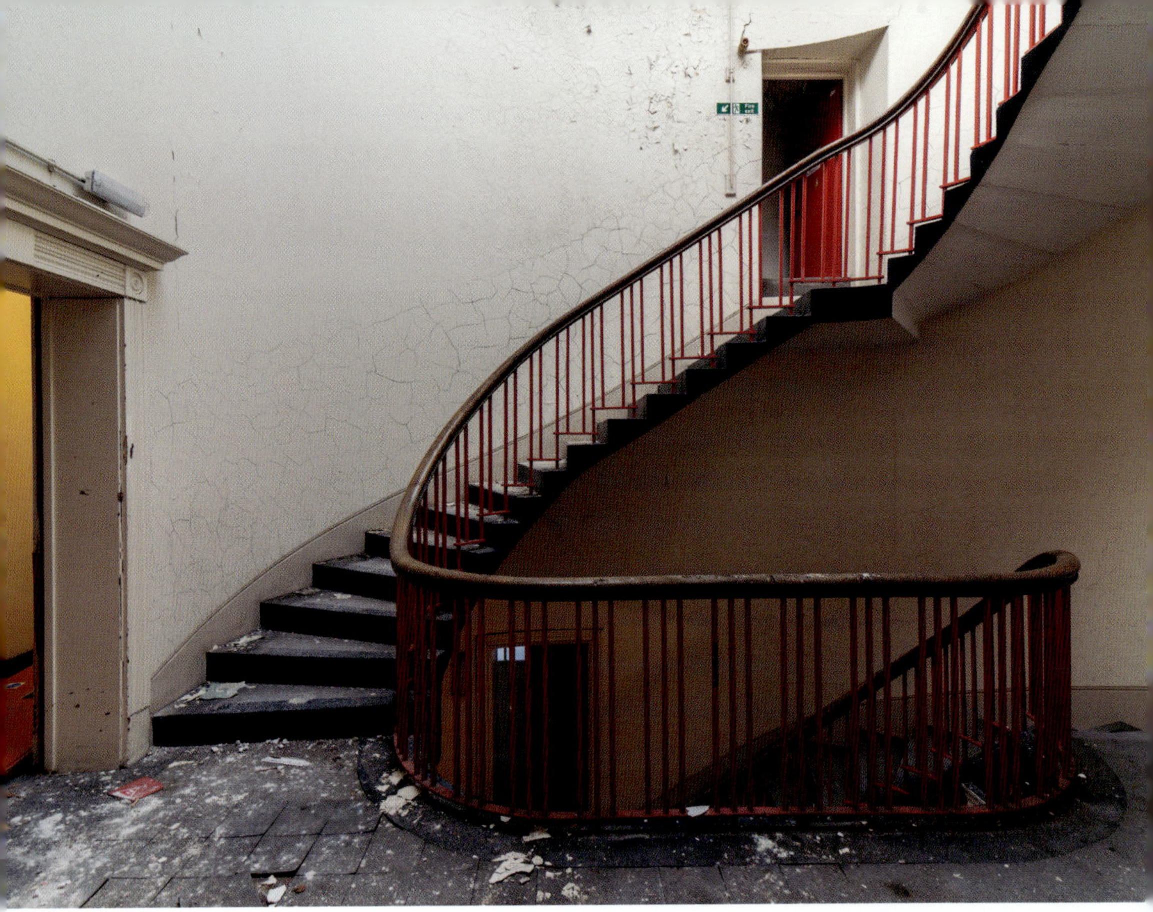

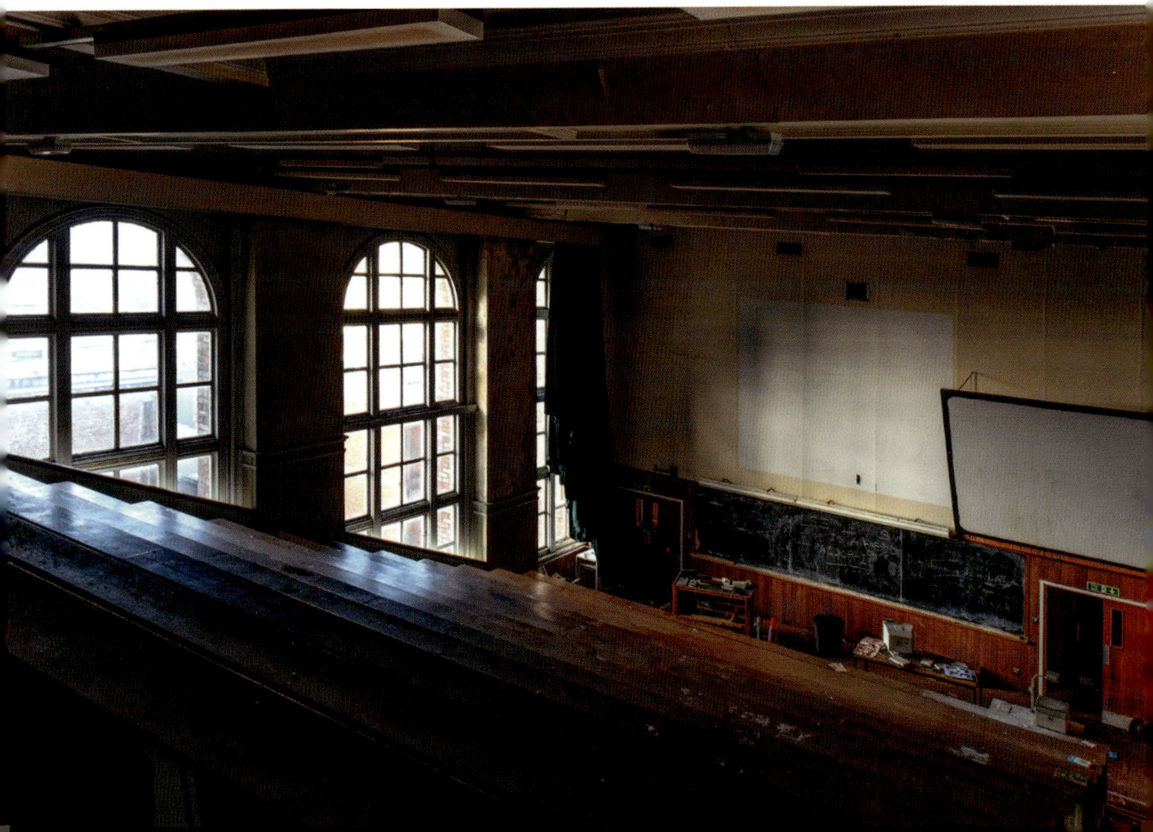

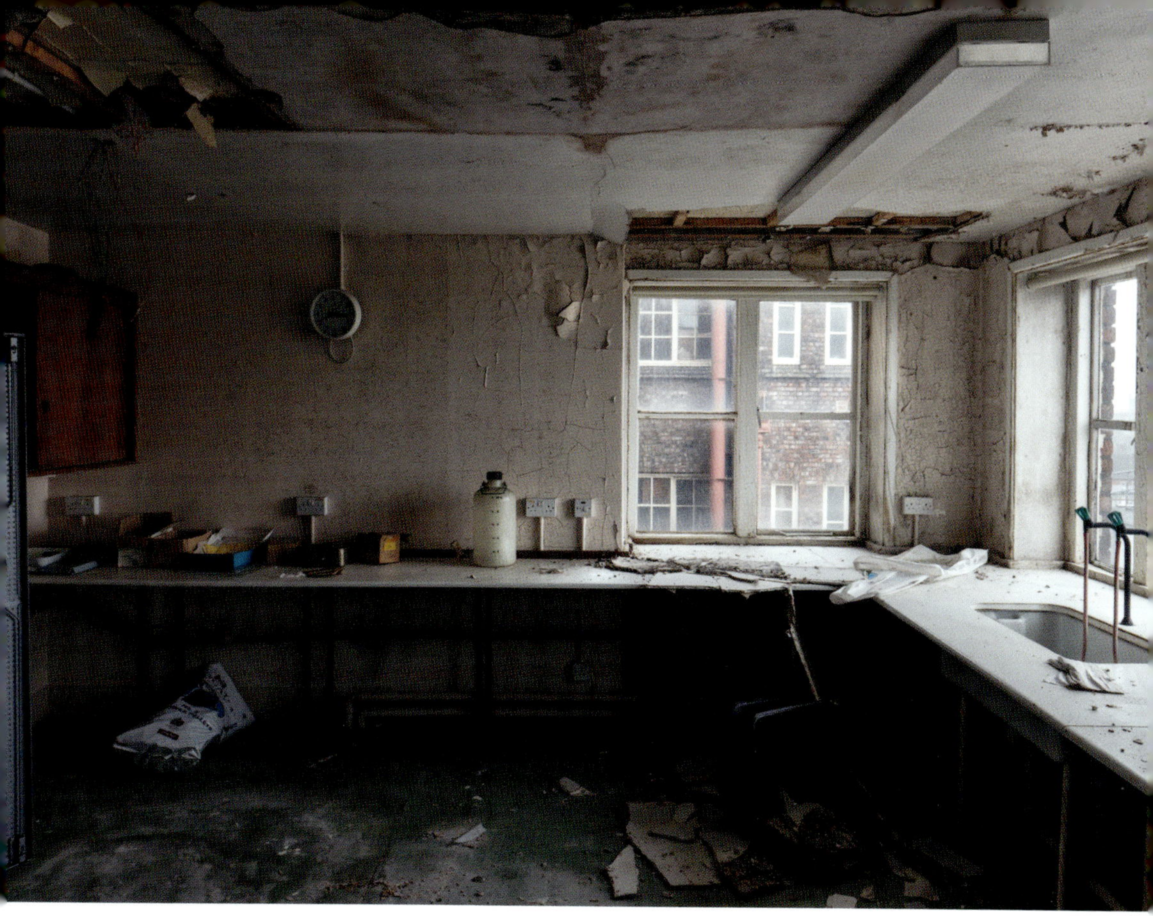

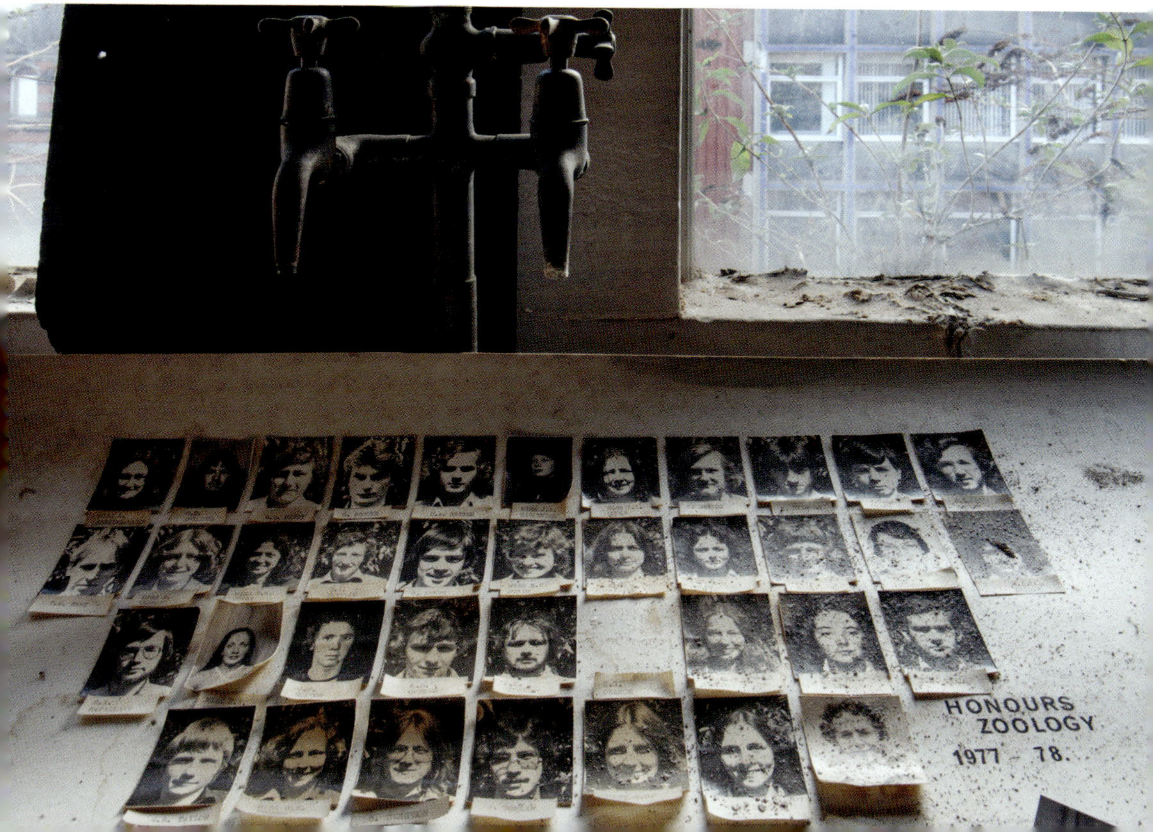
HONOURS
ZOOLOGY
1977 - 78.

MERSEYSIDE CENTRE FOR THE DEAF

The Merseyside Centre for the Deaf is a Gothic-style Grade II listed building that was originally built as a chapel for the deaf community of Merseyside. It was used from 1887 until 1986 as a church and then it became a community centre for the local Igbo community, promoting Nigerian culture until its final closure in 2007 due to the increasing age of membership and rising costs associated with the building. The building was added to the Victorian Society's Buildings at Risk register in 2018. (Images David Gooch)

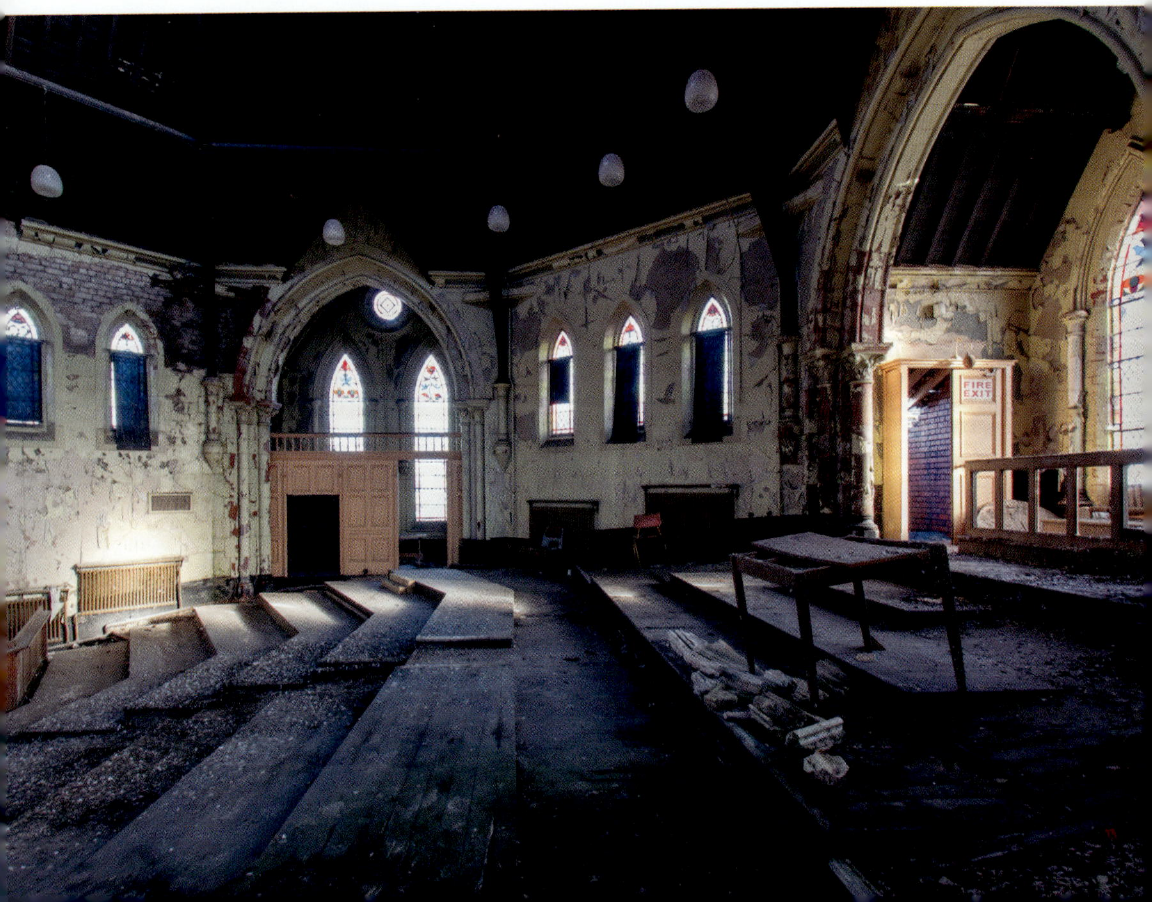

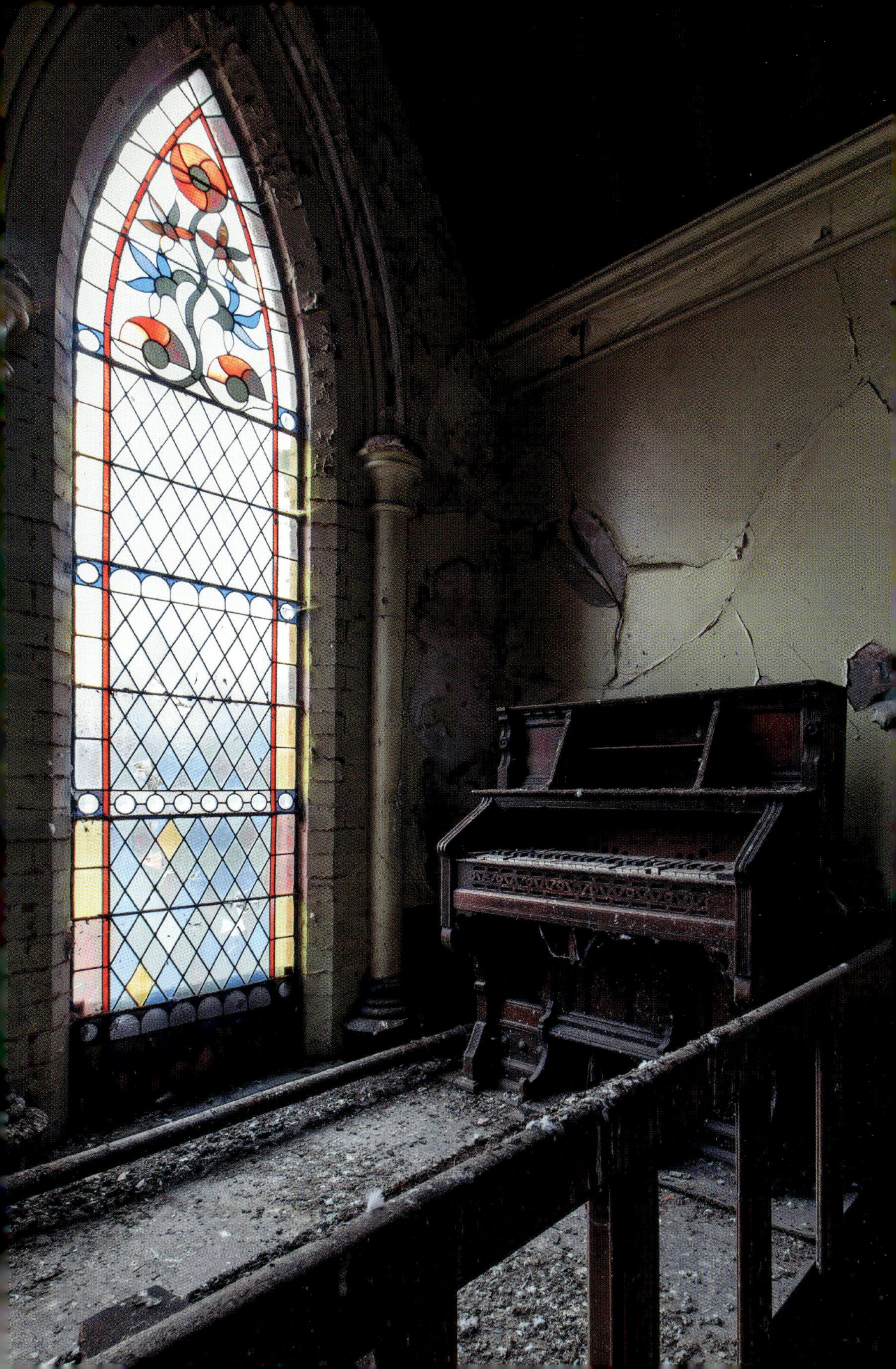

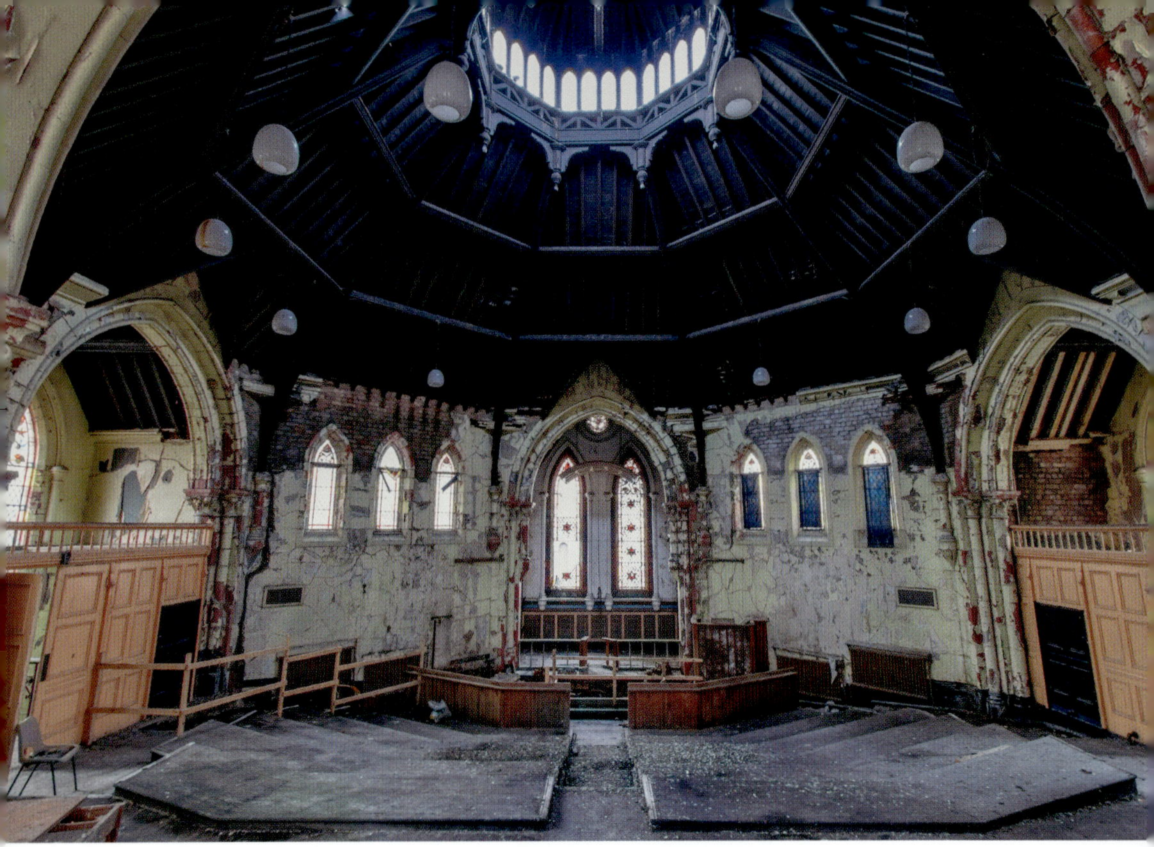

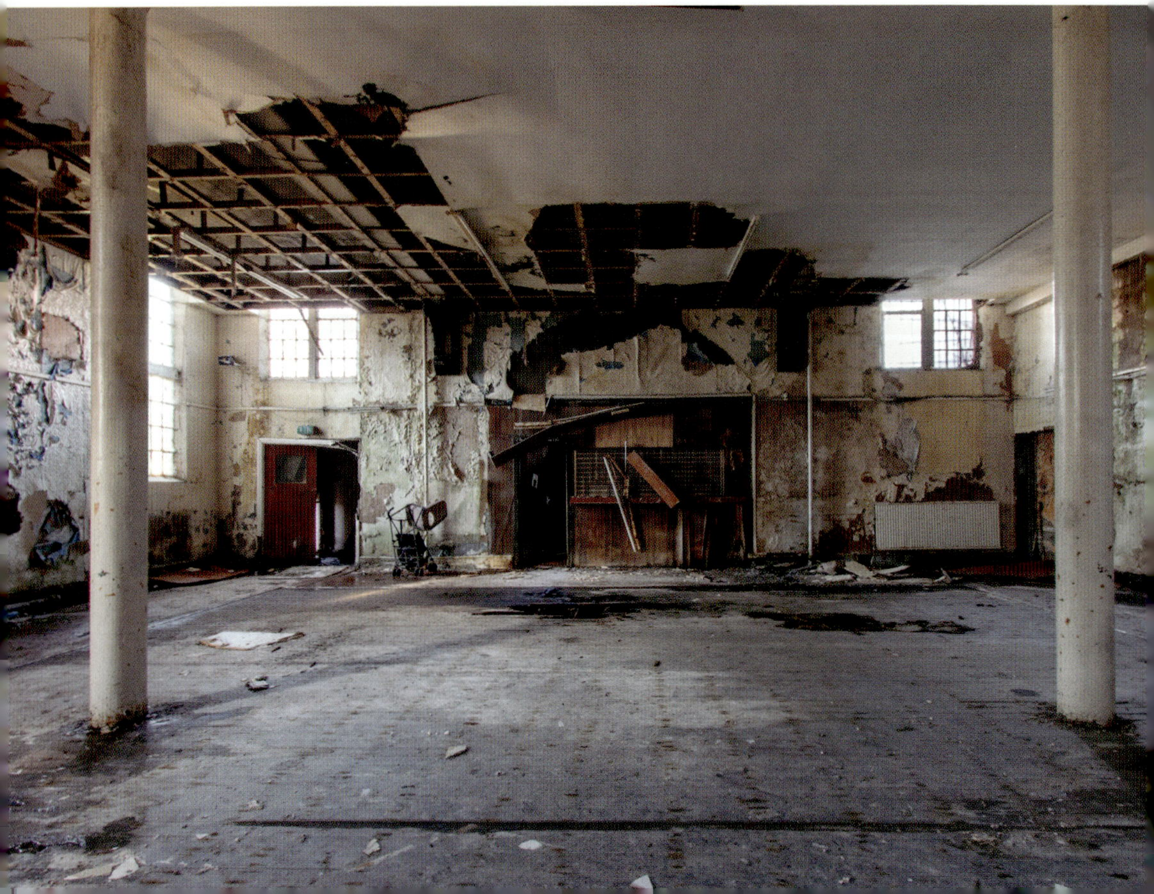

GARDNER & NEWTON GLASS FACTORY, ST HELENS

With the opening of the Sankey Canal in 1757, and its later extension to Ravenhead, goods flooded back and forth between St Helens and Liverpool. Local industries benefited from the flow of coal, copper ore, salt and limestone. By the late eighteenth century, the local landscape was changing dramatically in St Helens.

Many smaller firms thrived with the plethora of industries employing legions of men in the area. Such goods as mineral water and herbal beers, many of which were contained in locally made stoneware and glass bottles, were produced. The British Cast Plate Glass Company opened in 1776 and St Helens started its long history in the production of glass.

Gardner & Newton started blending glass in 1836, and this site in St Helens was one of many used in the production of glass. There is no history on this particular site from extensive searches online. It had been derelict for many years before these photographs were taken in 2015. (Images James Lacey)

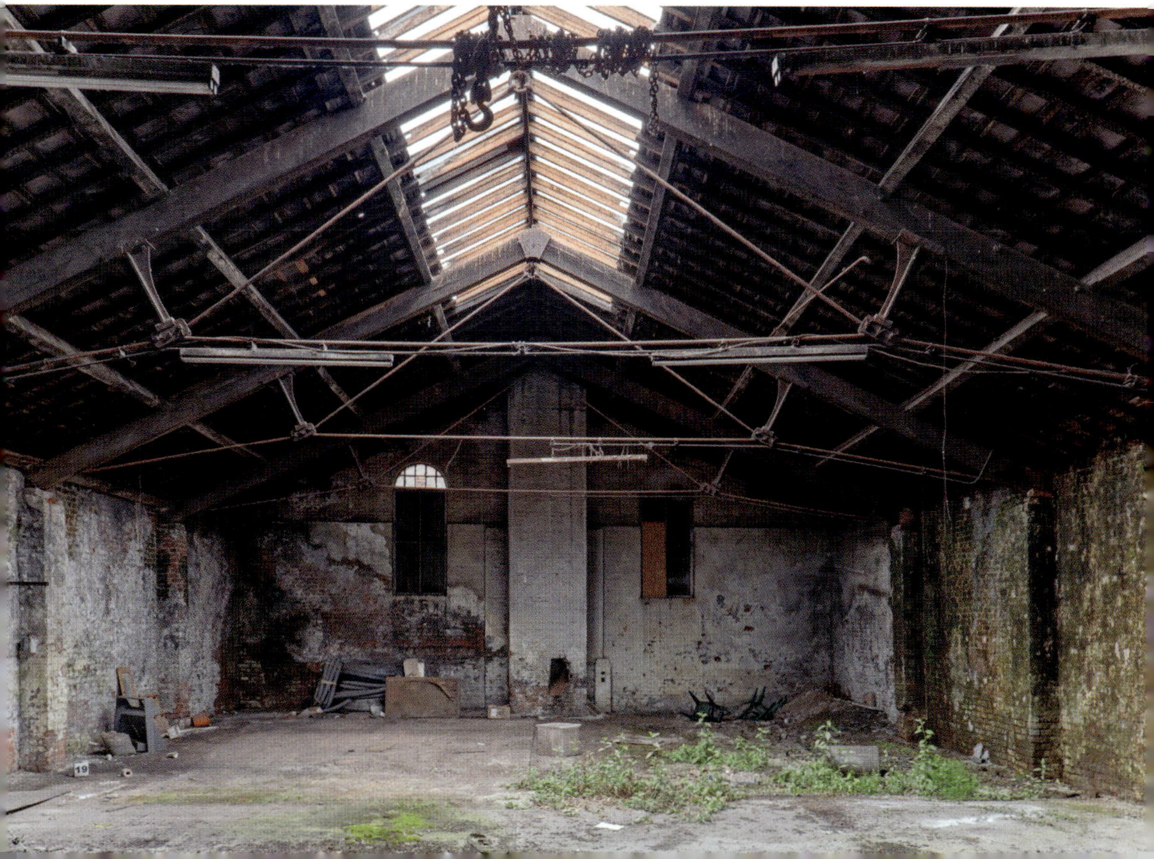

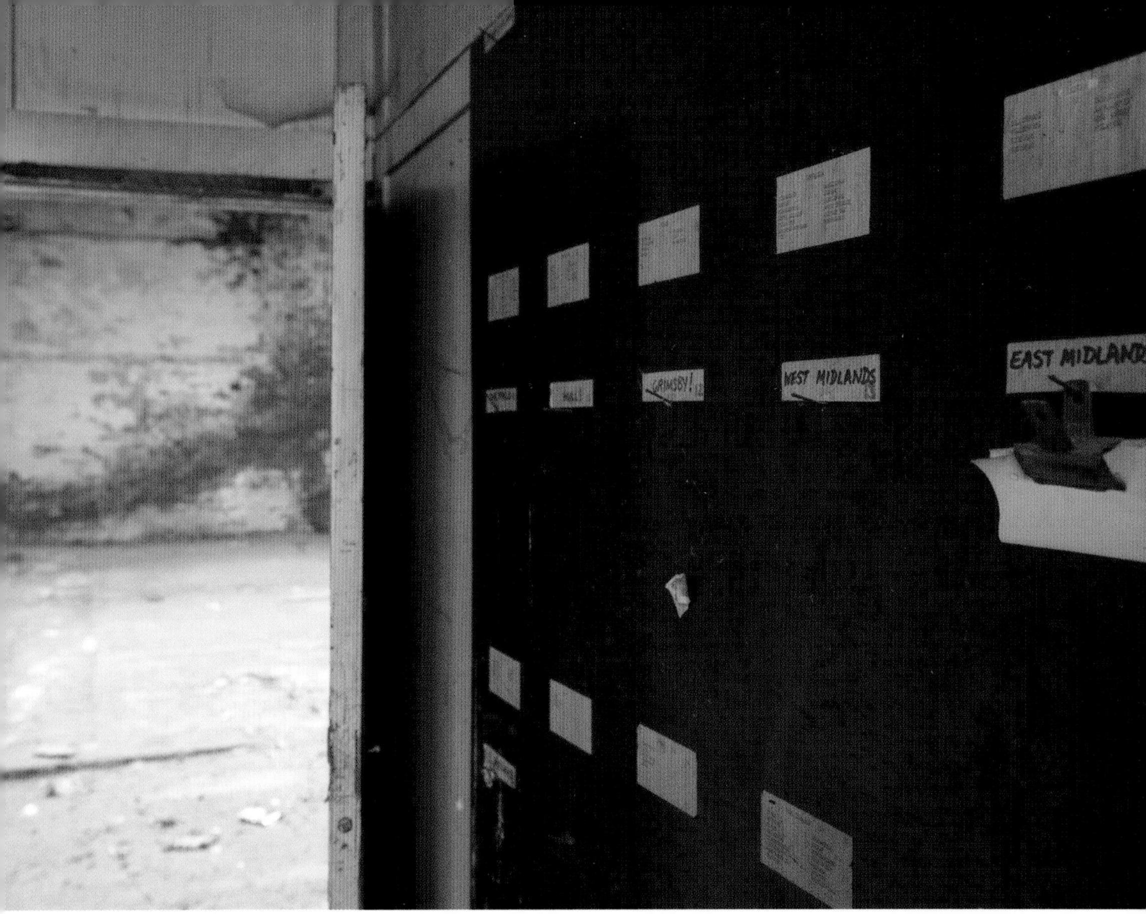
GRIMSBY!
WEST MIDLANDS
EAST MIDLAND

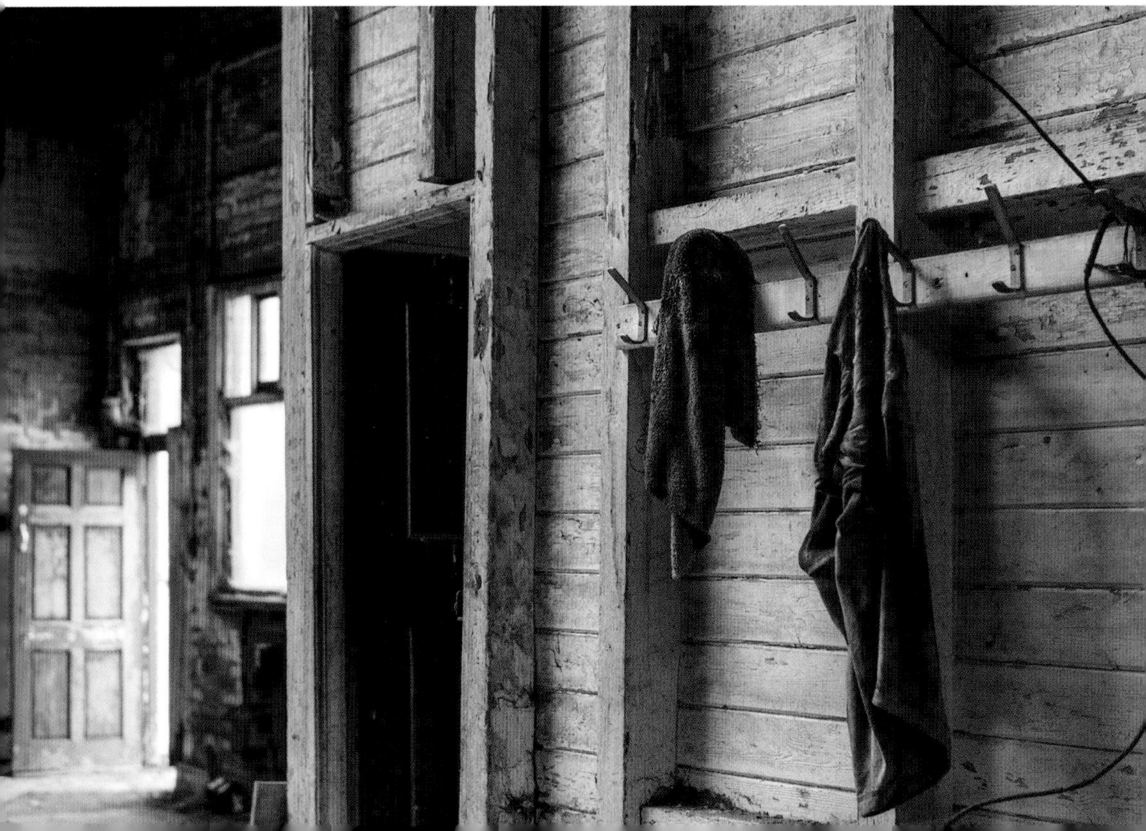

GARRICK THEATRE, SOUTHPORT

After the Opera House burnt down in 1929, the site was used to build the Garrick Theatre, which opened in 1932. It was built with a large stage to be able to provide a wider range of acts, such as touring drama groups and musicals. In 1957 it was converted to show films with a projection box being added. This only lasted until 1963 when it then became a bingo hall.

The Garrick closed in 2020 due to the Covid-19 pandemic and never reopened. While it operated as a bingo hall it still had the projectors and the many disused changing rooms from its theatre days. In 2022 it was added to the Theatres at Risk register by the Theatre Trust. (Images David Gooch)

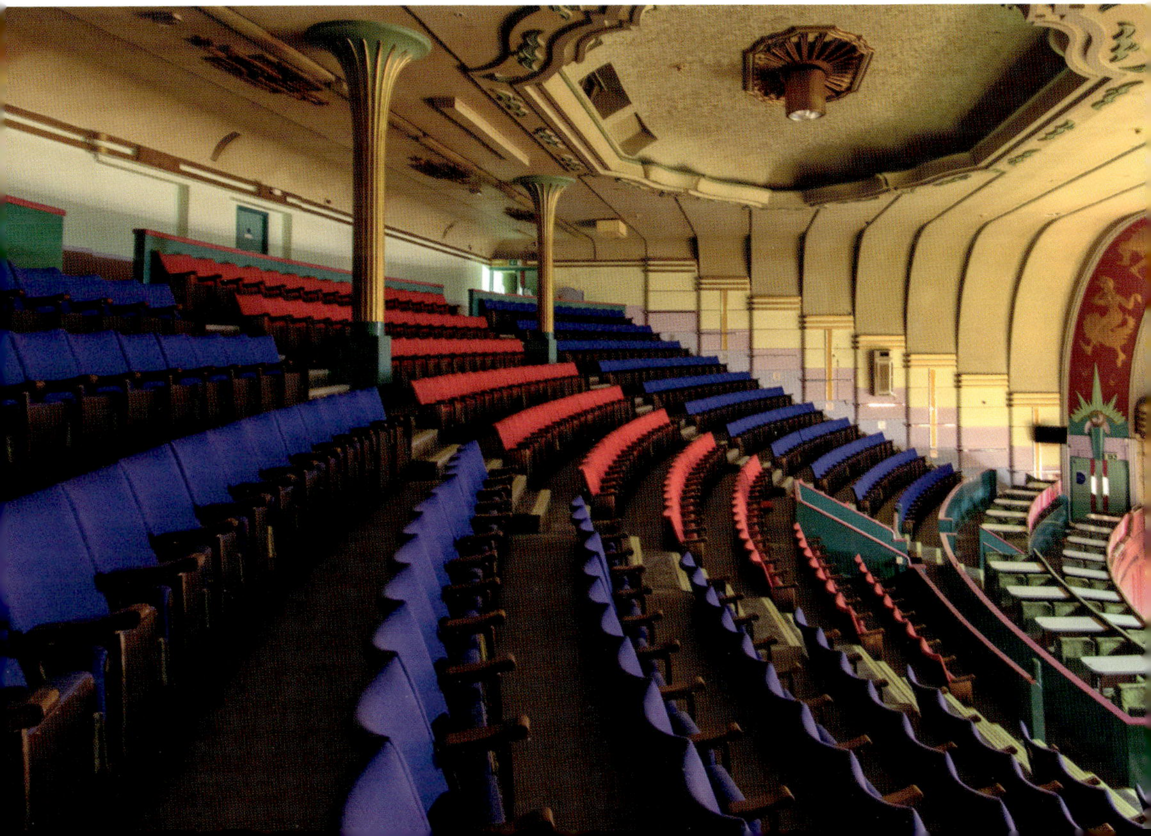

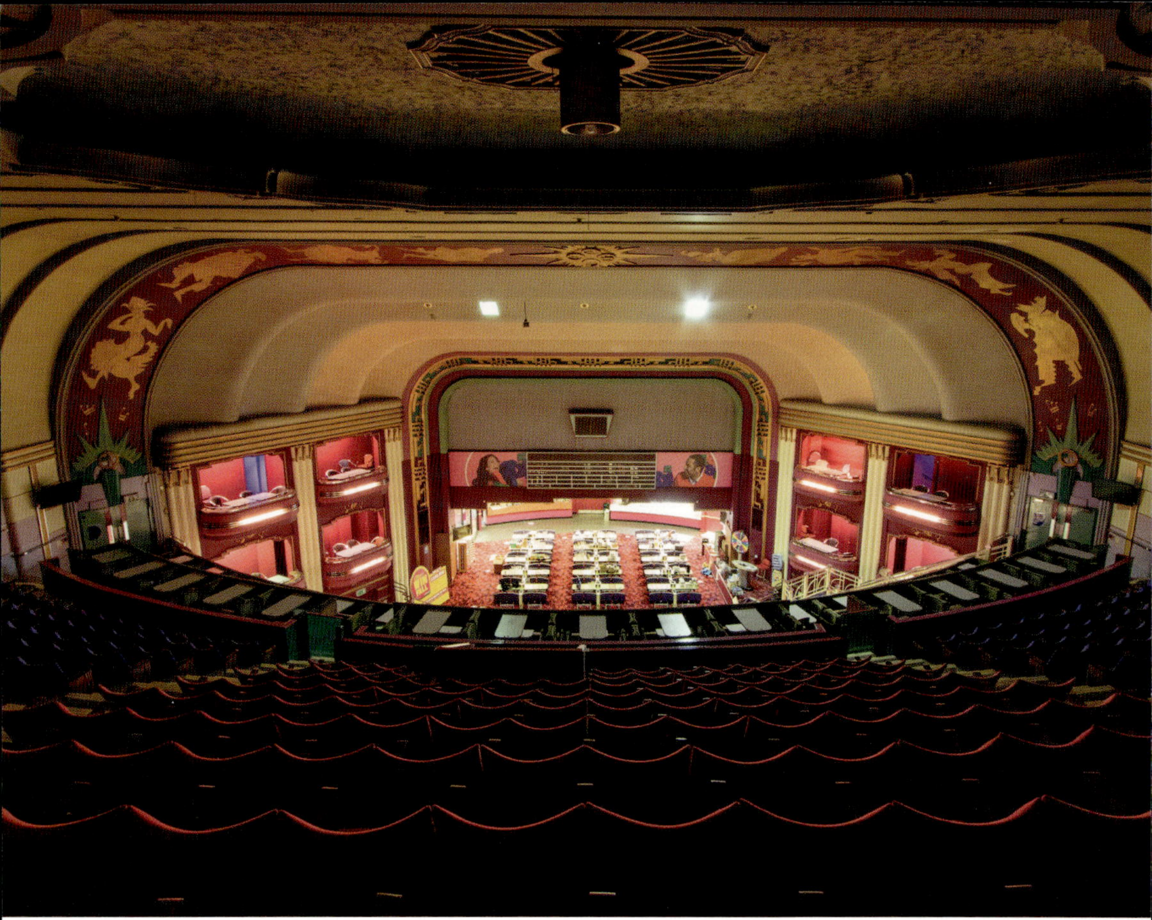

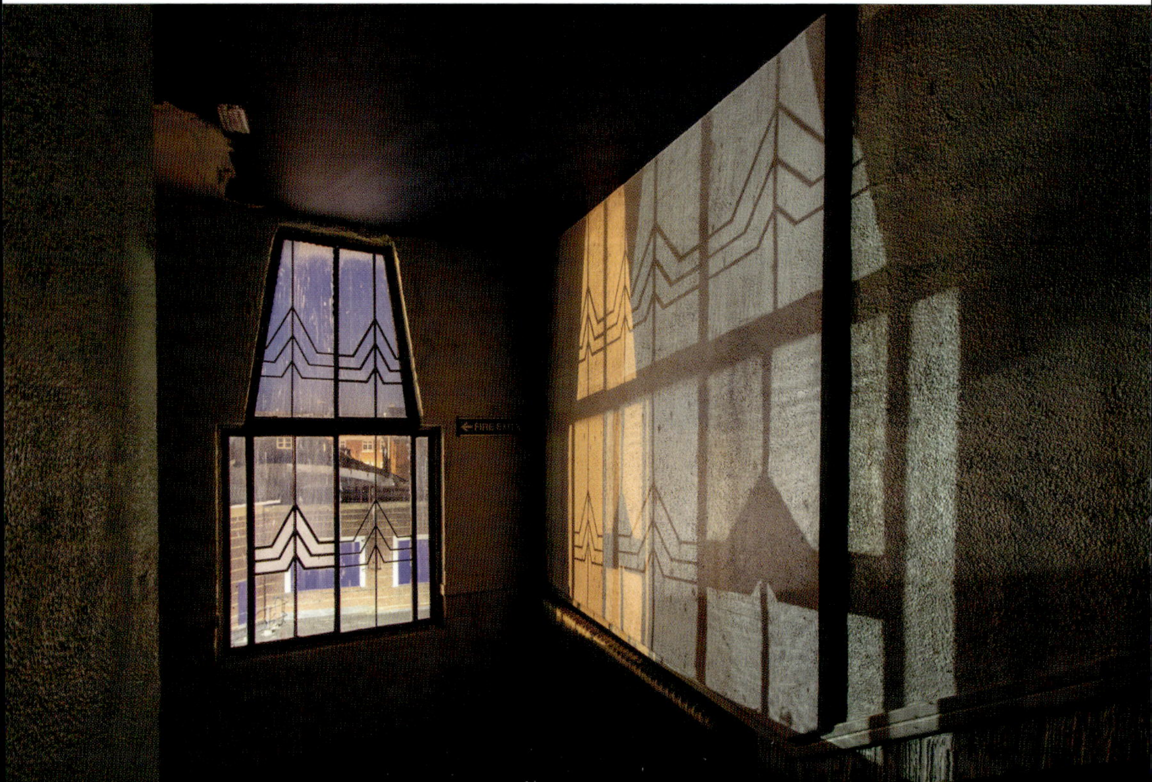

QUEENS STORES COMPANY

This historic Grade II listed building was originally constructed in 1857 for Stewart & Douglas and was designed by William Culshaw in the Baltic triangle area of Liverpool, in a once thriving industrial area. Stewart & Douglas were prominent shipowners, coopers, sail makers and chandlers, trading with Africa. This building was their head office and merchandise store.

In 1909, it was renamed Queens Store Company, trading as a ships chandlers and sail makers, and was recorded in 1919 as suppliers for the Cunard and White Star lines. In 1934 it was then sold to S. R. Manufacturing Company who made turbine bags, life belts and soaps and continued to trade as Queens Store Company.

The building closed for good sometime in the 1980s and has been left to decay ever since, awaiting its fate. (Images James Lacey)

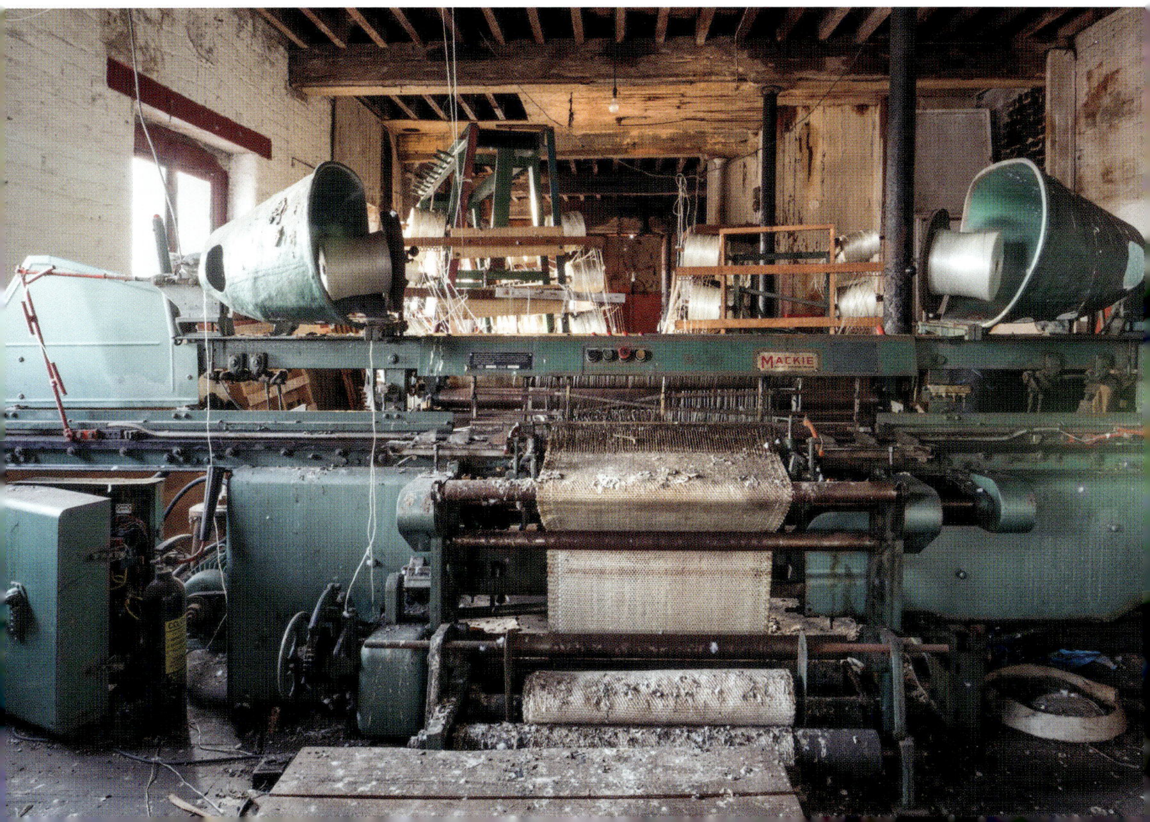

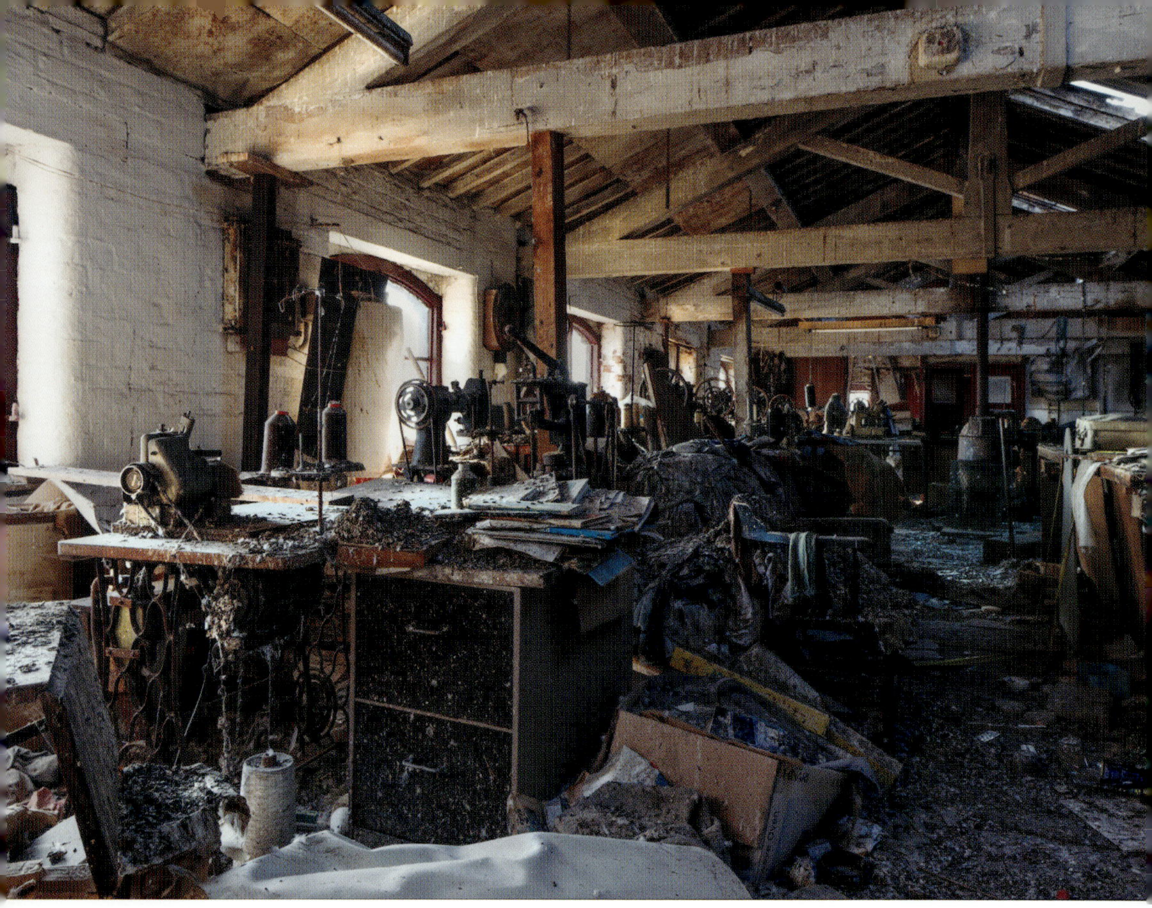

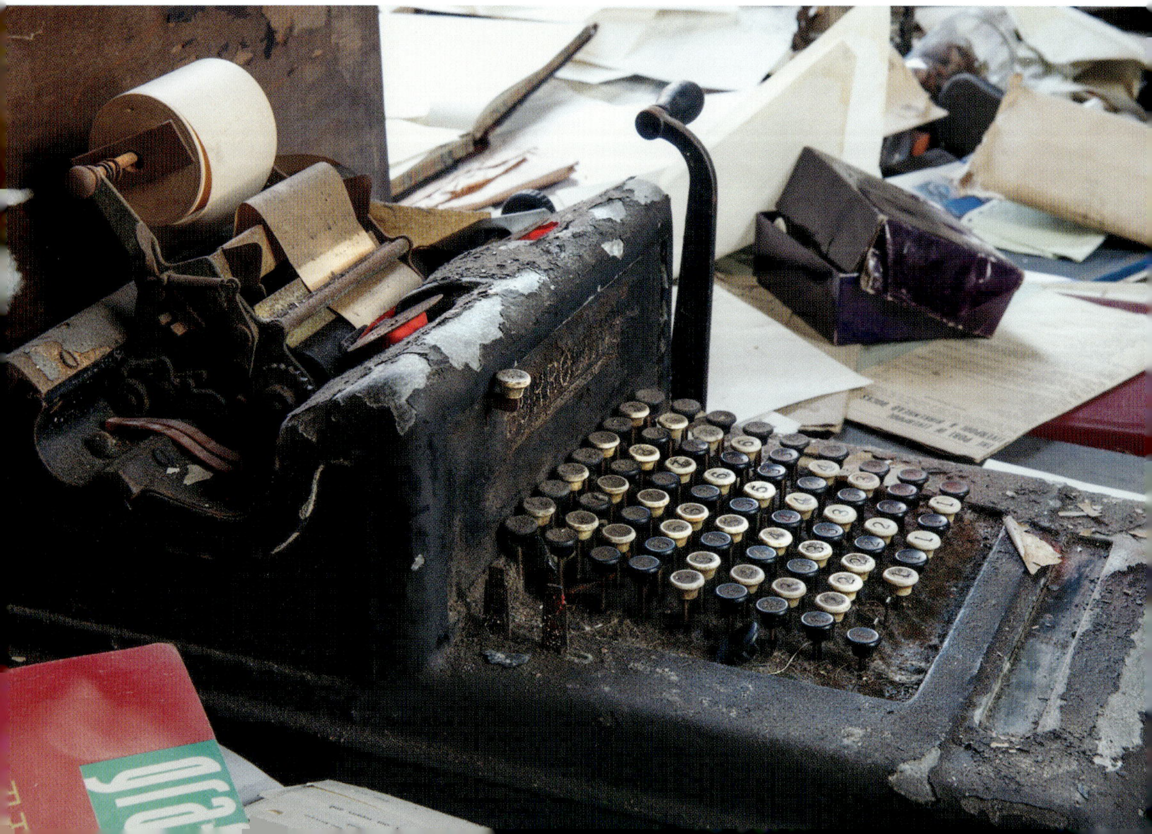

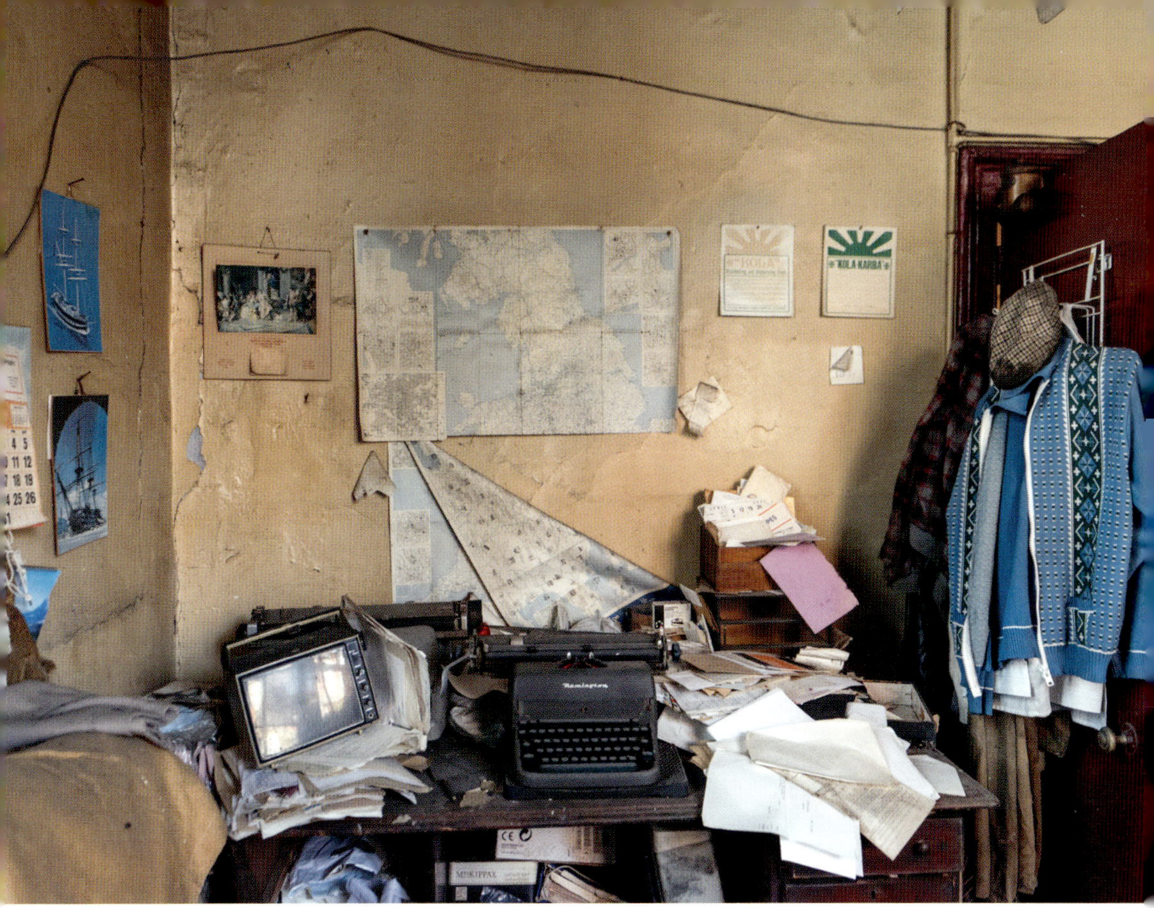
'KOLA KARBA'
Remington

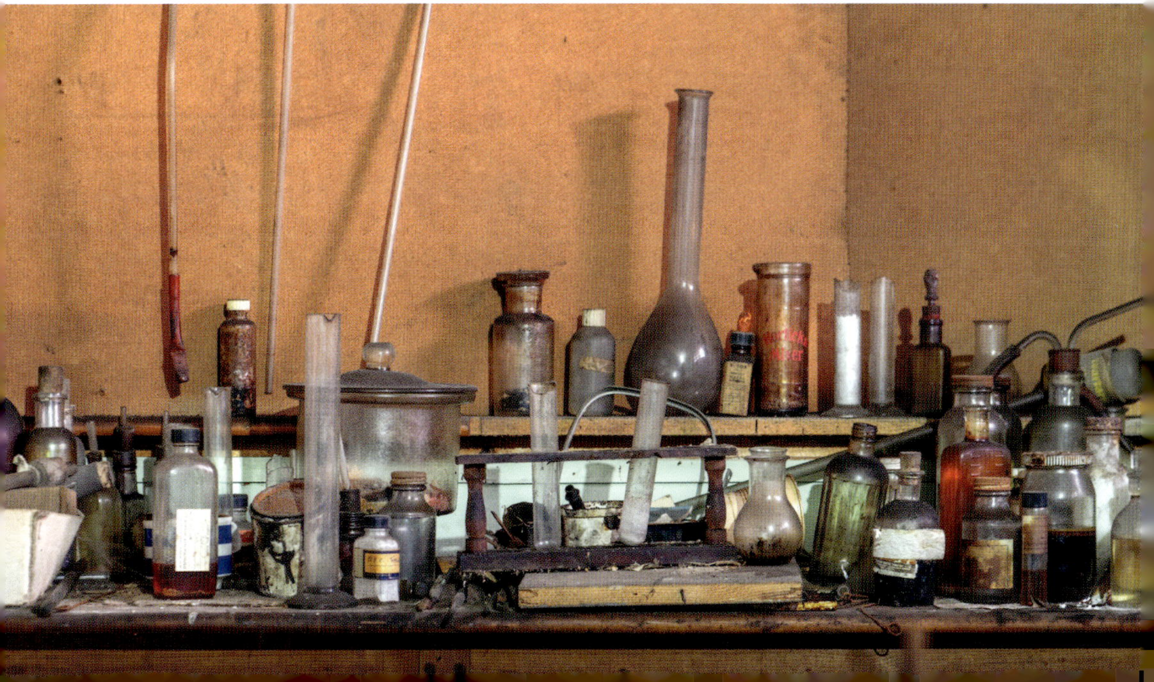

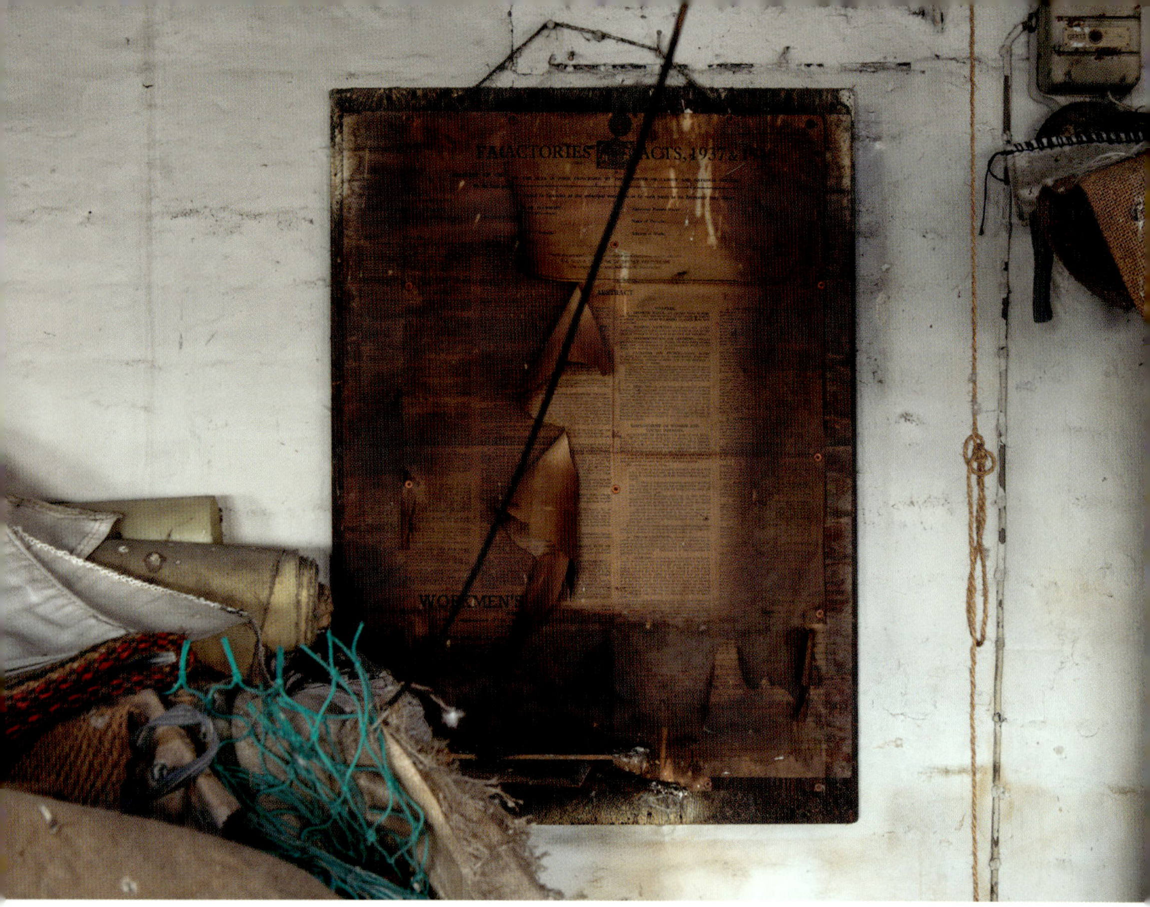

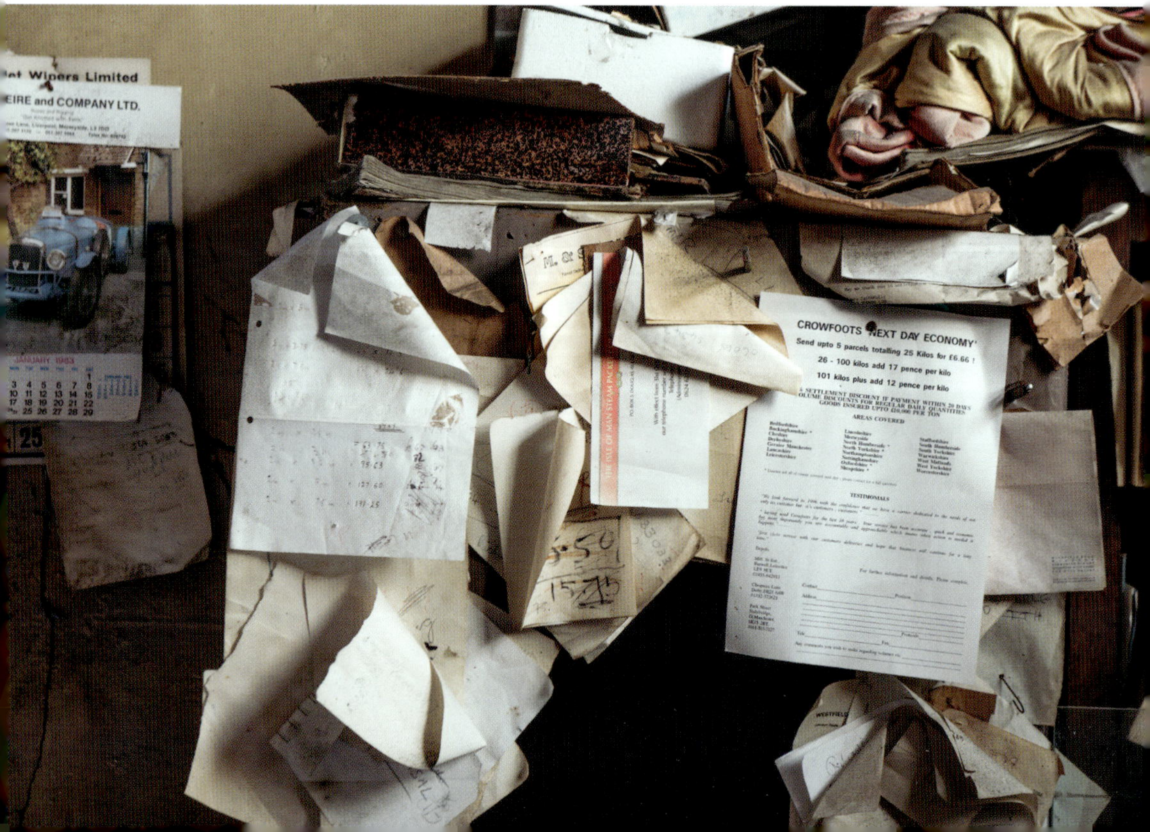
EIRE and COMPANY LTD.
JANUARY 1983
CROWFOOTS 'NEXT DAY ECONOMY'
Send upto 5 parcels totalling 25 Kilos for £6.66 !
26 - 100 kilos add 17 pence per kilo
101 kilos plus add 12 pence per kilo
AREAS COVERED
TESTIMONIALS

LISTER DRIVE LIBRARY

The library originally opened in 1905 as The Andrew Carnegie Library, taking its name after the wealthy man who donated £13,000 towards its construction. He donated the money after being impressed with the spirit of Liverpool. The library closed in 2006 and fell into disrepair.

In 2012 a group was set up to campaign for the building to be saved and used again. It eventually reopened in 2020, being run by a value-led community charity. (Images David Gooch)

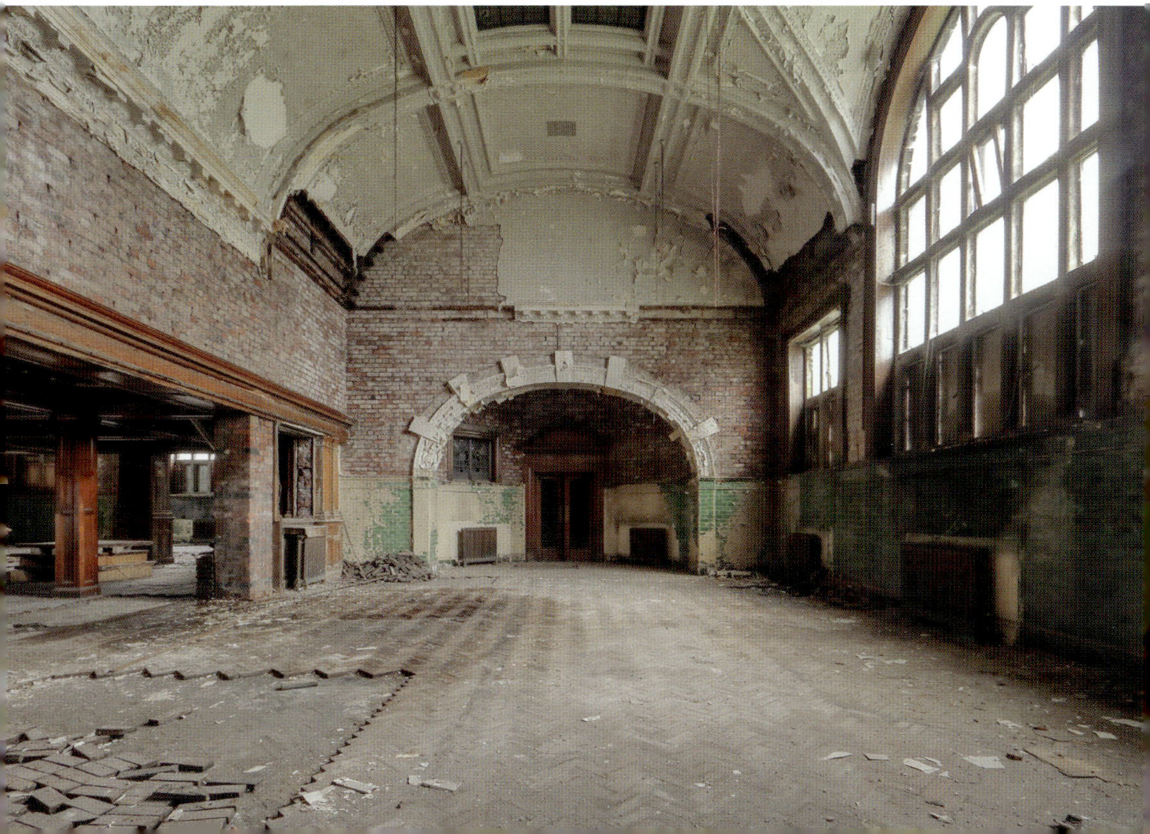

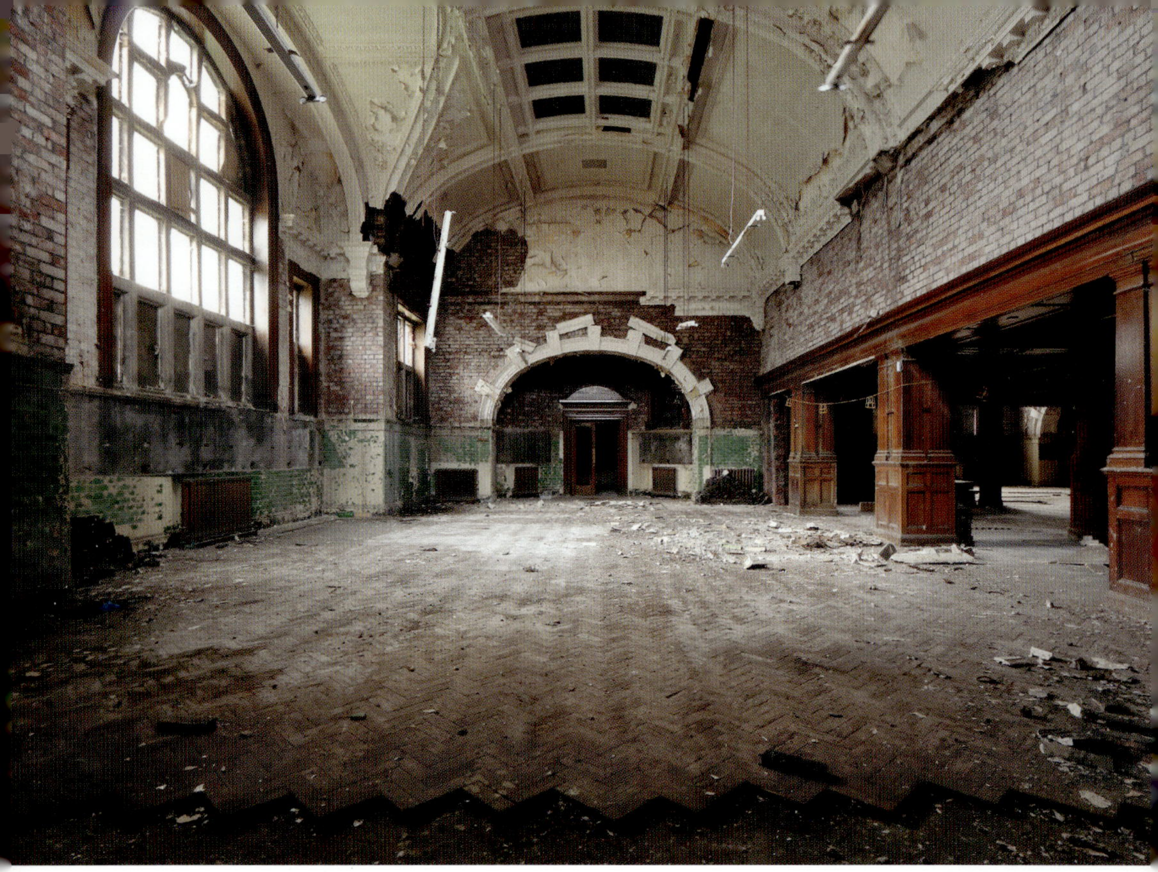

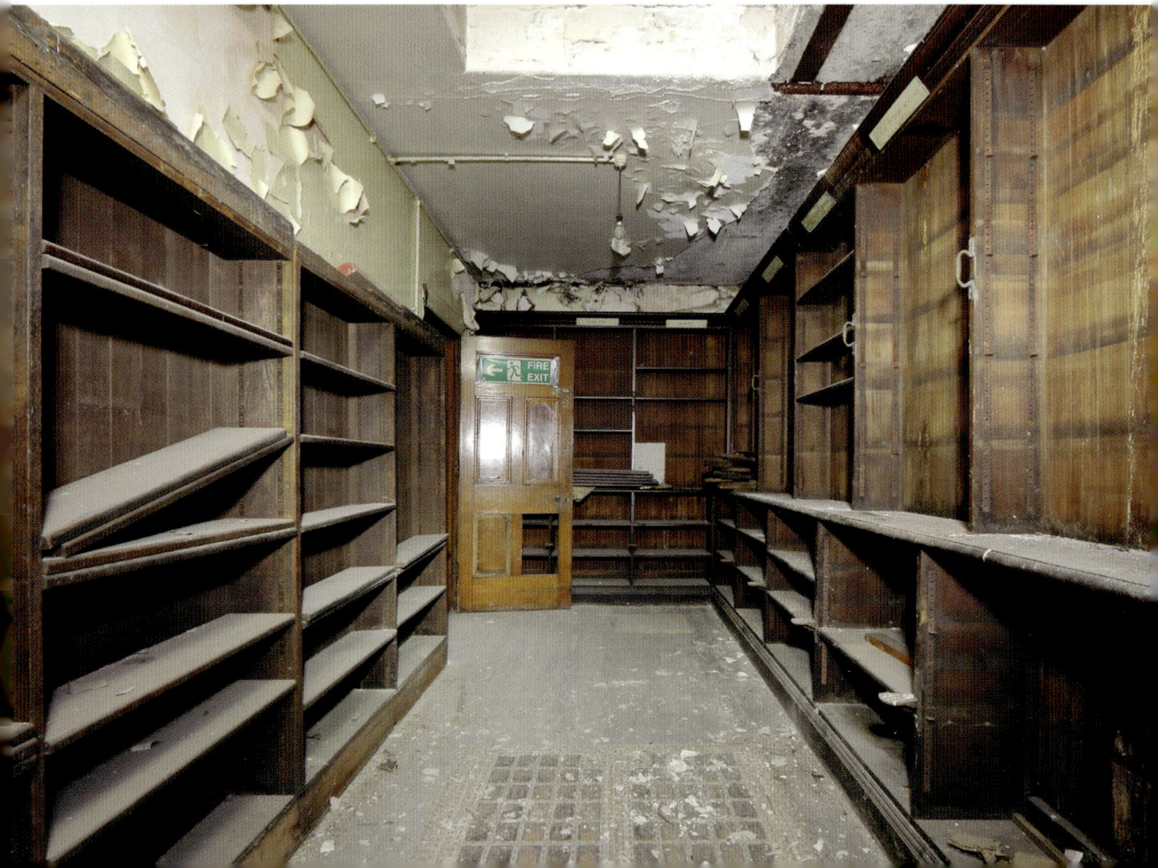
FIRE
EXIT

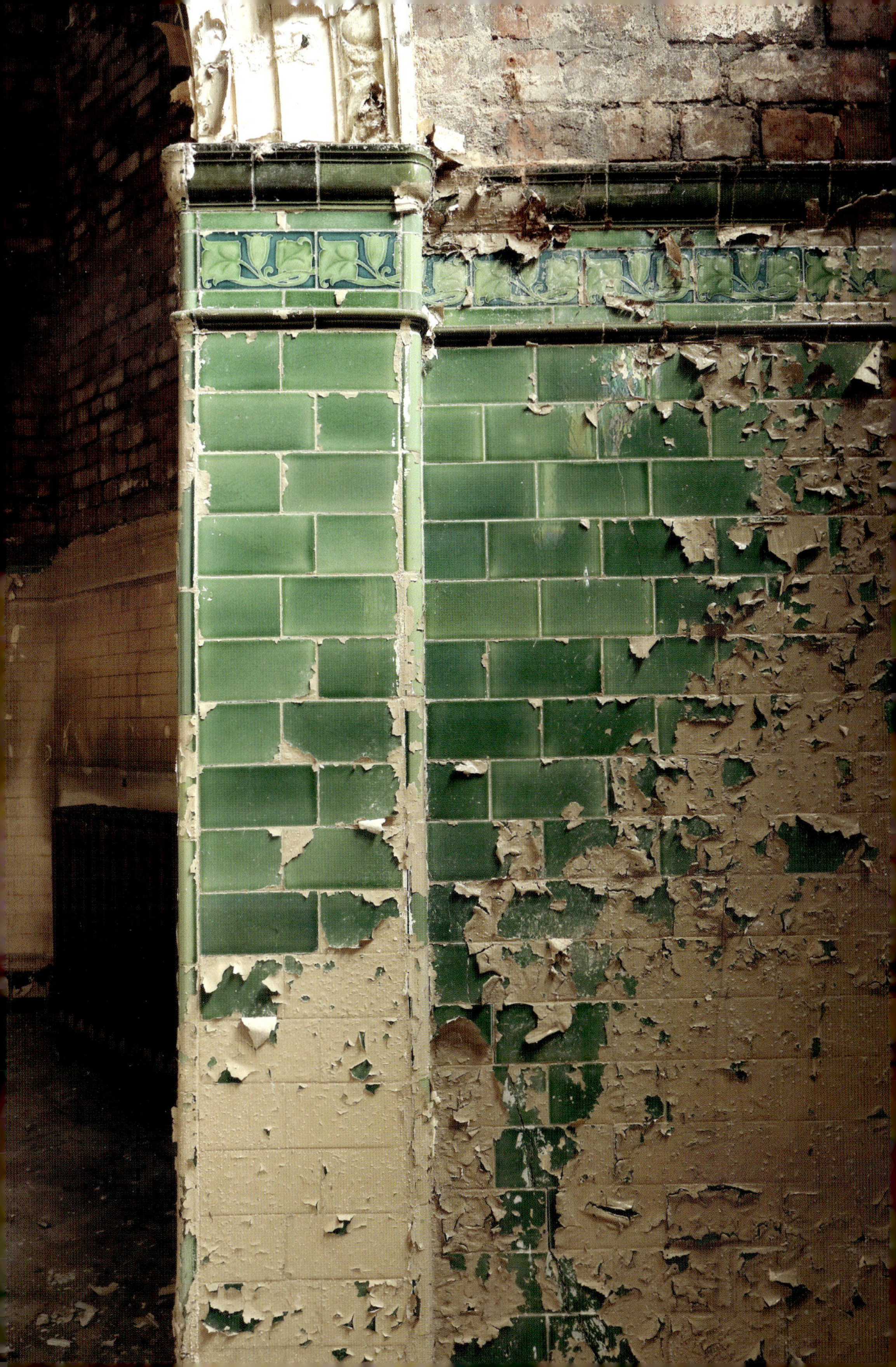

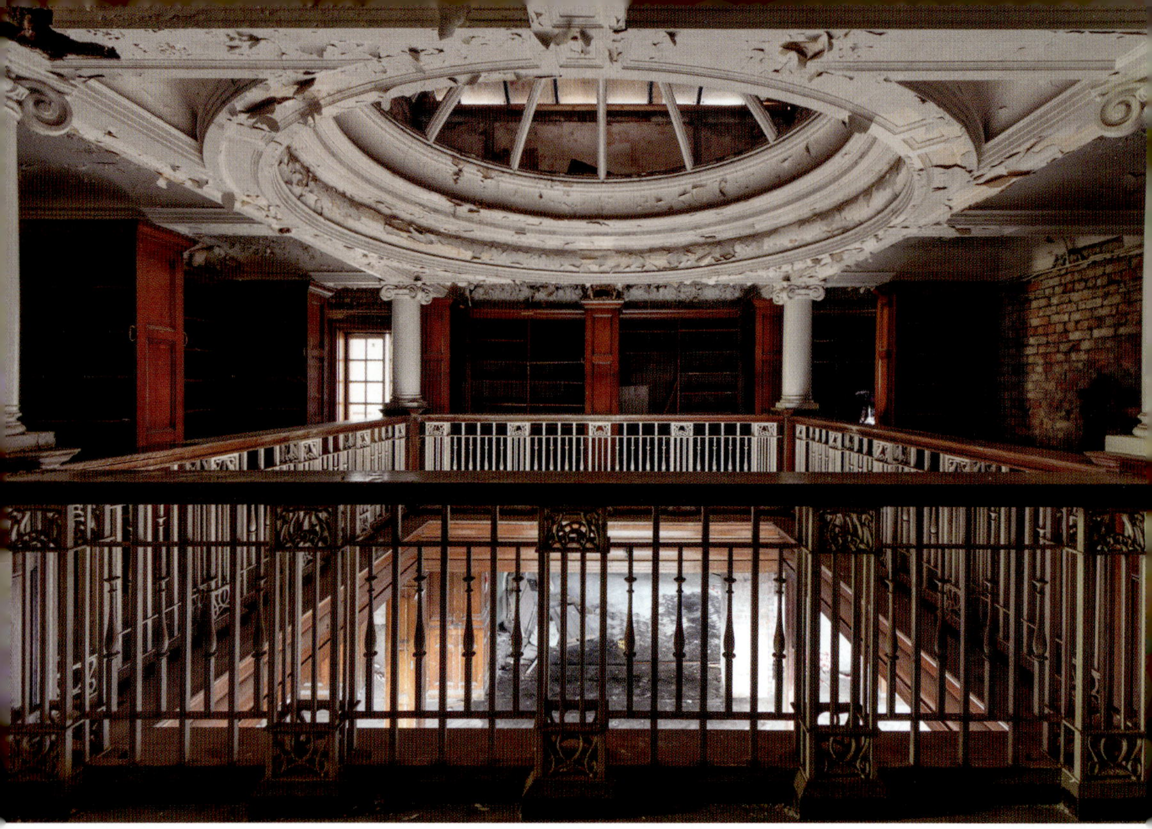

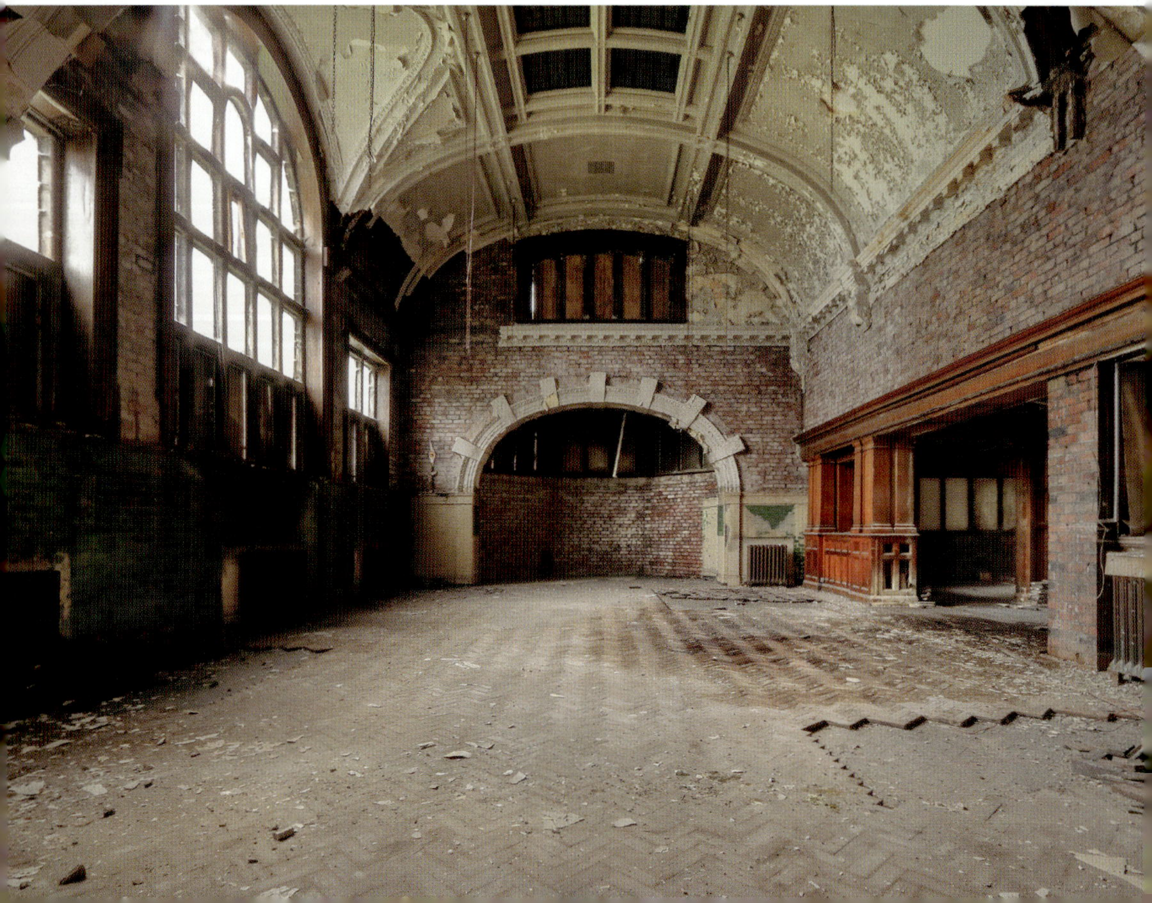

STANLEY DOCK TOBACCO WAREHOUSE

The Grade II listed Tobacco Warehouse was designed by the dock engineer A. G. Lyster. It was constructed in 1901 with a net floor area of 1.6 million square feet and built using twenty-seven million bricks. It was claimed that at the time of its construction the warehouse was the world's largest building in terms of area. The warehouse was a late addition to the Stanley Dock complex and was built on land reclaimed from the dock. The docks were at the heart of the thriving trade in Liverpool in the 1900s and connected Liverpool with far-off places around the globe, allowing the import of goods to fuel the city's economy.

With the decline of trade going through Liverpool, the warehouse fell into disuse in the 1980s and gradually into disrepair.

In 2014, Stanley Dock Properties put forward a proposal for the warehouse to be converted into 550 apartments accompanied by businesses, cafes and retail outlets on the ground floor. Between 2015 and 2021 Tobacco Warehouse was redeveloped into several hundred apartments as part of a larger development of the whole Stanley Dock site. The plans involved hollowing out the centre of the warehouse to create a garden-filled courtyard and the building welcomed its first residents in 2021 into their Manhattan-style apartments, with artwork of The Beatles being utilised as part of the interior designs of the rooms. (Images James Lacey)

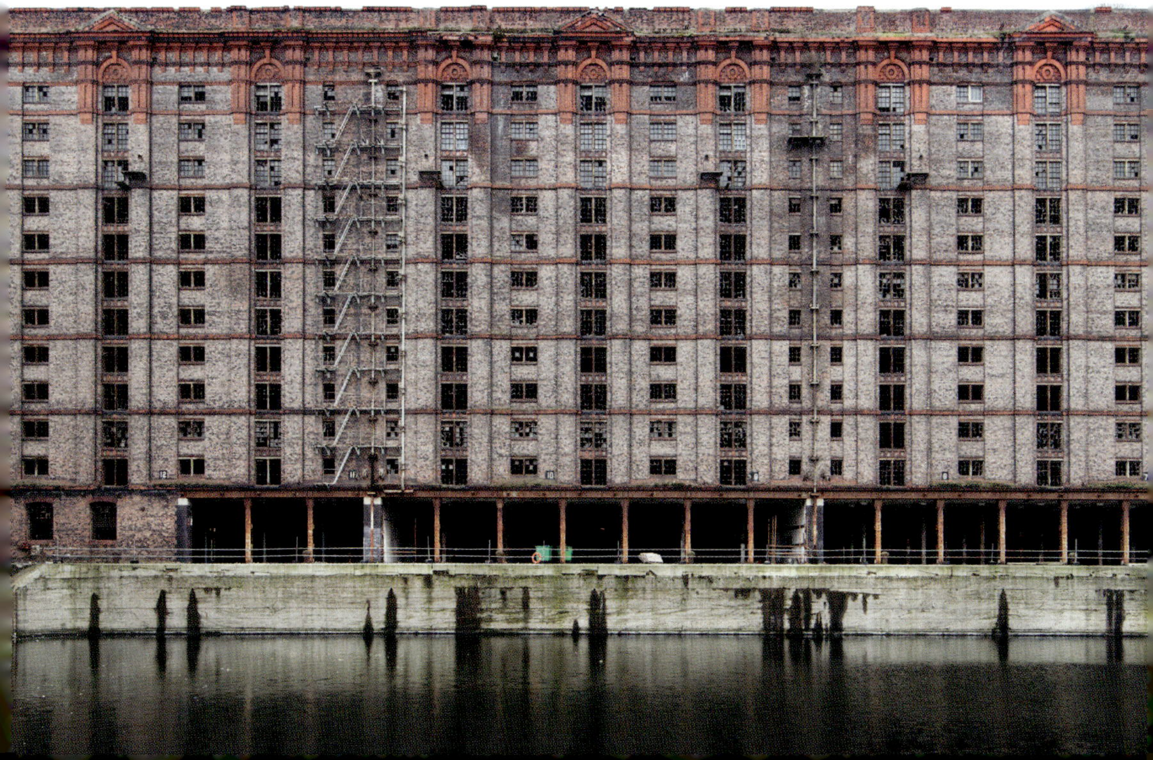

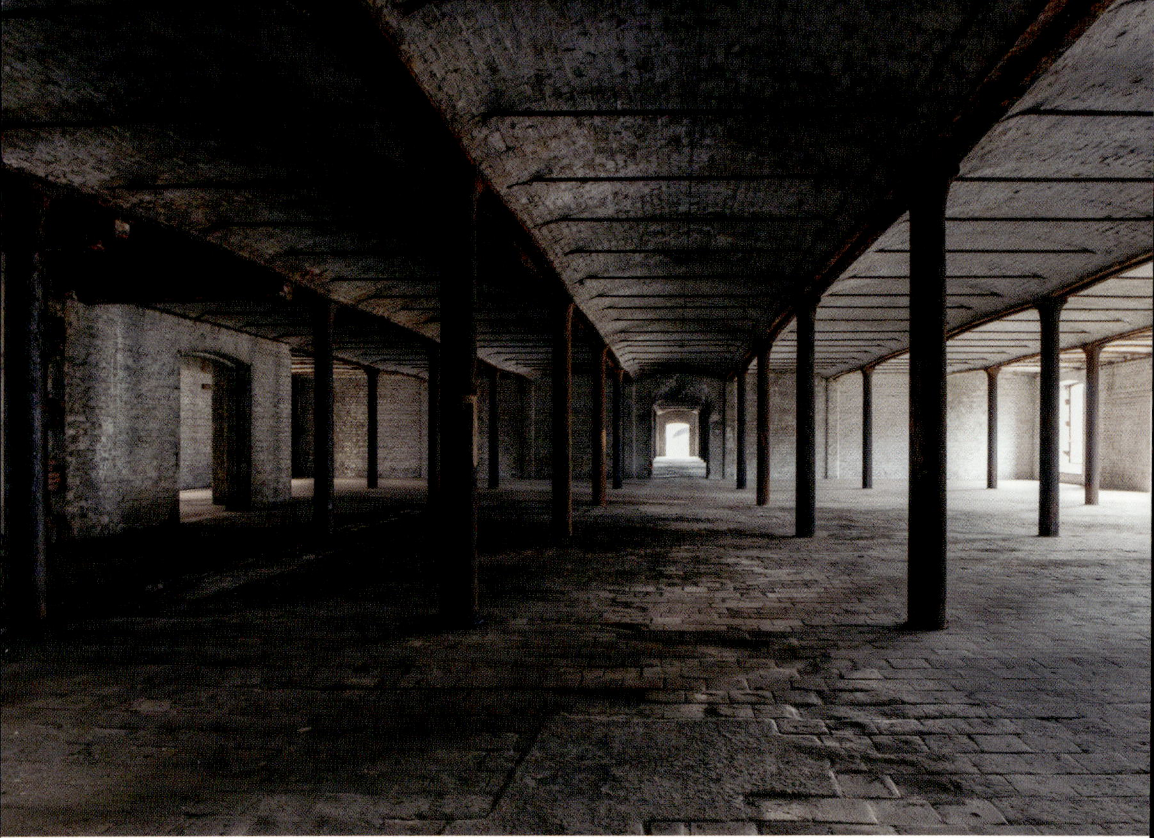

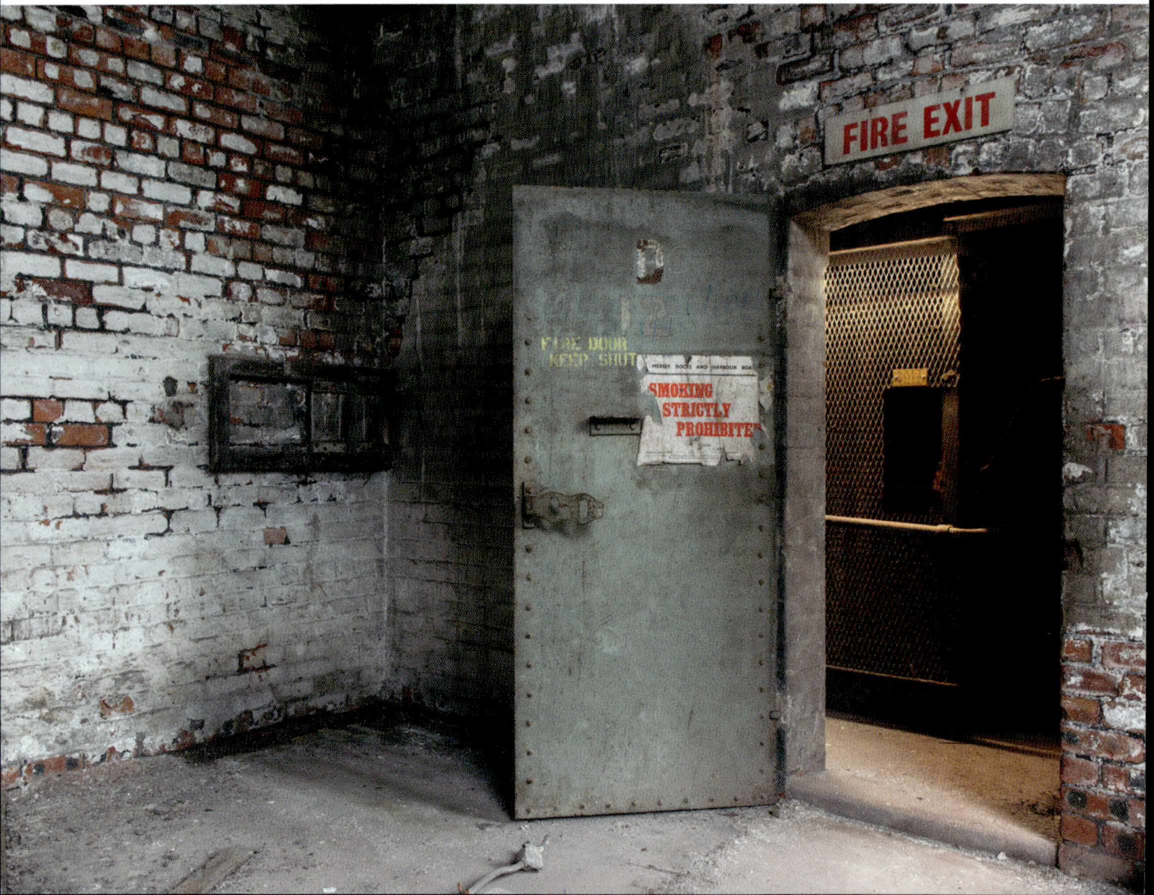
FIRE EXIT
FIRE DOOR
KEEP SHUT
SMOKING
STRICTLY

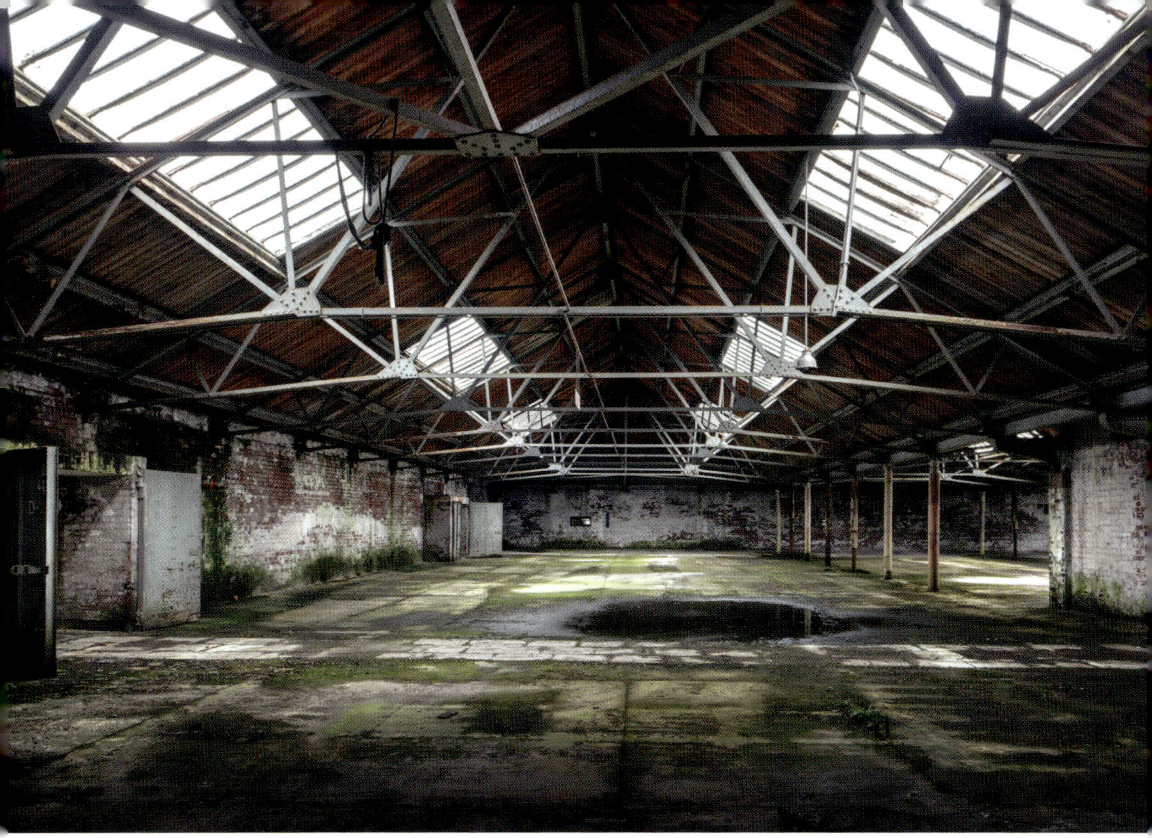

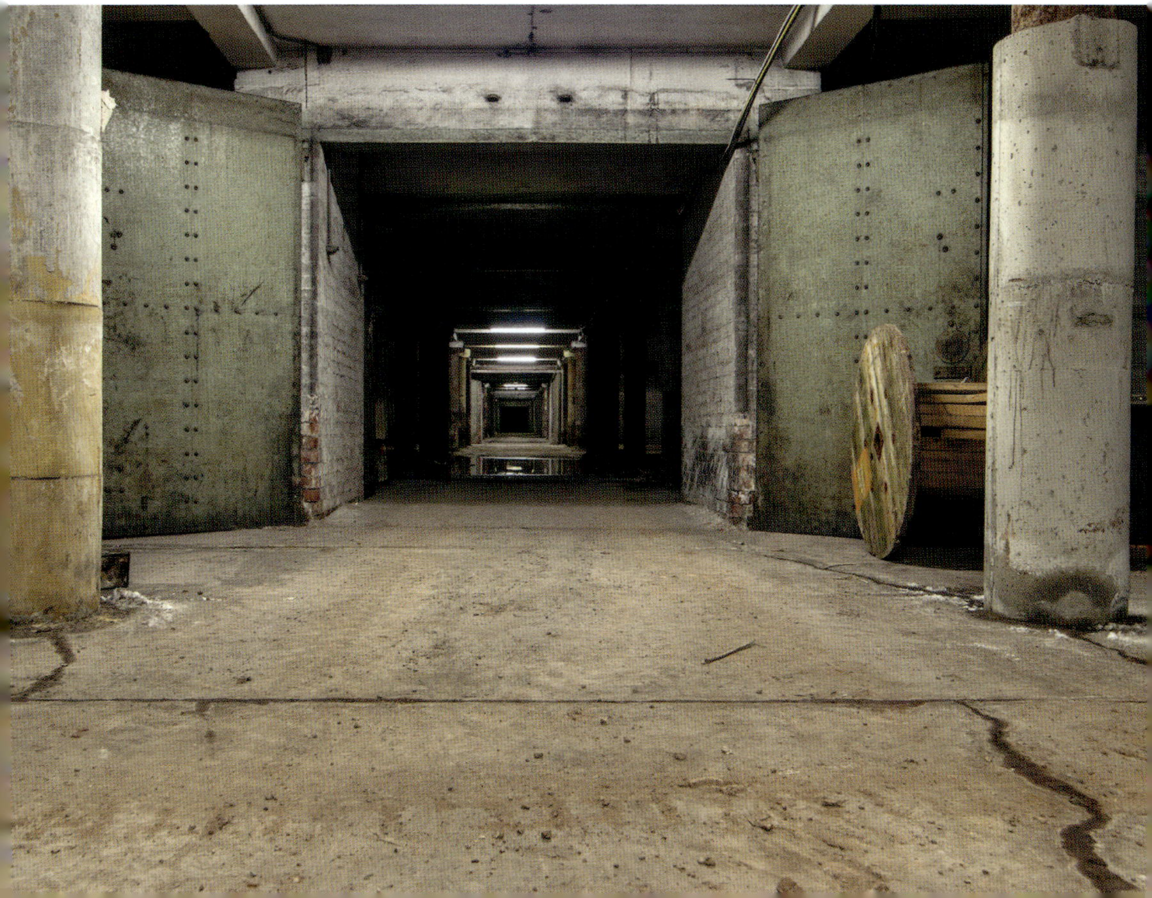

ALDER HEY CHILDREN'S HOSPITAL

Alder Hey was originally used as a military hospital by the Americans in 1914, during the First World War. During the Second World War, parts of the hospital were again used to treat the injured men of conflict.

In 1990 Myrtle Street children's hospital was closed in the city and the A&E unit was absorbed by Alder Hey. After 100 years of use, the old hospital closed its doors and was replaced with a new purpose-built hospital nearby. The original hospital buildings were mostly demolished, and the area turned into parkland for the local community. Alder Hey is one of the largest children's hospitals in the UK. (Images David Gooch)

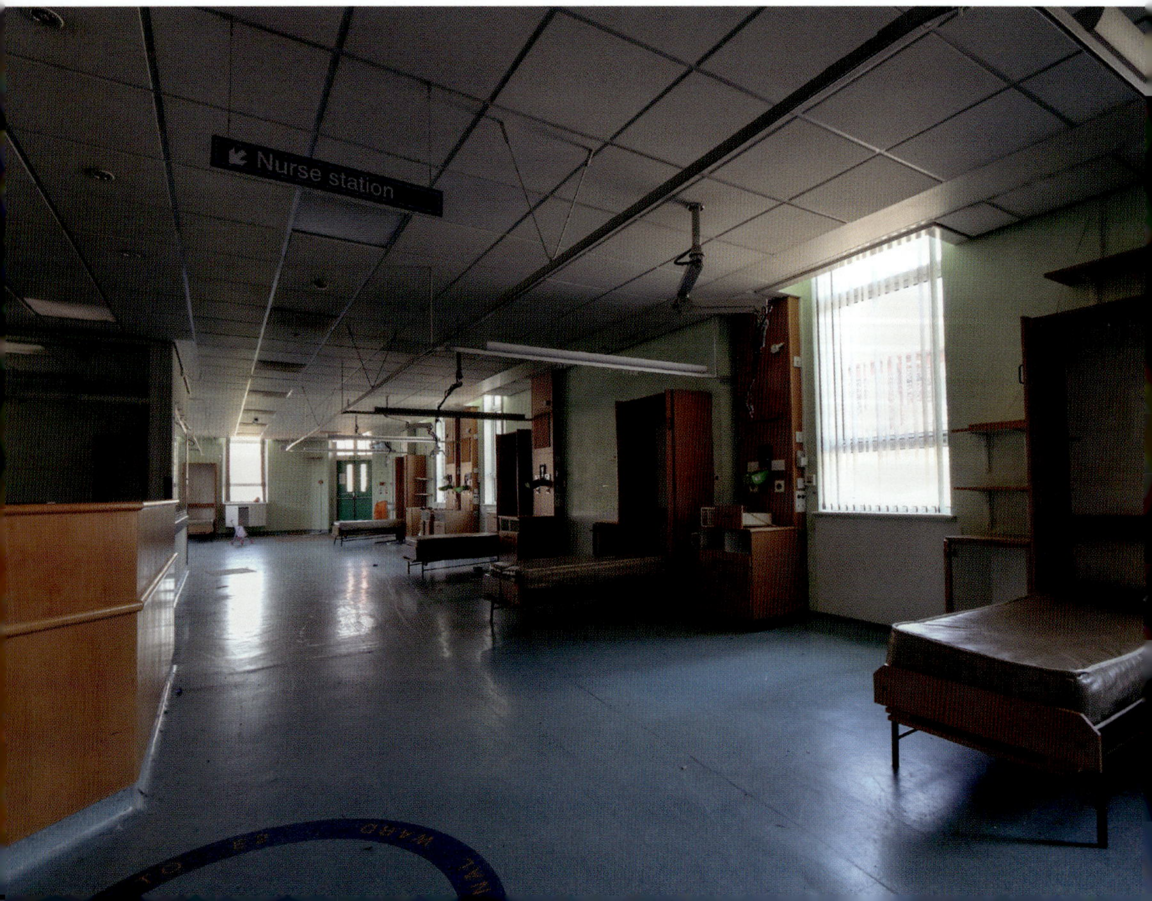

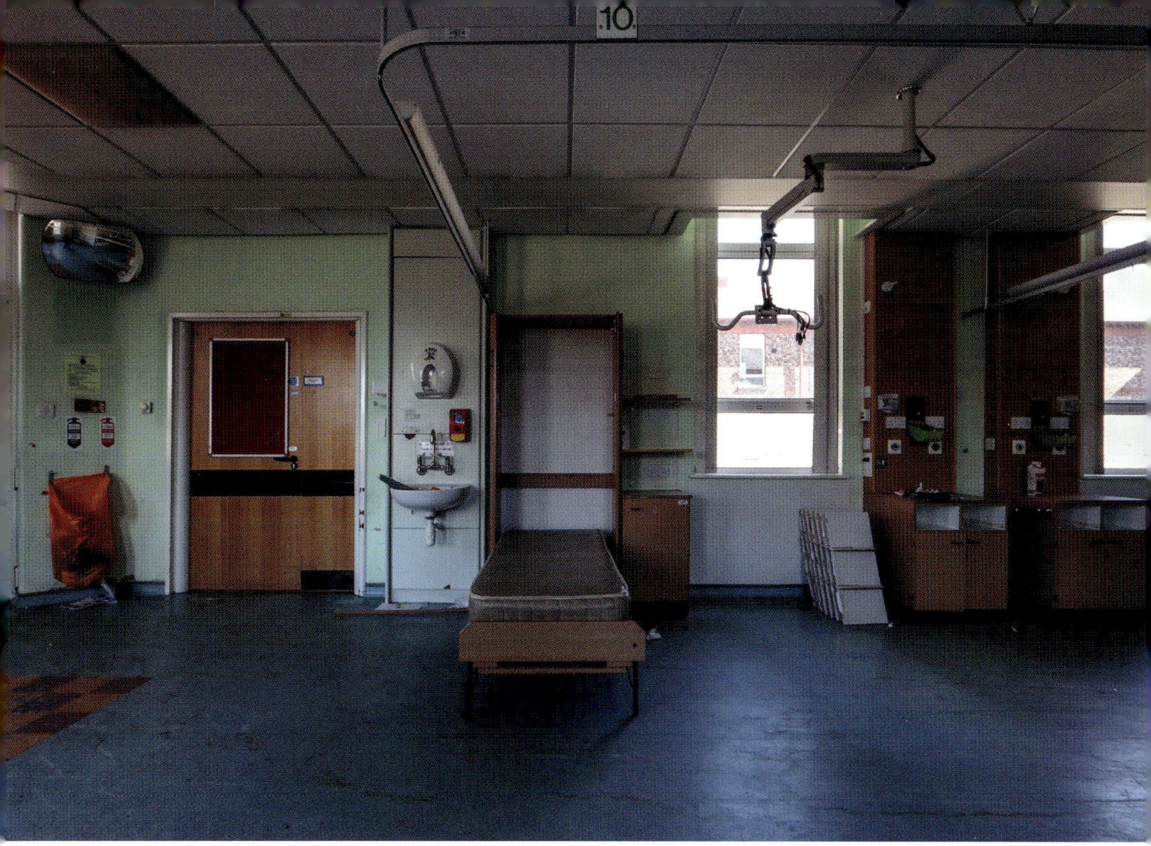
10

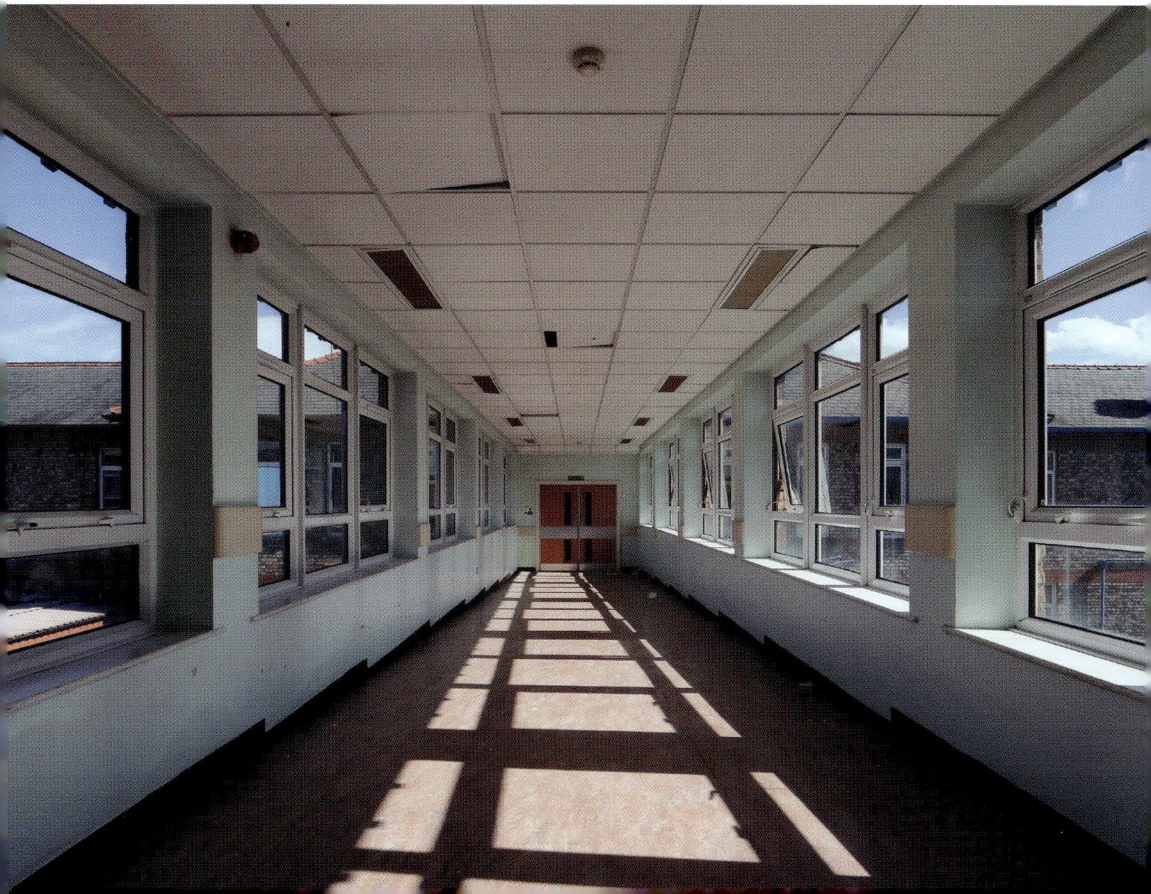

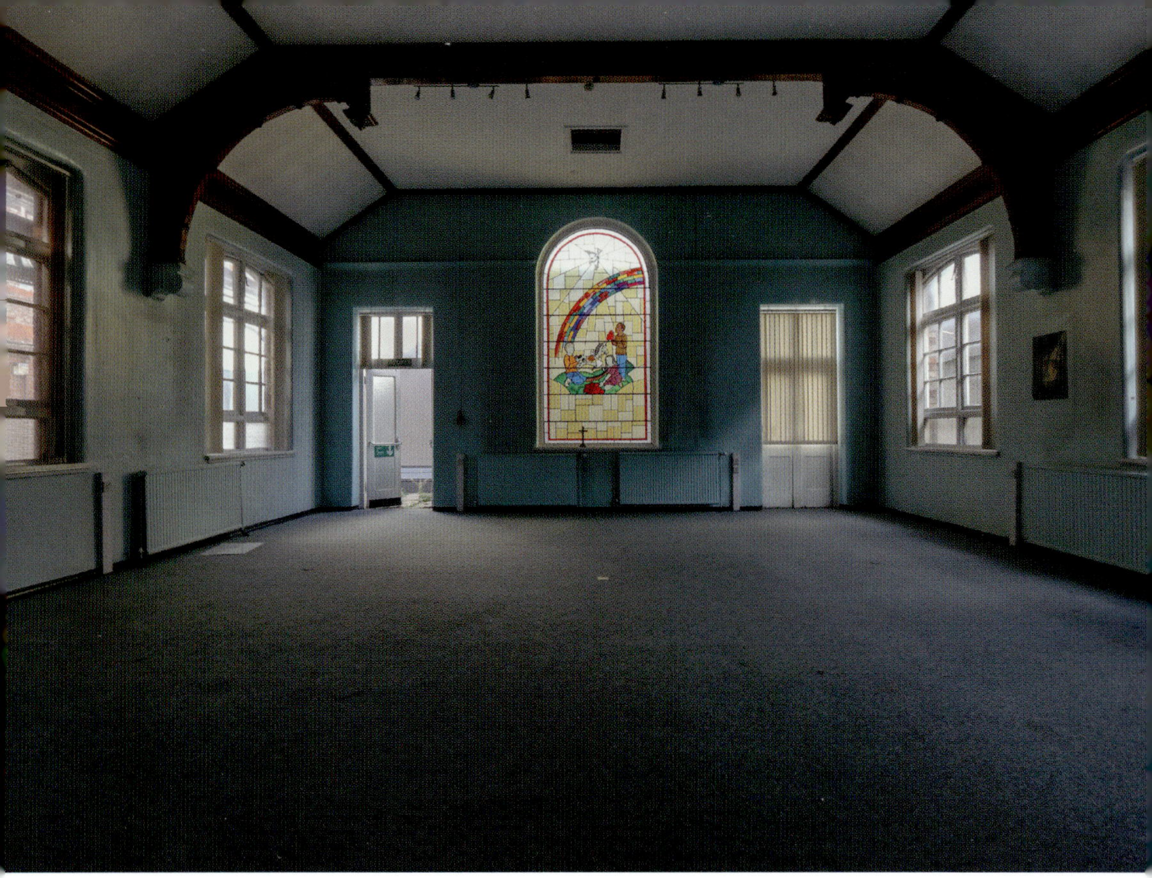

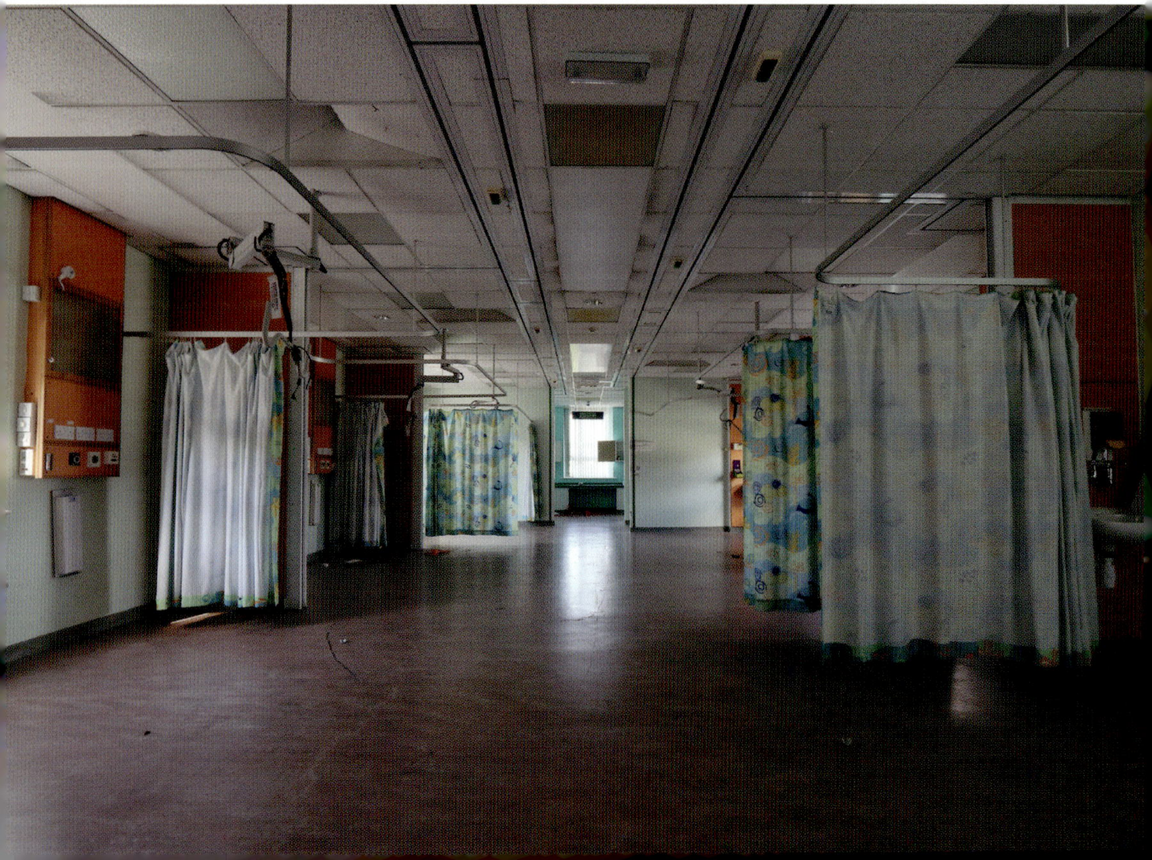

LIME STREET ABC CINEMA

Originally named The Forum, the cinema opened in May 1931, showing Clifford Mollison in *Almost a Honeymoon*, at a cost of £200,000 for an audience of 1,835. Because of the restricted width of the site, the capacity was achieved by having a huge circle containing 750 of the seats.

Being six storeys tall and made of Portland stone, the building is a prominent feature of Lime Street. It was renamed ABC (Associated British Cinemas) in 1971 and remained this way until 1982 when it was converted into a three-screen location. In 1986 it was renamed Cannon until it closed in 1998 with a special screening of *Casablanca*.

There have been several proposals for renovation over the last few years, but none have seen the light of day, and this historic Grade II listed building remains empty and in a perilous state of decay. (Images James Lacey)

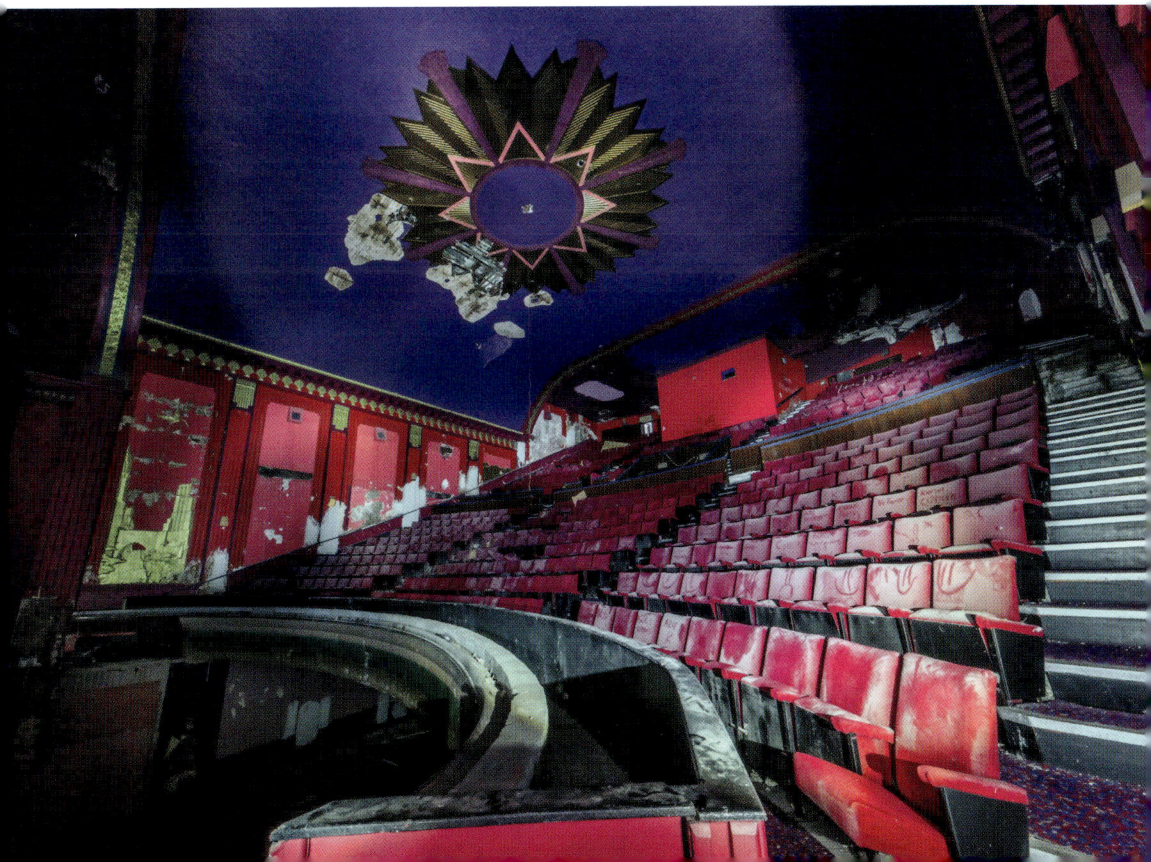

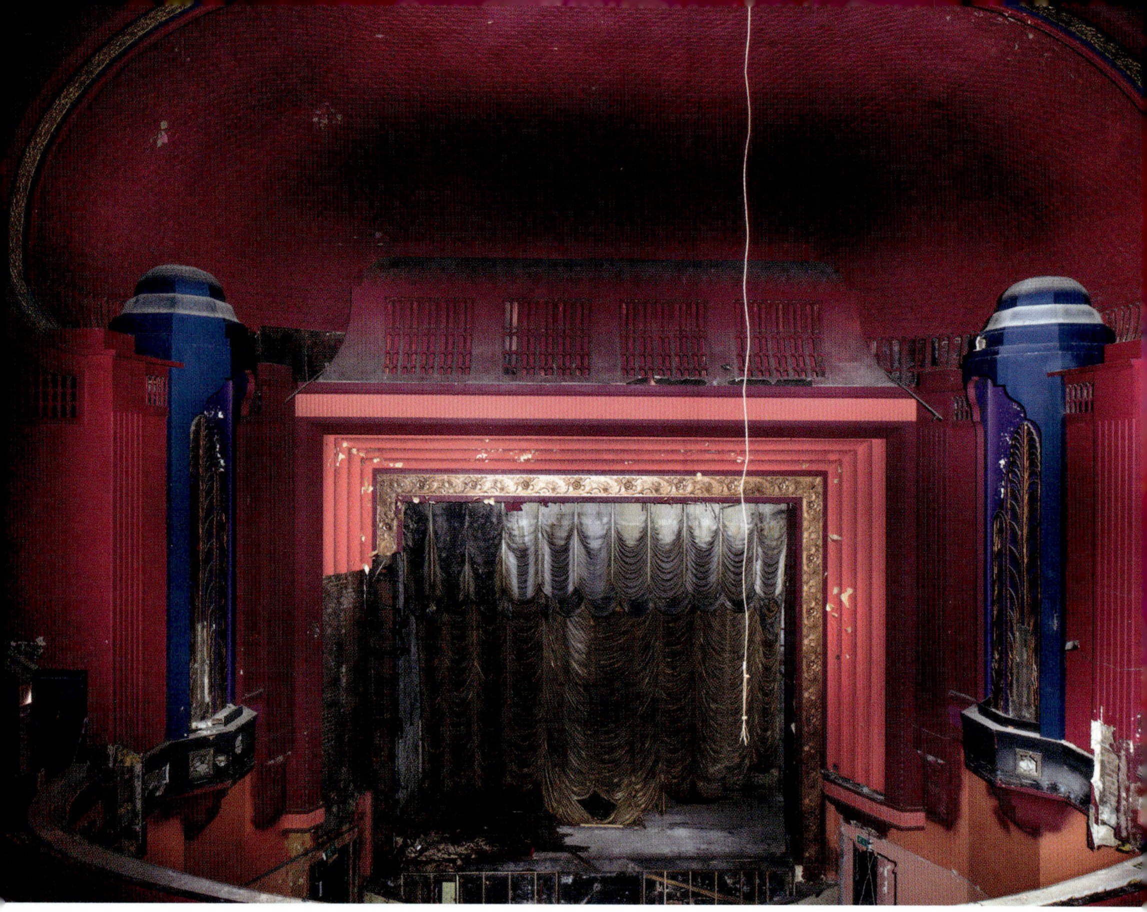

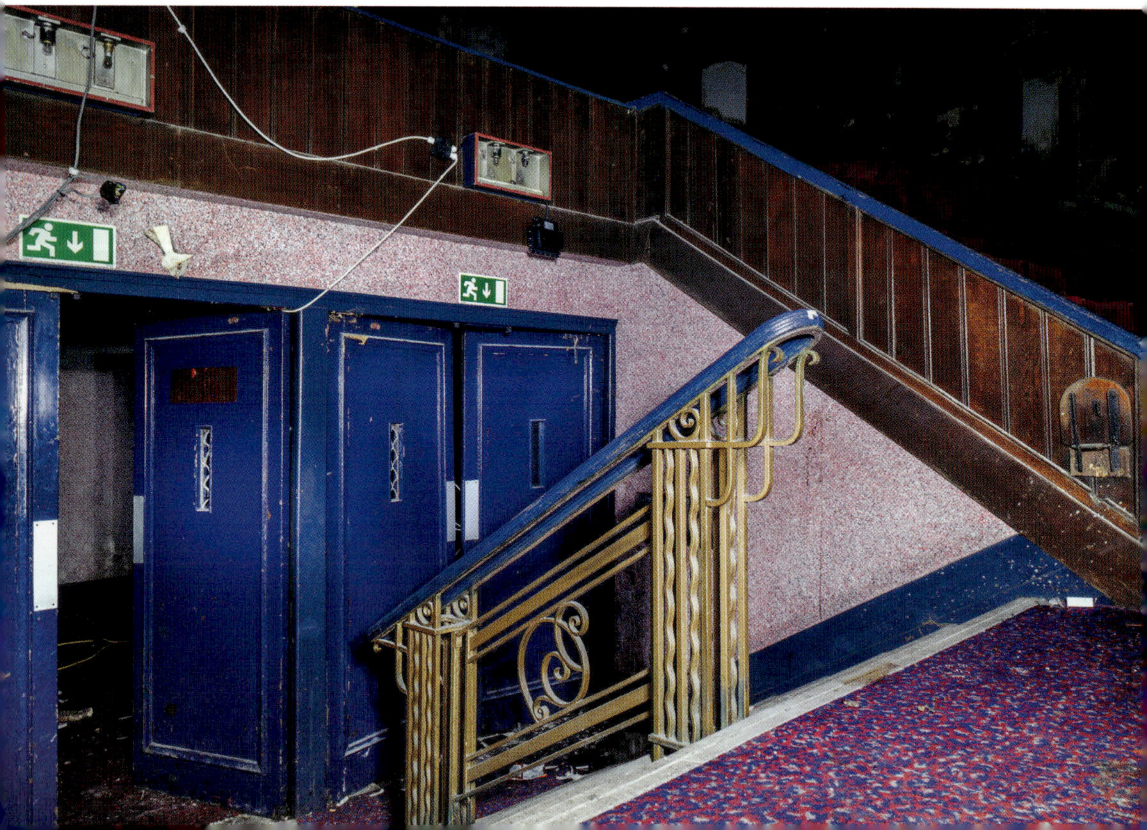

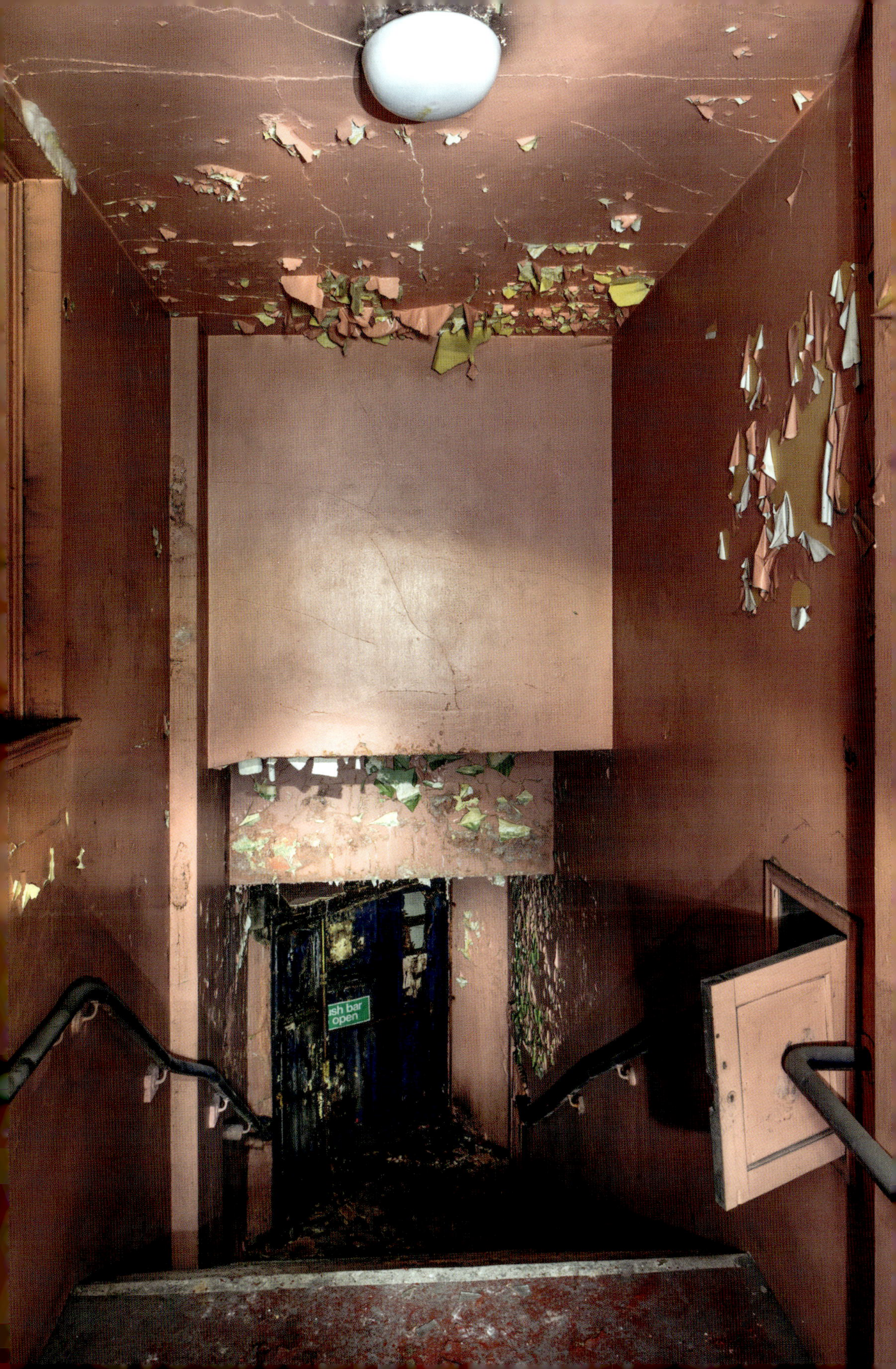
ush bar
open

LITTLEWOODS BUILDING AND AIR-RAID CENTRE

Littlewoods Pools was founded in Liverpool by John Moores in 1923. With the rapid expansion of the company in the early 1930s, a purpose-built space was needed. The art deco Littlewoods Pools Building opened in 1938 as the headquarters of the company. During the years of the war the building was used as the government's censorship department. The printing machines normally used for the thousands of coupons each week were switched to printing seventeen million call-up papers. The building was used until 1994 when there was a decline in playing pools.

The air-raid shelter was built along the eastern edge of Wavertree Park at the Littlewoods site in Edge Hill, parallel to the factory, with several entrances to aid in a speedy access by the staff. During the Second World War, factories would have an external shelter to protect from a collapsing building if bombed. Liverpool was the second most bombed part of the UK after London. What adds poignancy to the shelter are the portraits which are still visible – albeit faded by time – on the walls, possibly drawn by a single person and were most probably depictions of co-workers as they waited in the shelter for the bombing to stop. The bunkers are around 300 metres in length. (Images David Gooch)

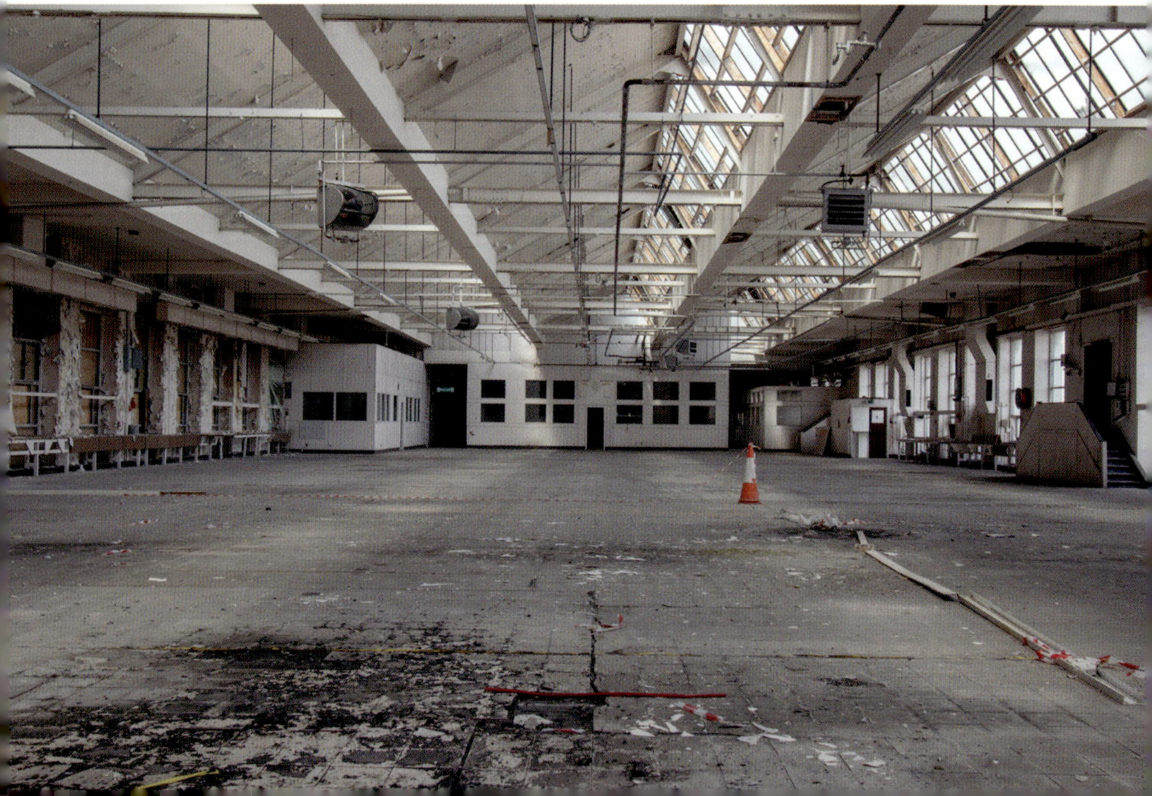

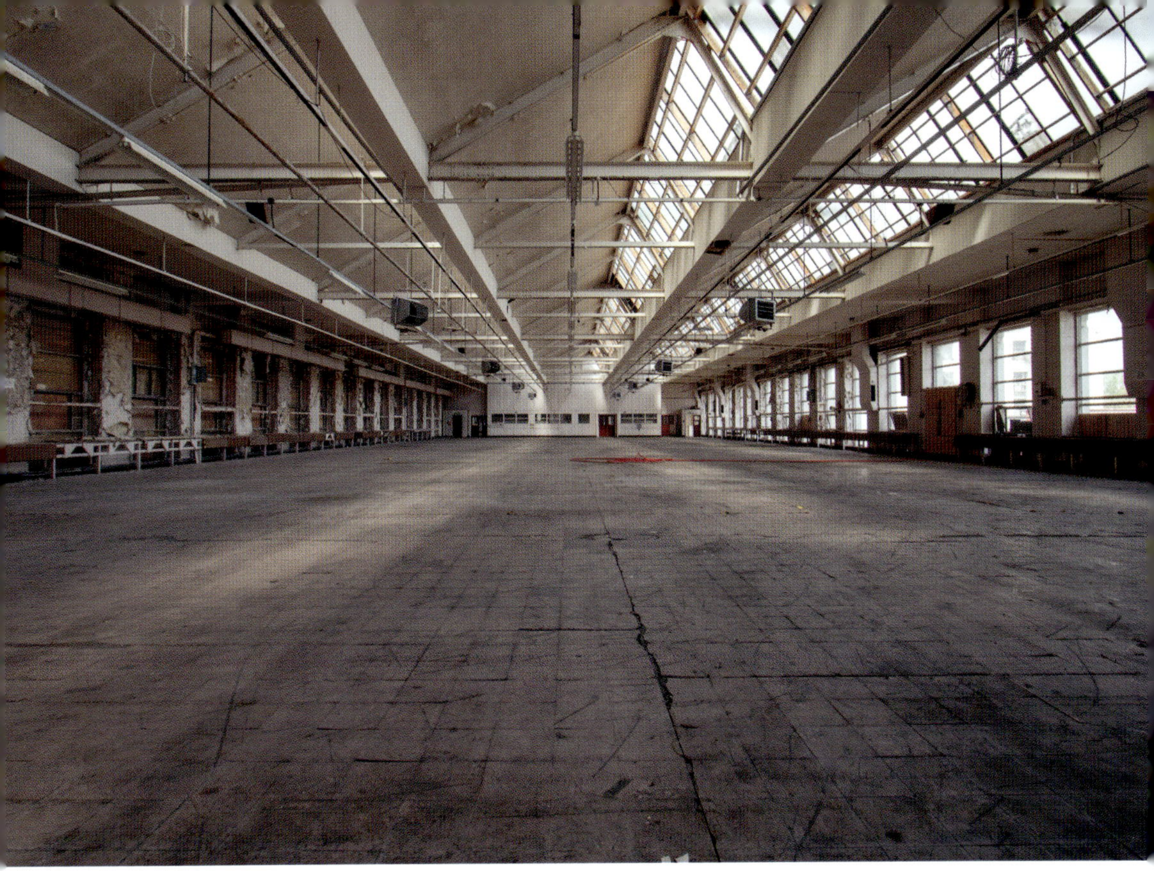

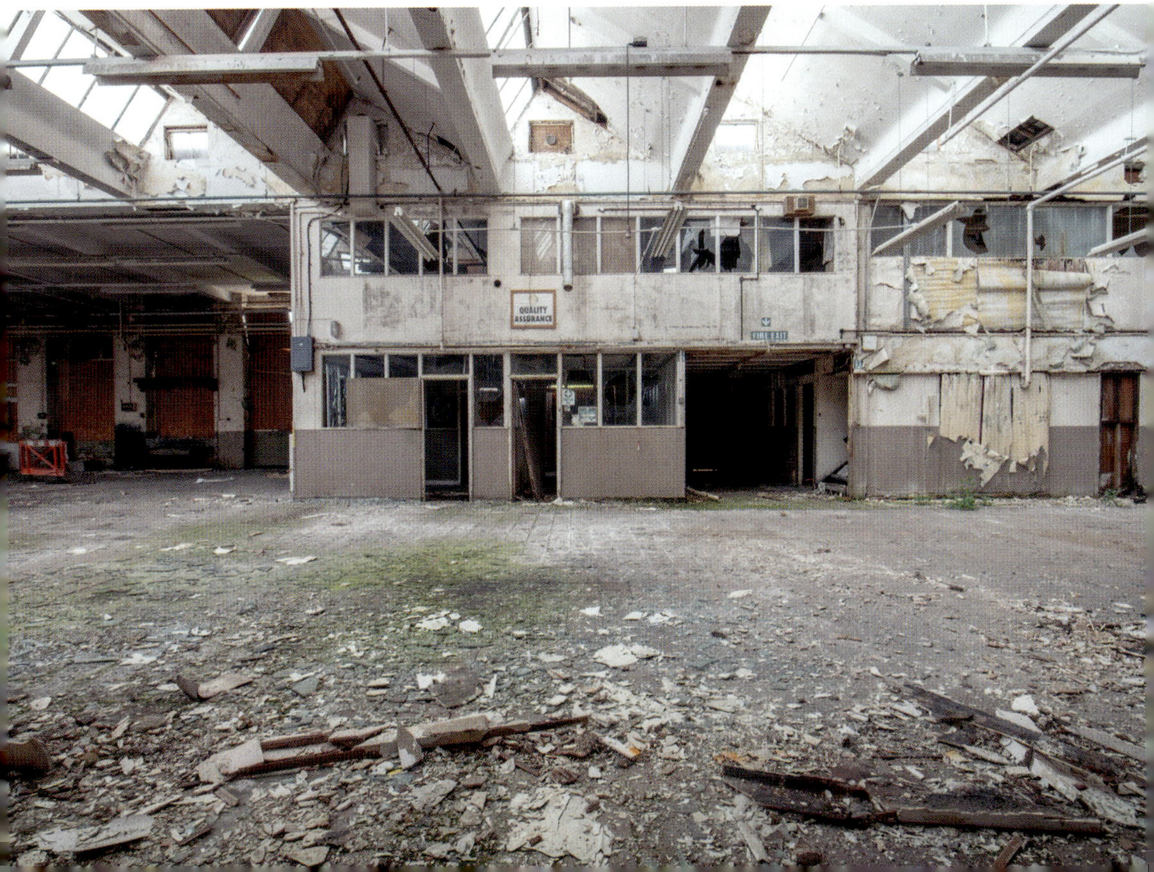
QUALITY
ASSURANCE

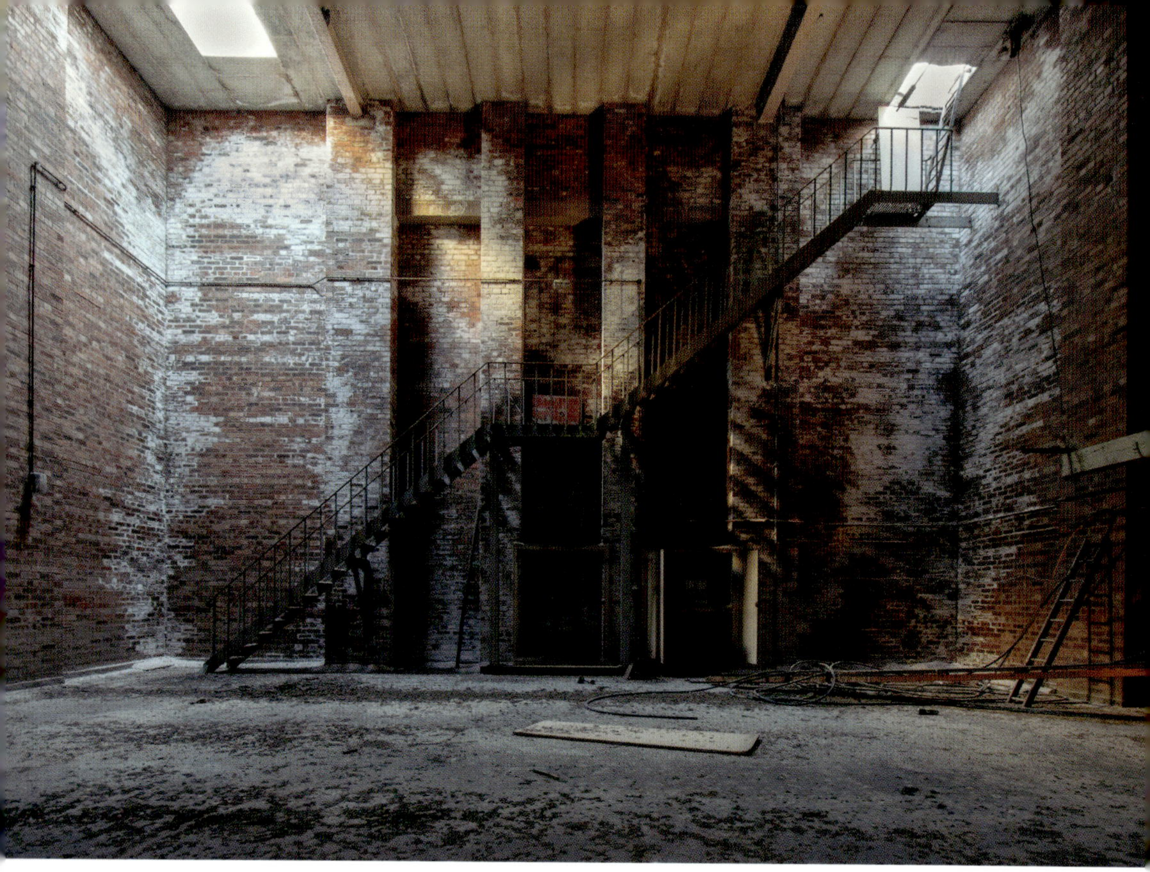

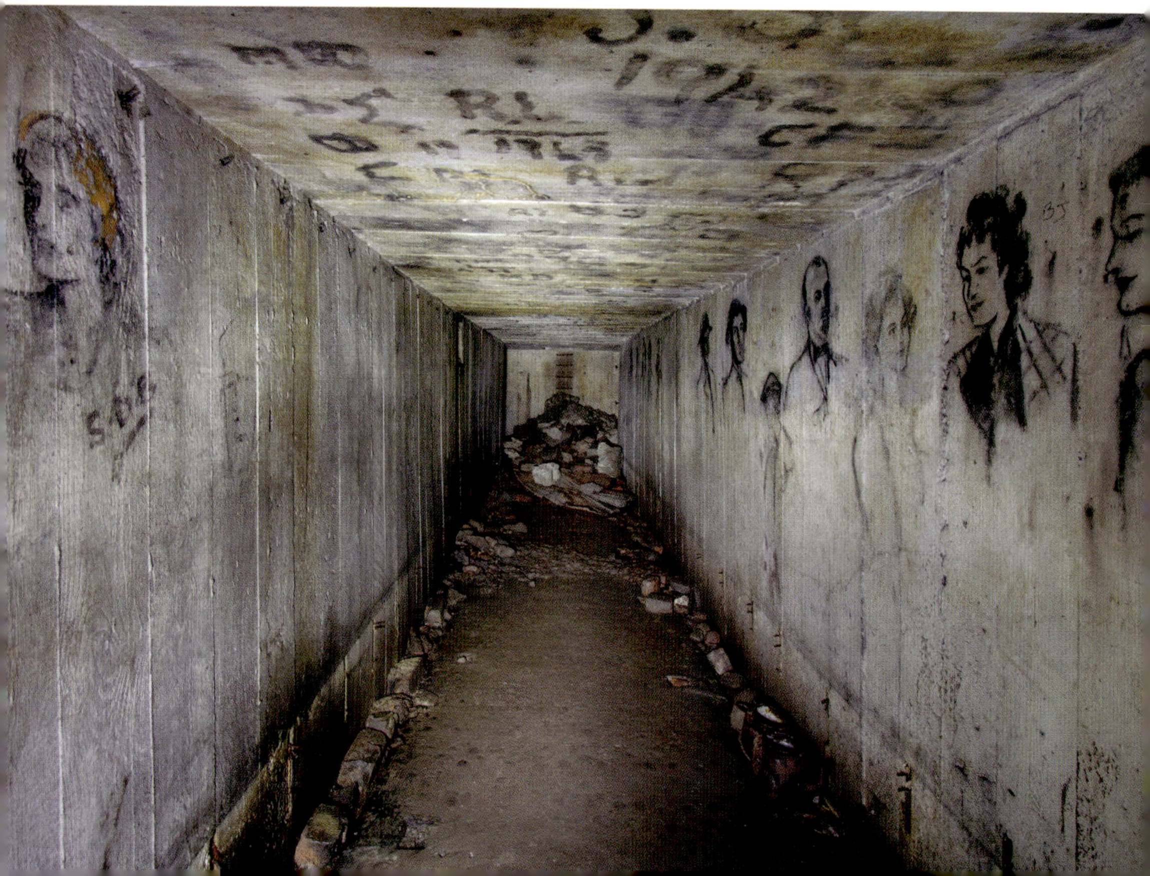

KELTON CONVENT

The convent was originally built around 1800 as a private residence called Kelton with extensive land and gardens and a lodge. Around 1900, the Catholic Church purchased it as a home for penitents and children. It was part of the Sacred Heart Convents, and was also known as the Kelton (House of Providence). In essence, the building was a home for unmarried mothers whereby the children were adopted off and the mothers were effectively in servitude – usually working in laundries. Later, the two hall extensions and chapel were built, and another large building was erected on the land which may have been a laundry. The convent appears to have closed in the early 1980s and the site left idle since 2006.

In 2020 a planning application was approved to carry out partial demolition of the Grade II listed Kelton Grange, with alterations and extensions to the existing convent, in order to convert the site into luxury private apartments. (Images James Lacey)

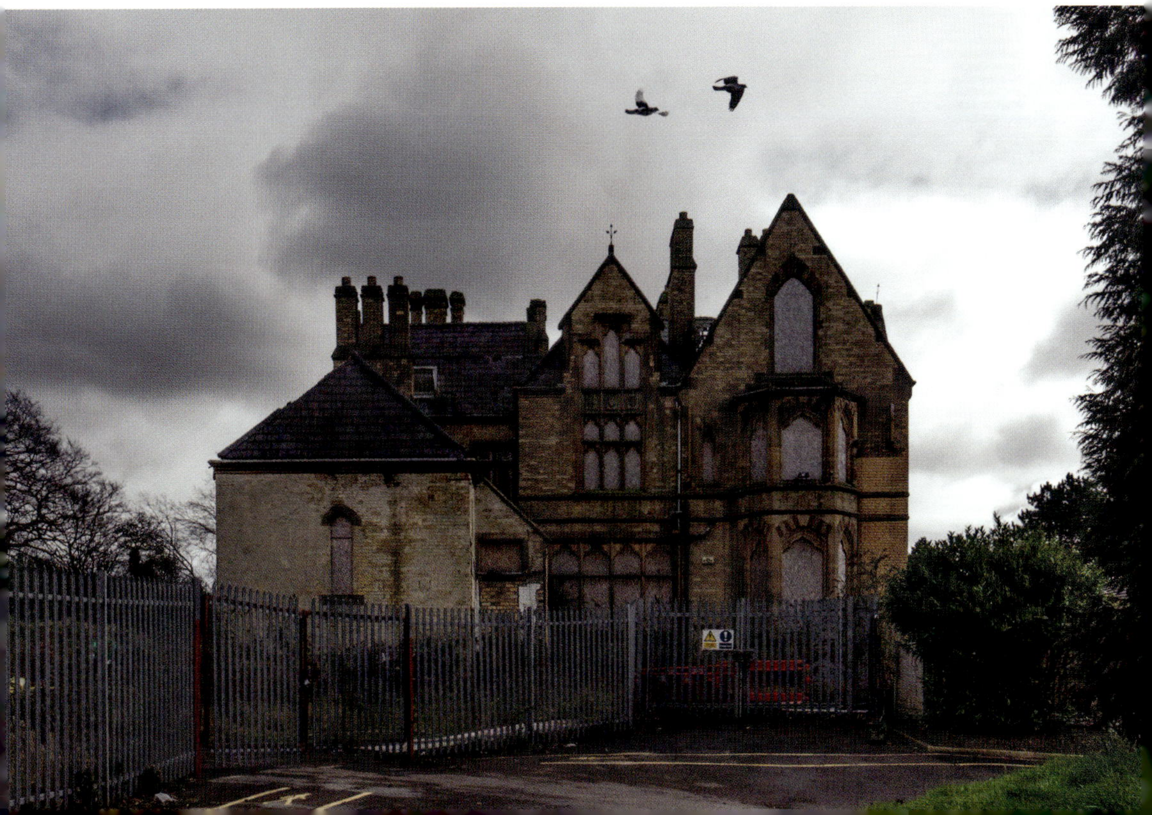

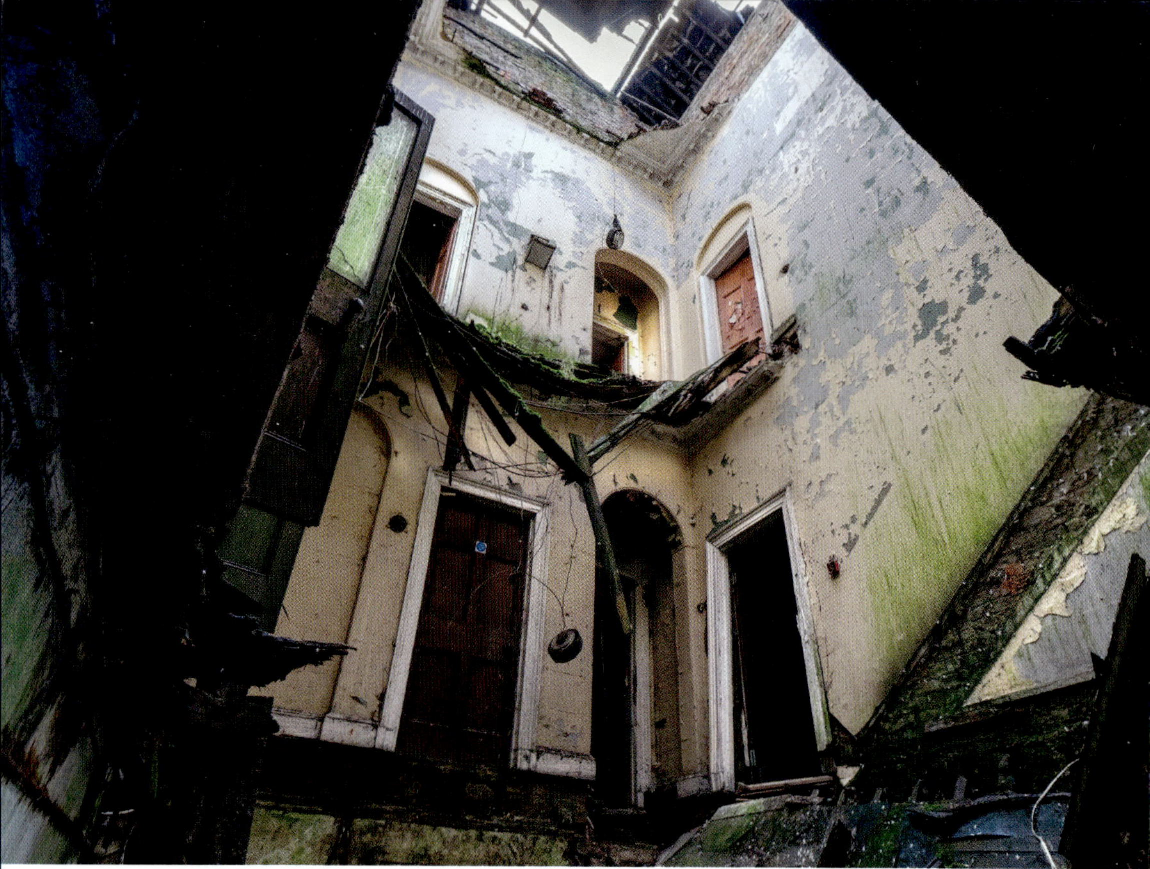

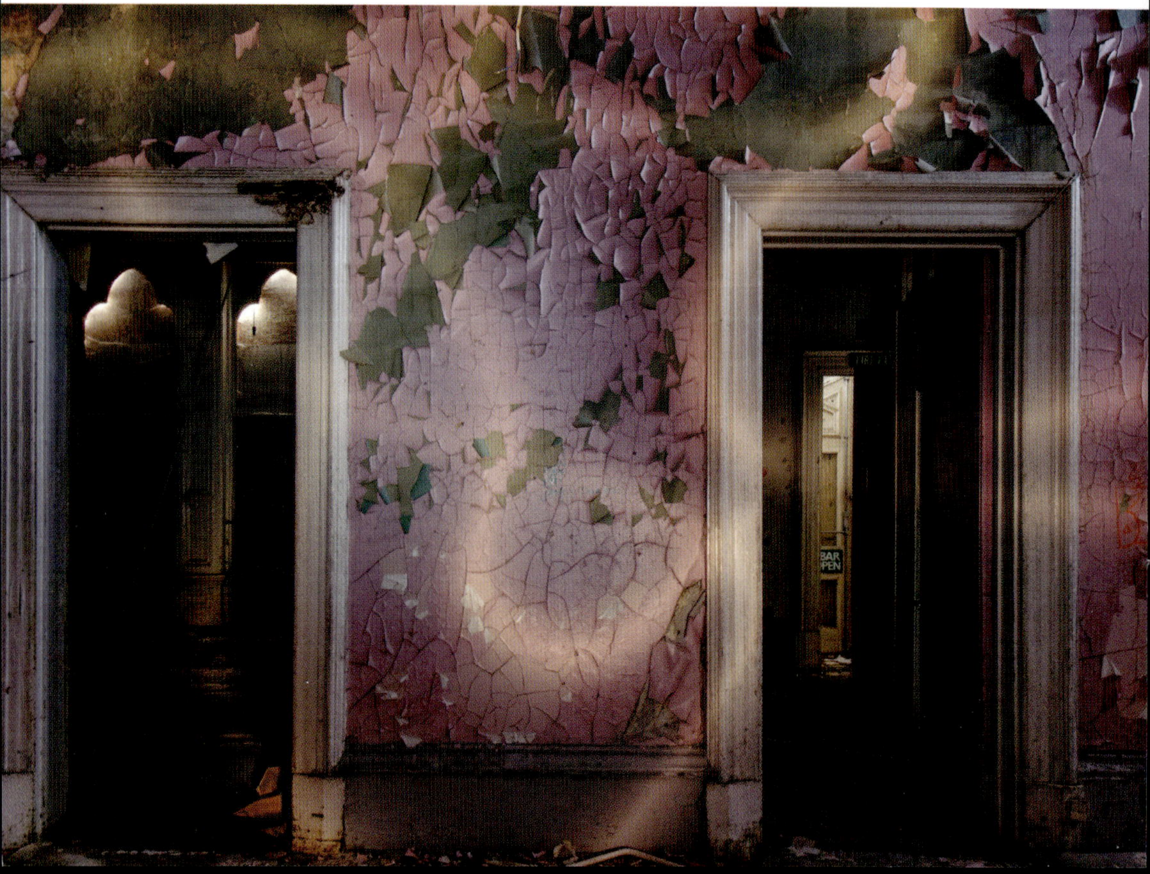
BAR

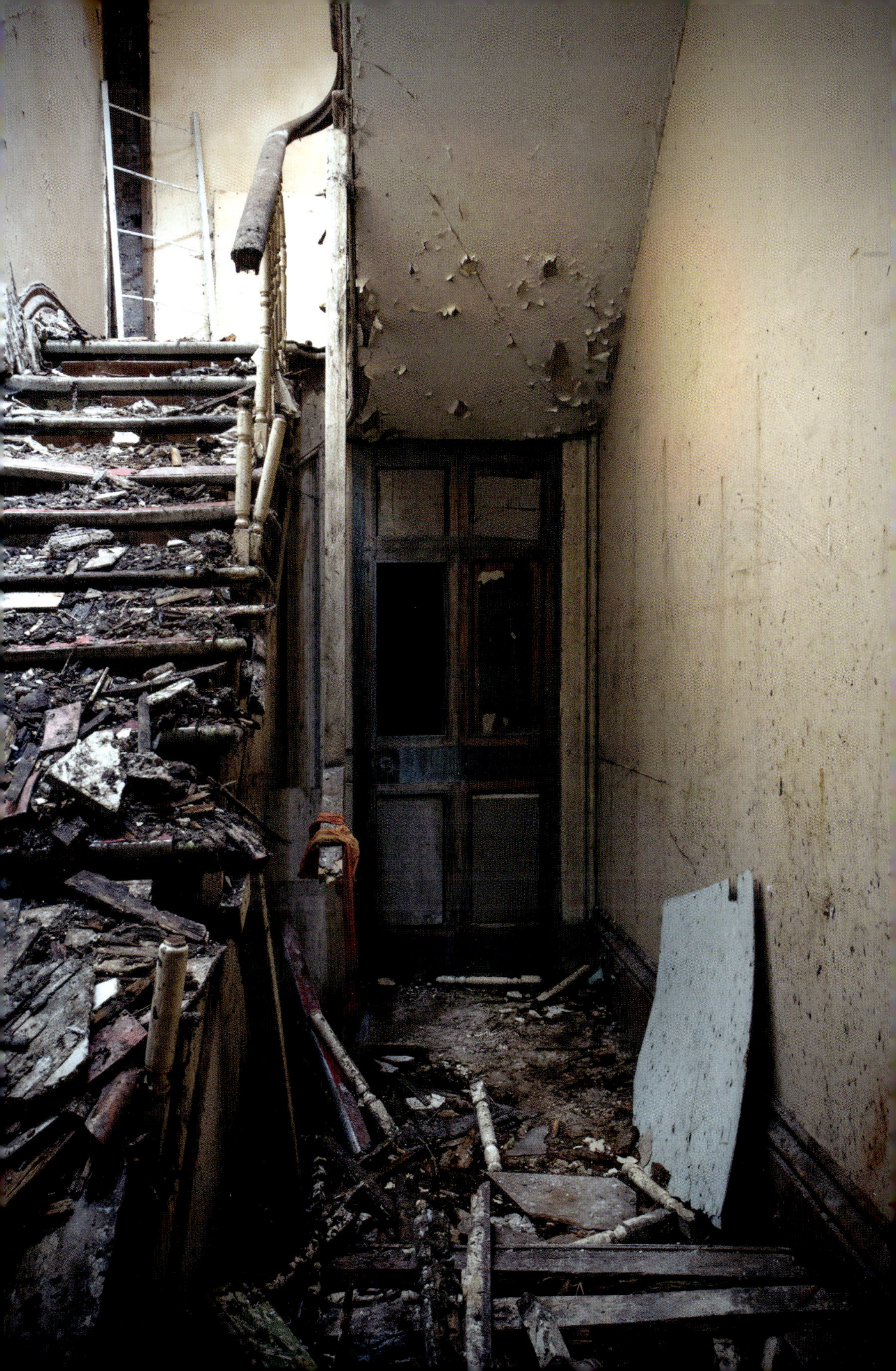

SUNNYMEDE SCHOOL, SOUTHPORT

Sunnymede was the last independent school in Southport and after fifty years it has been marked to close. Partly to blame was the falling numbers of pupils being admitted to the school. The school in its day took children from the age of three to eleven years, costing the parents around £5,100 a term. The buildings are planned to be turned in luxury apartments. (Images David Gooch)

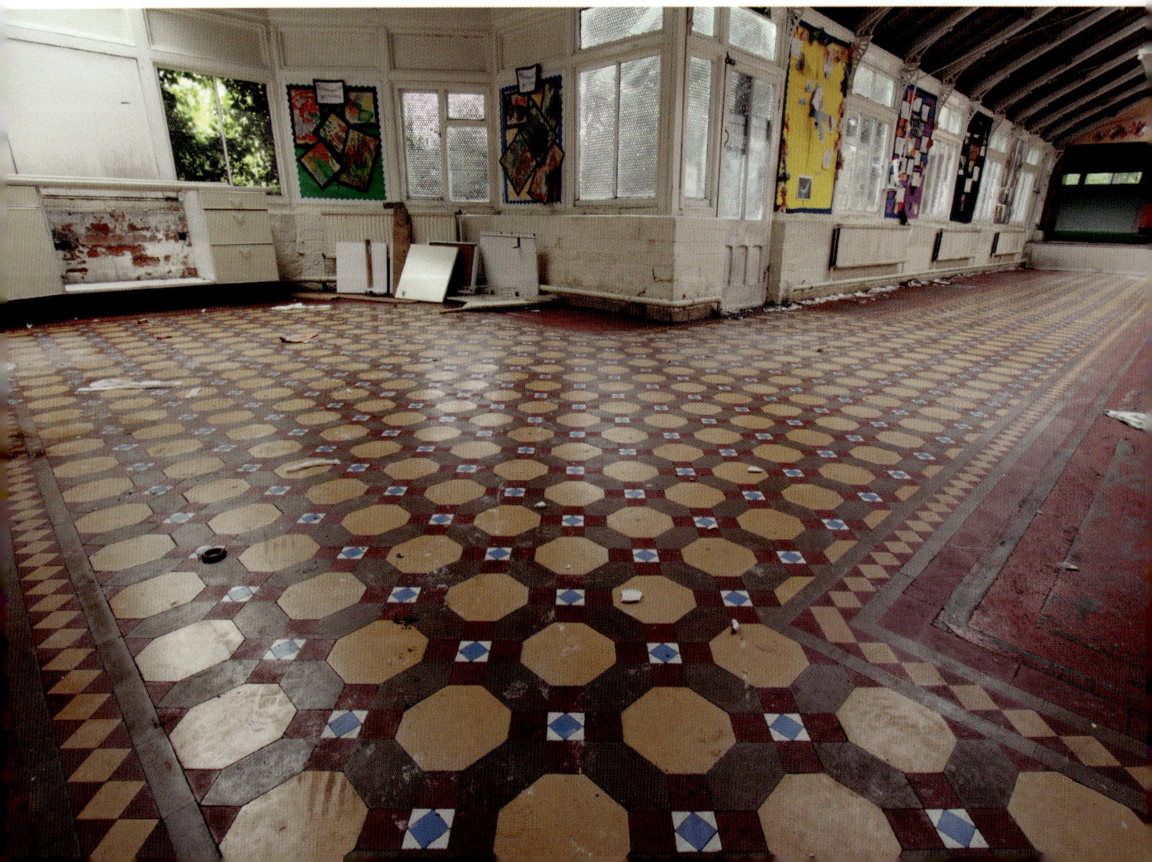

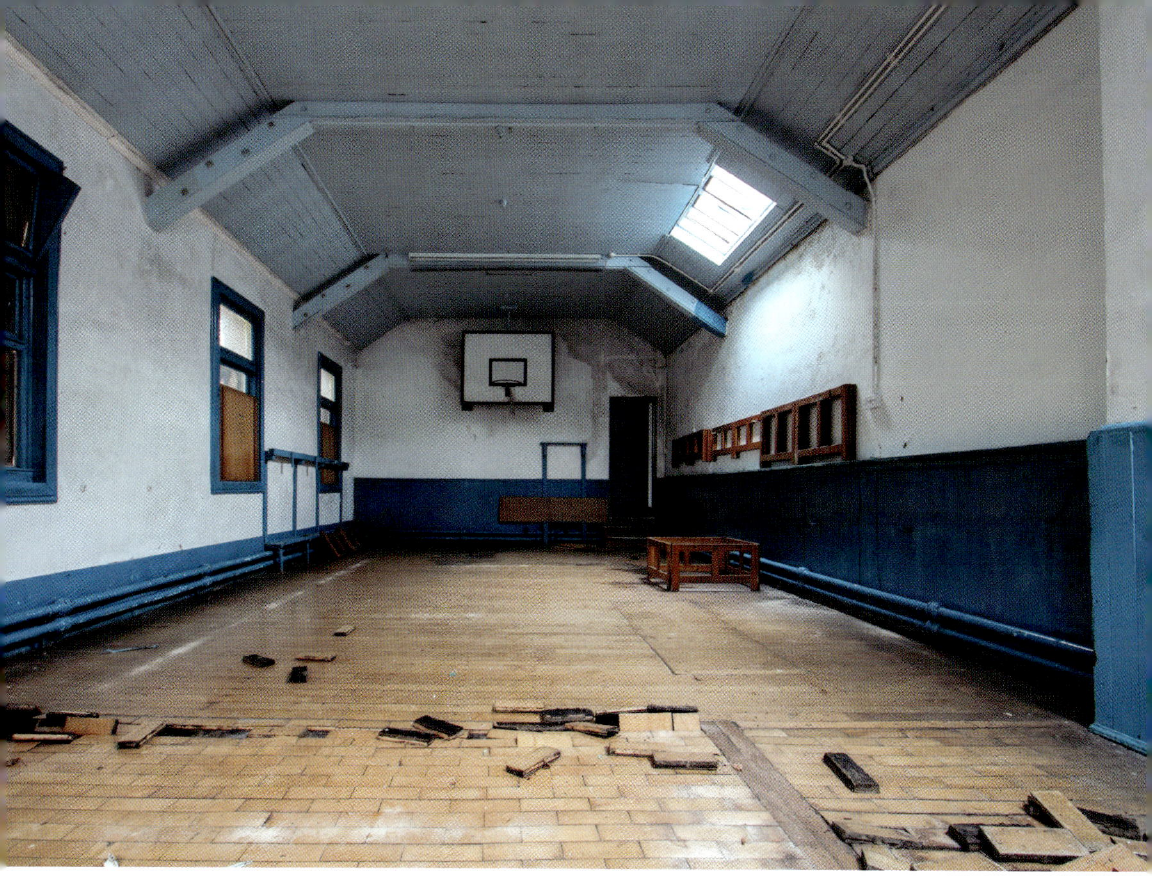

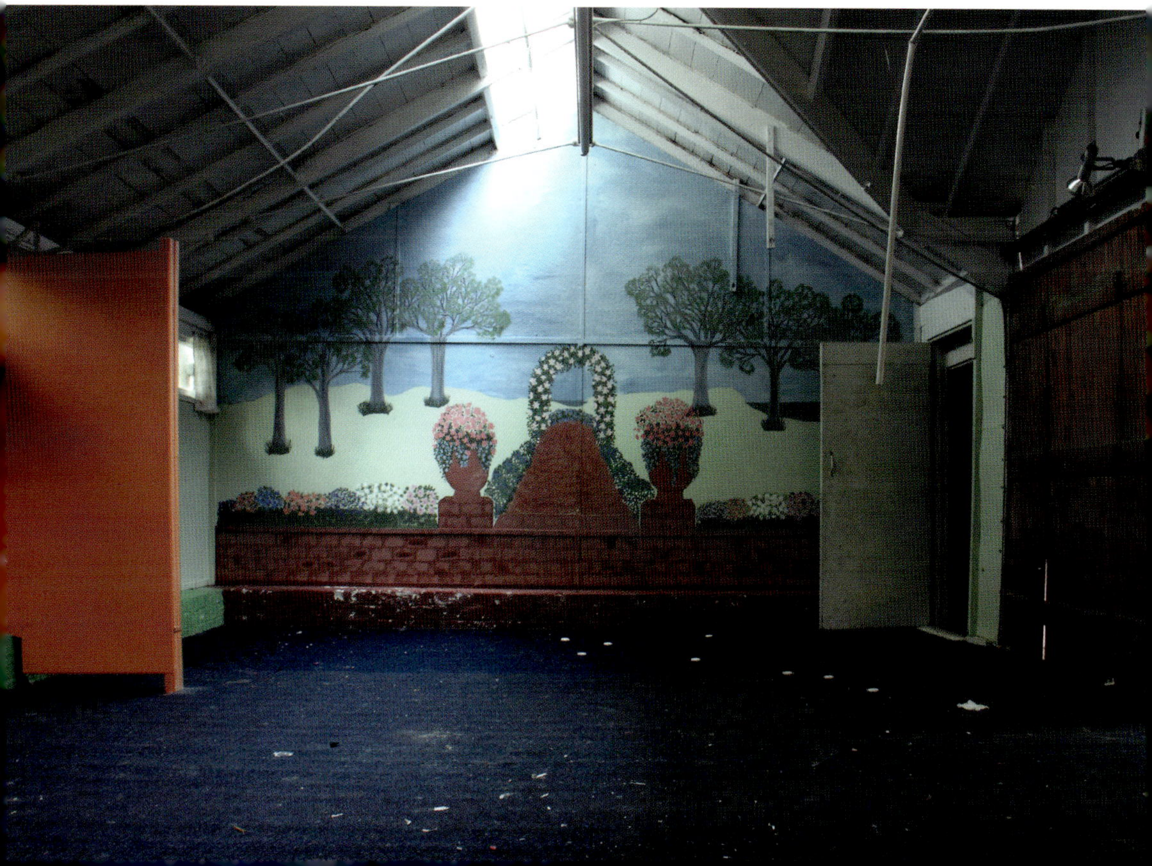

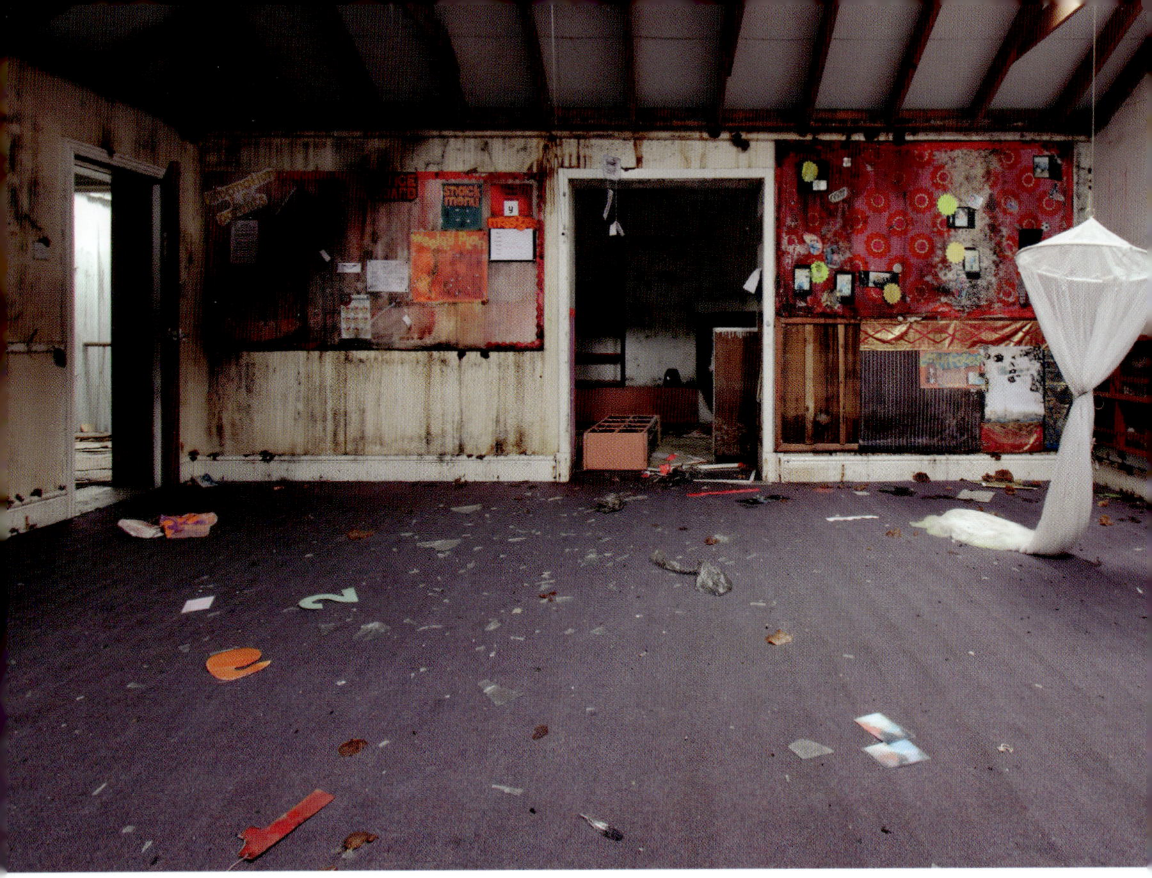

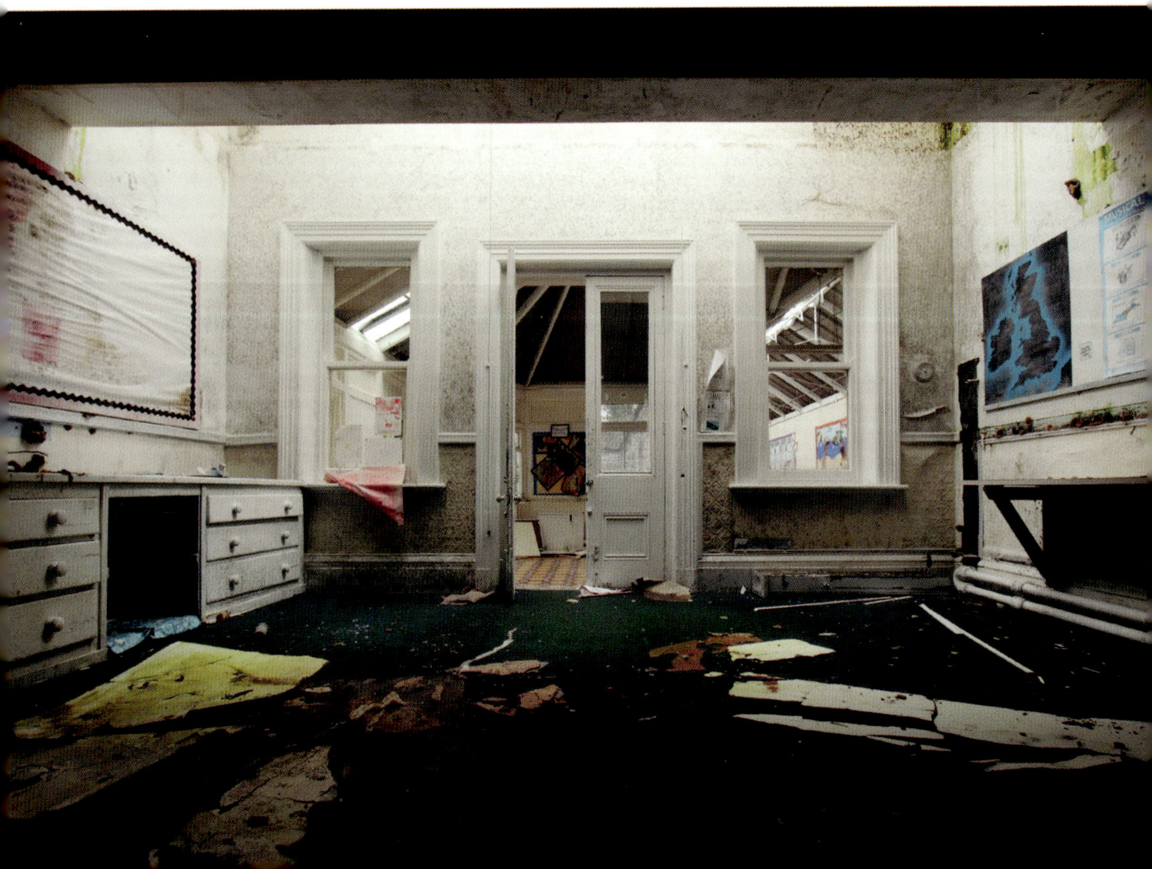

HOLLY LODGE GIRLS' SCHOOL

The history of Holly Lodge in West Derby, Liverpool, goes back to 1828. The original building on the site was a detached Georgian lodge which subsequently opened as a girls' school in 1922 after the original private residence had undergone some alterations. In 2015 a replacement Holly Lodge was built within the grounds to replace the original buildings, which were themselves demolished in 2016 after a long campaign to save it by the West Derby Society. Two Grade II listed lodges, Fremont and Sandheys, were saved; however, Holly Lodge was inspected by English Heritage who deemed it had lost too many of its original features to warrant being saved. (Images James Lacey)

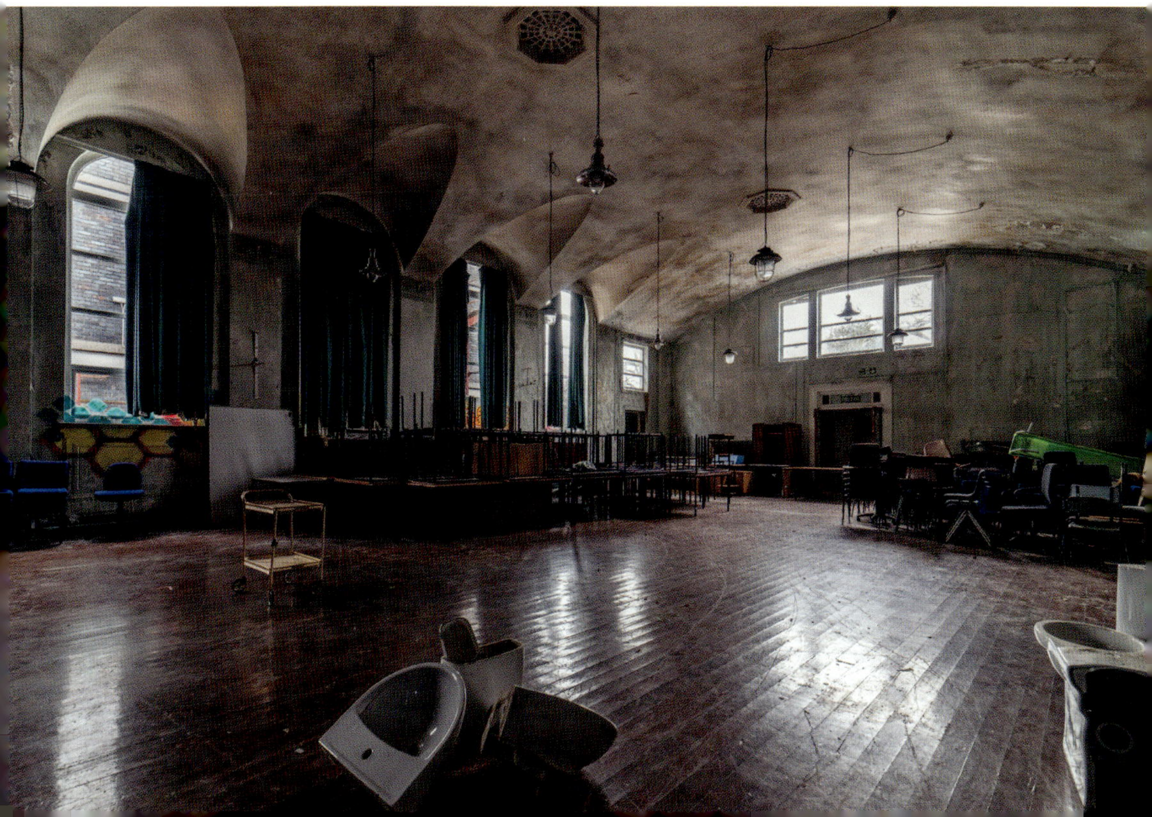

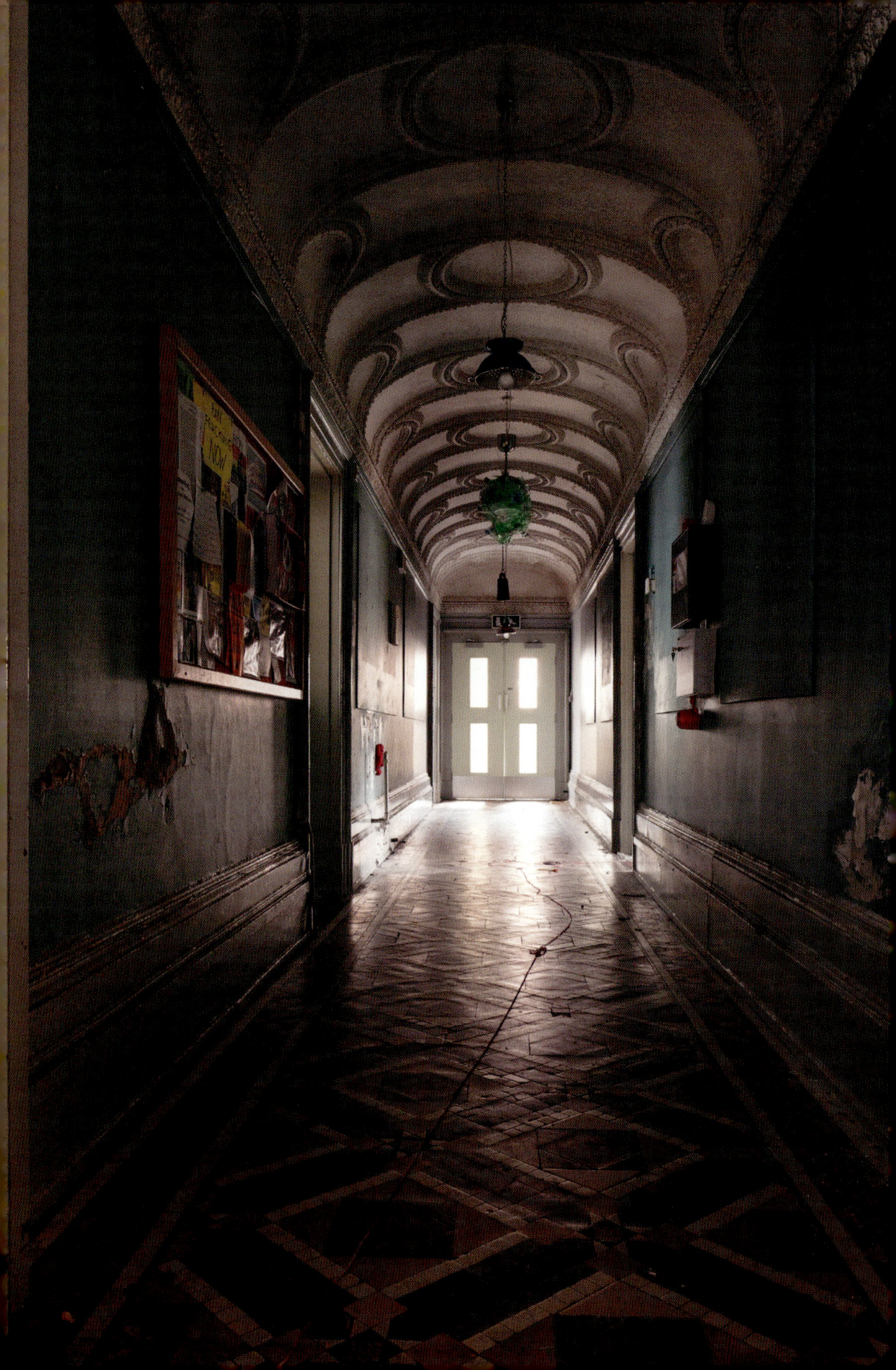

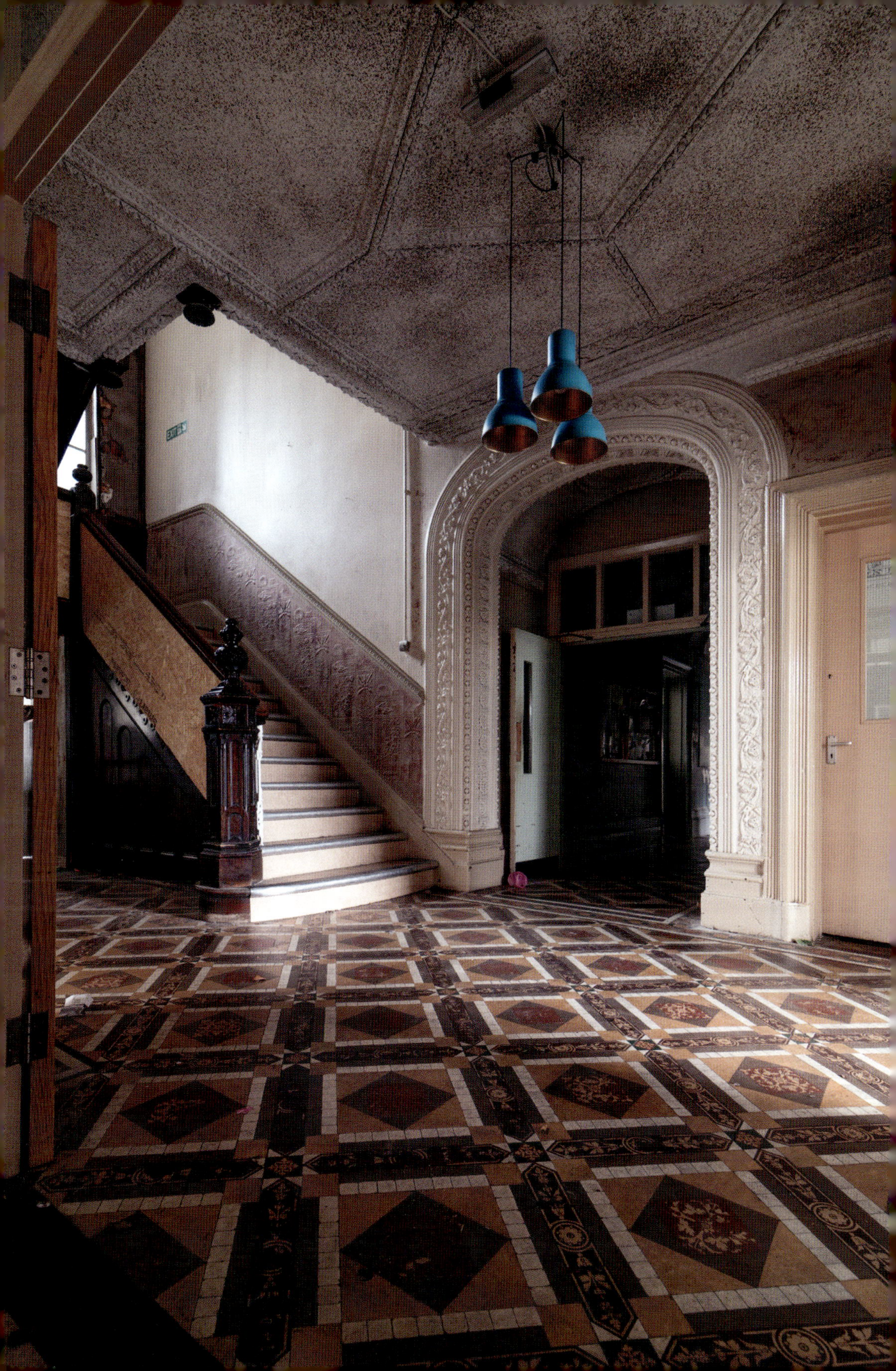

BURTONS FOODS COMPANY

Burtons announced the closure of its site in the town of Moreton, costing around 342 jobs. The factory made some of the biggest of the Burtons brands such as Wagon Wheels and Jammy Dodgers before its closure around 2011. The loss of jobs was blamed on the cost of ingredients and over-capacity. The site has been sold and work has already begun demolishing the buildings and turning the site into new houses. (Images David Gooch)

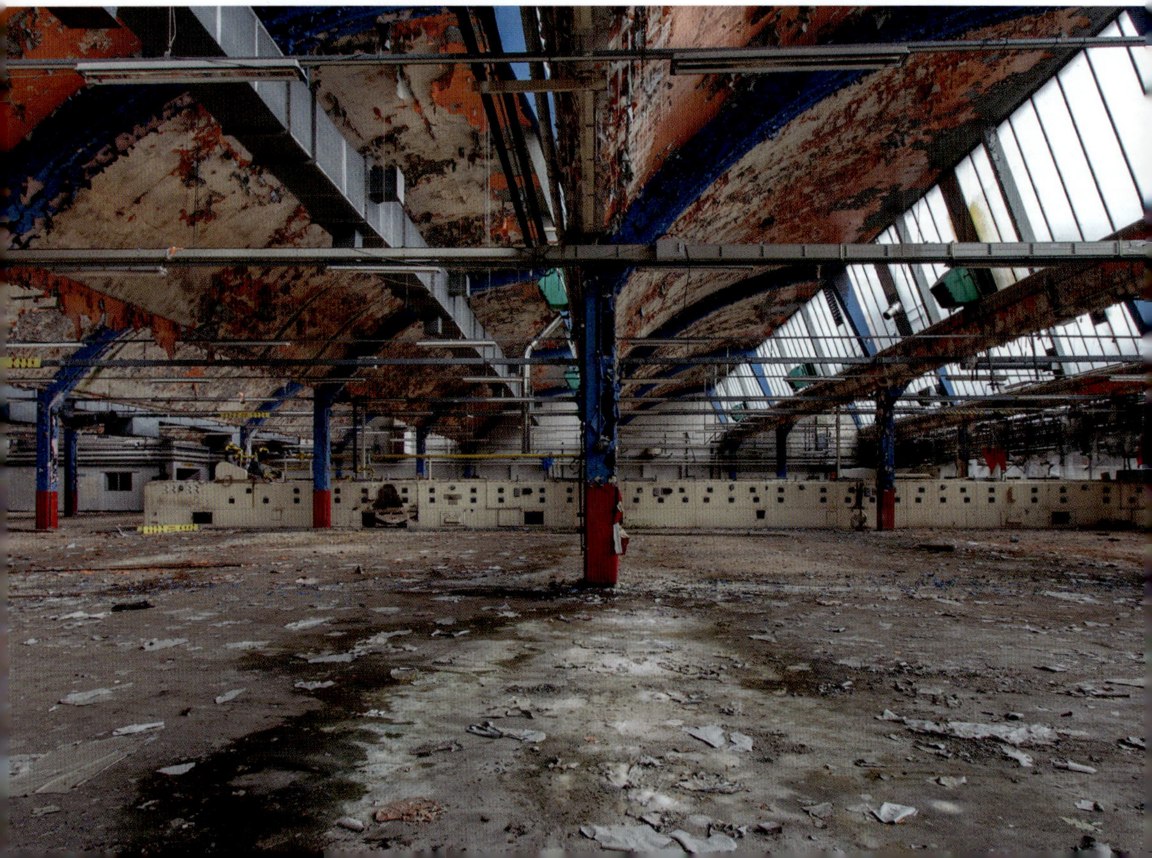

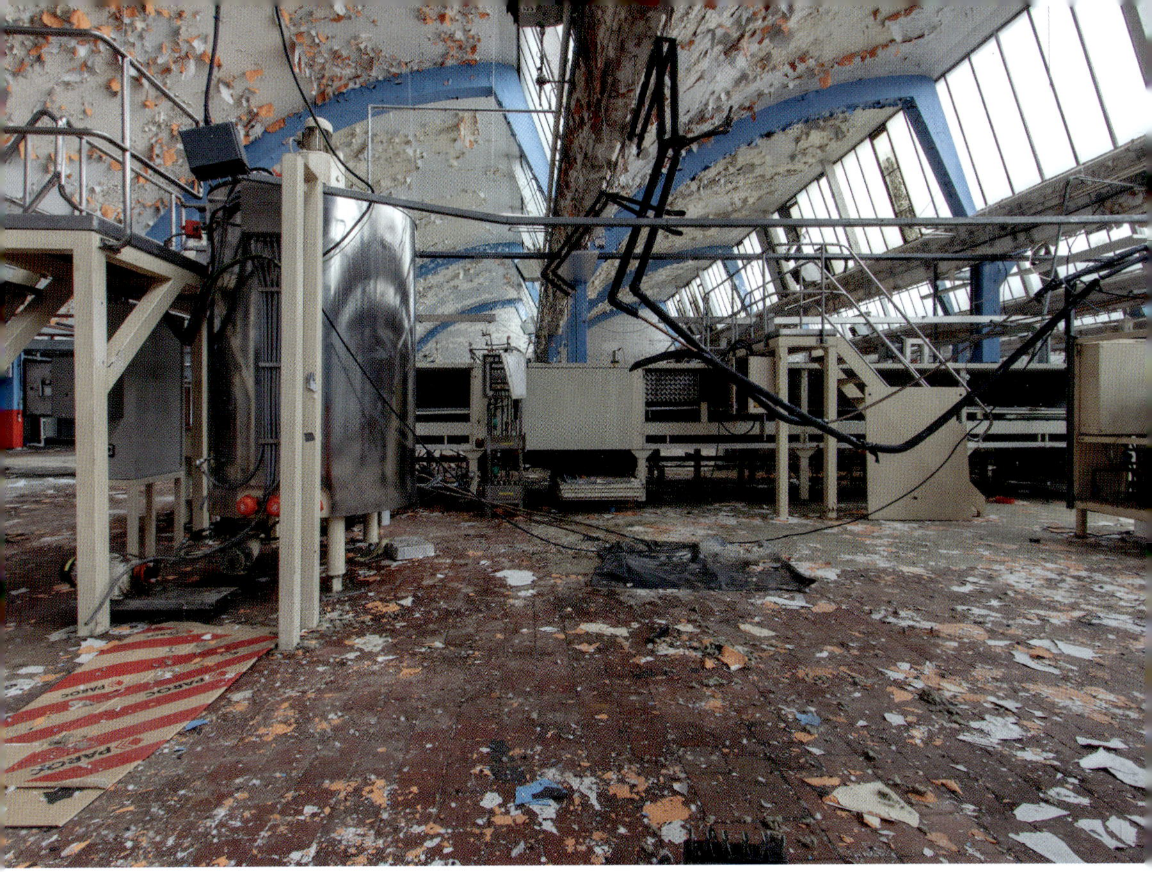
PAROC

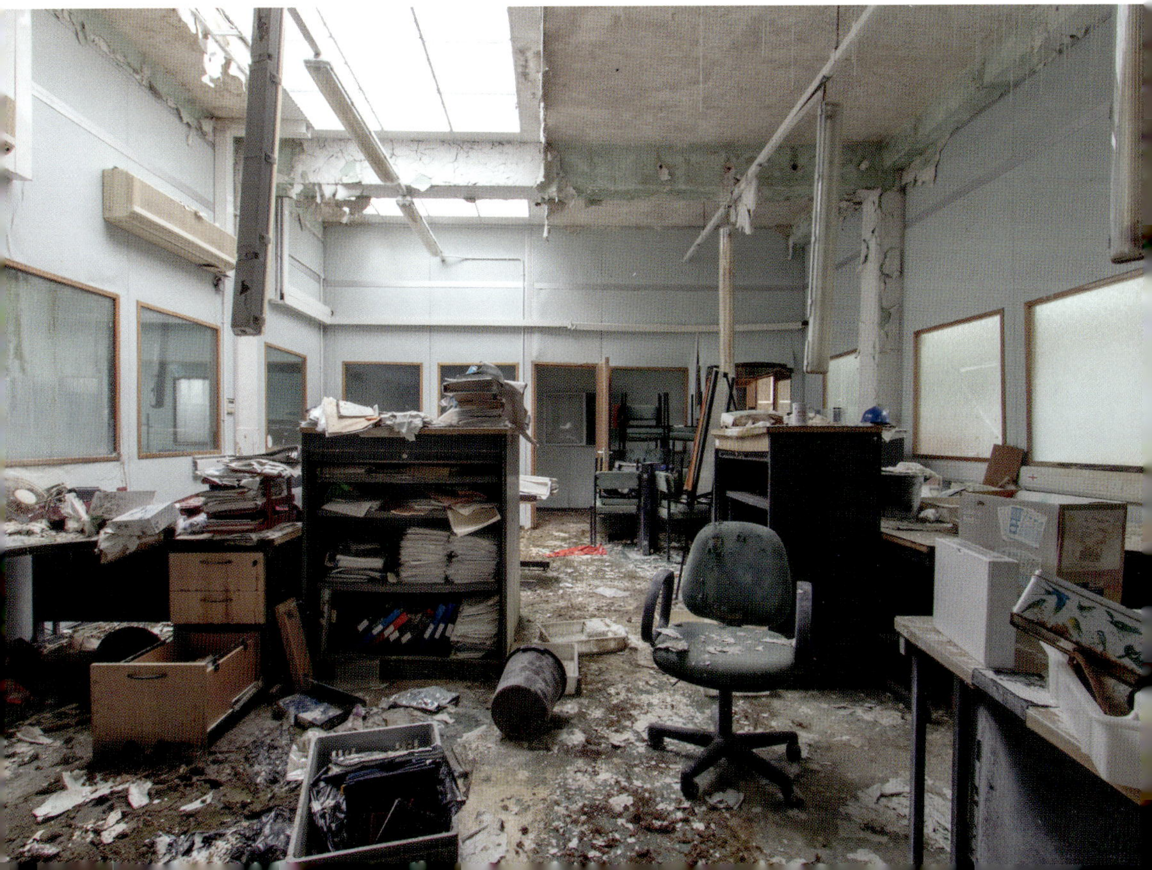

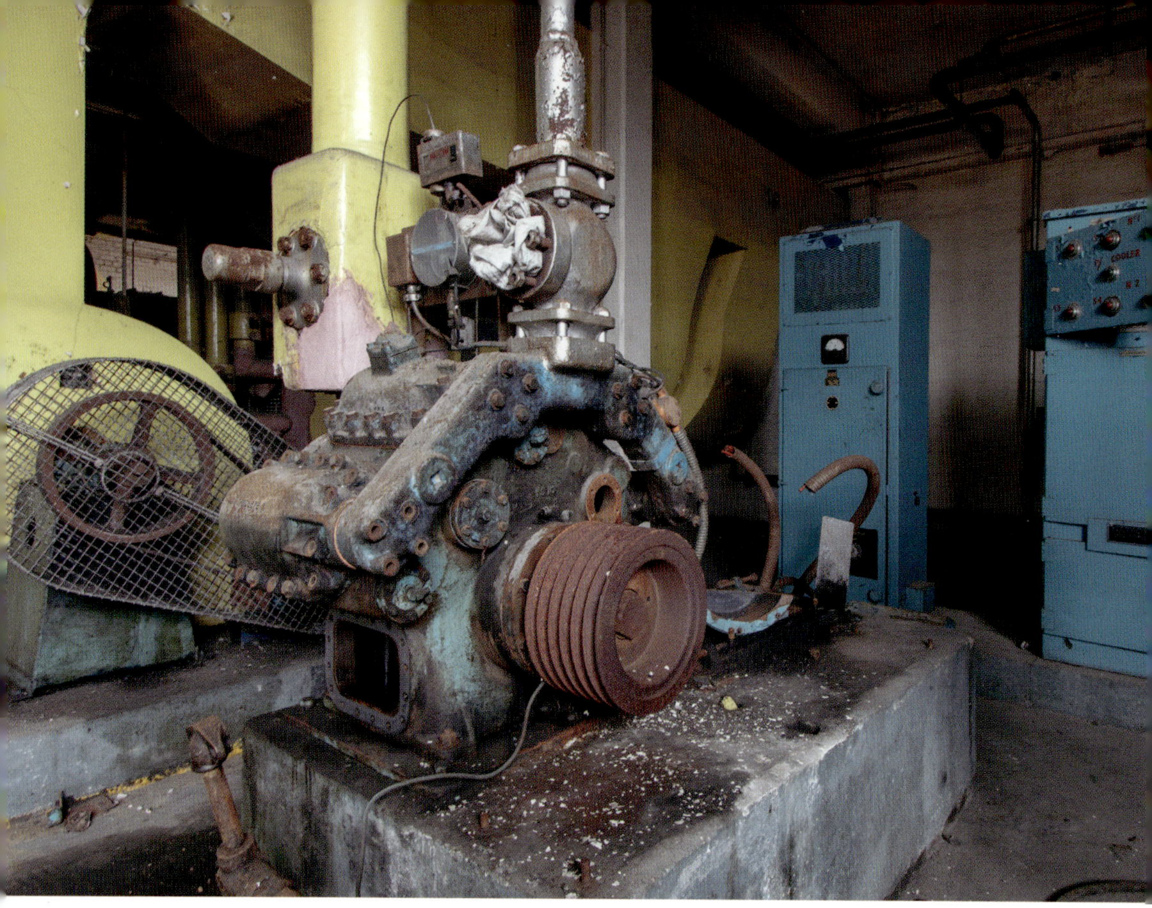

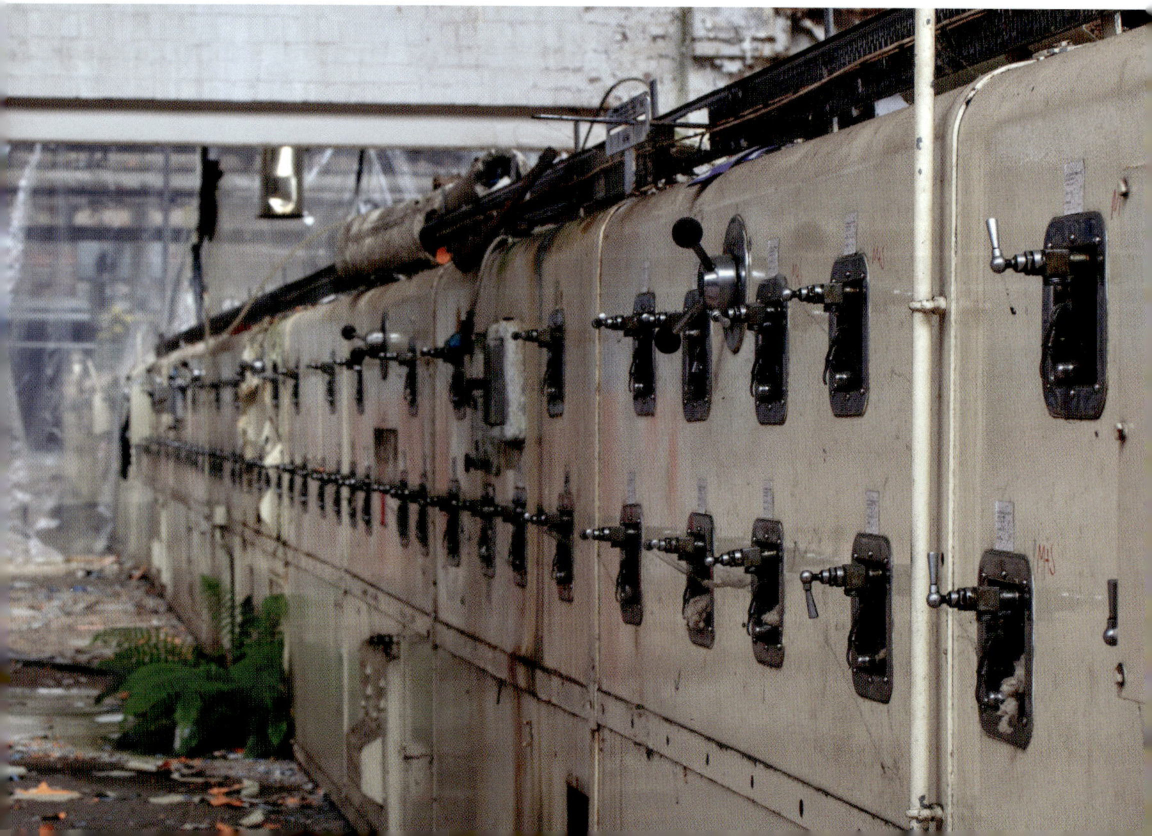

PILKINGTON GLASS HQ CANTEEN

Pilkington Glass was founded in 1826 as a partnership between members of the Pilkington and Greenall families, under the name St Helens Crown Glass Company. The first glass-making furnace in St Helens was operational by 1700, so by the time St Helens Crown Glass Company was established there was already competition.

The building photographed here was the HQ canteen and was completed in 1964 in a distinctive modernist style. The well-being of the staff who worked there was at the forefront of the design plans, with the site sitting in a mini modernist utopia. The canteen was a bright and spacious area and overlooked the adjacent lake which could be viewed through a series of oversized windows installed specifically to utilise these views and promote well-being.

Pilkington was acquired by the Japanese firm Nippon Sheet Glass in 2006 and in 2015 the sale of the former St Helens HQ was agreed, with the 125 remaining staff being transferred to the Lathom facility near Ormskirk. (Images James Lacey)

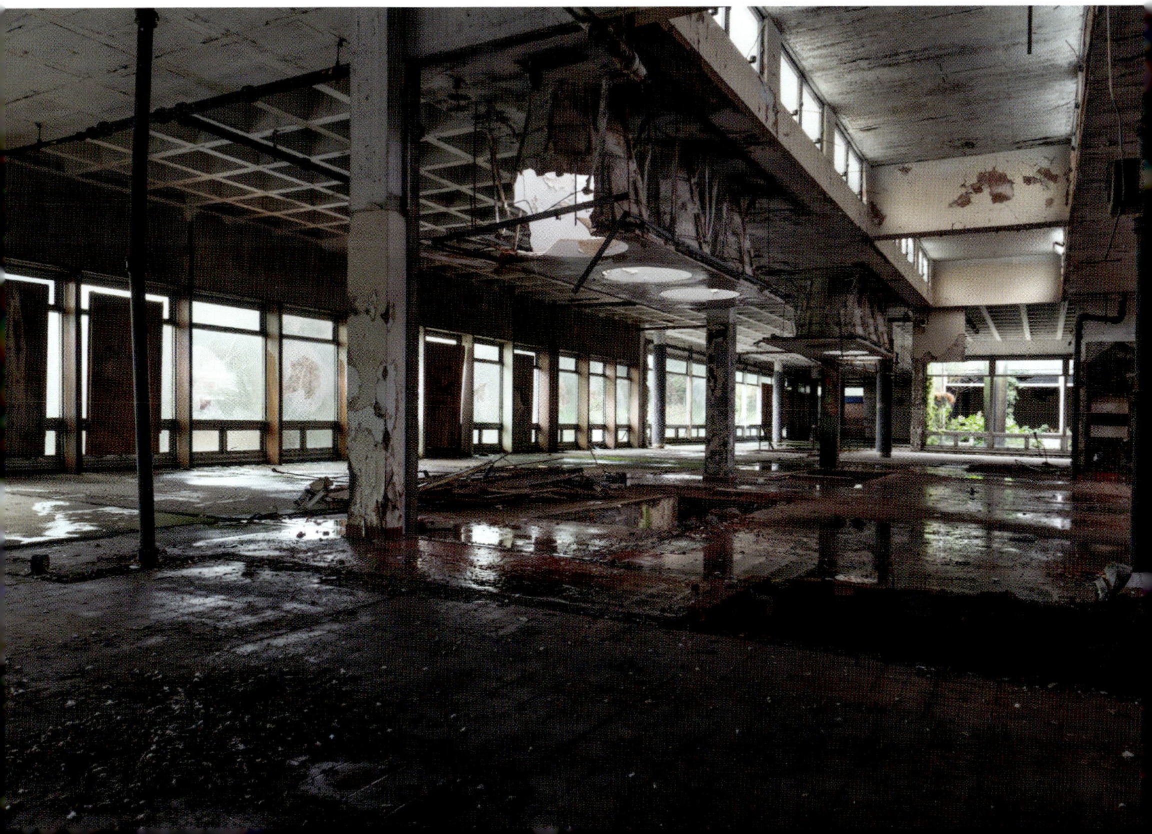

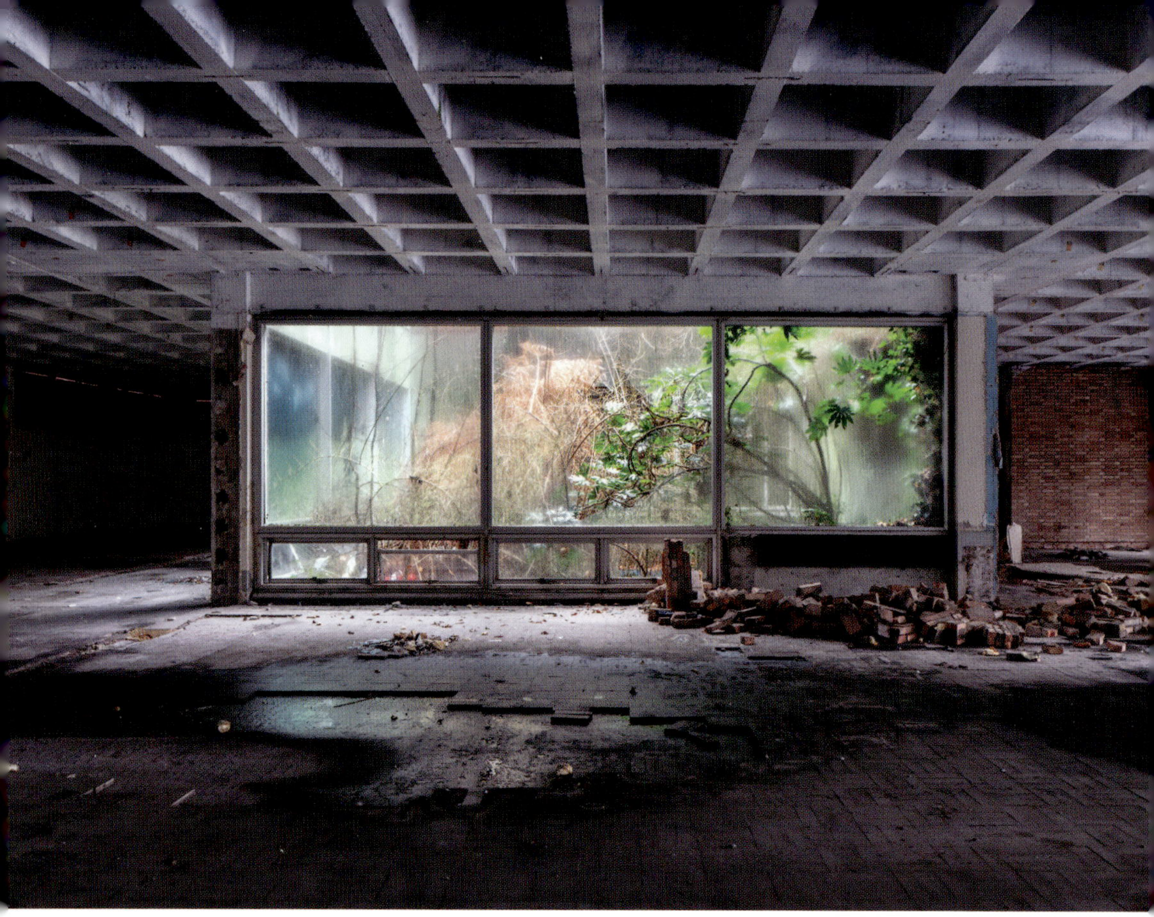

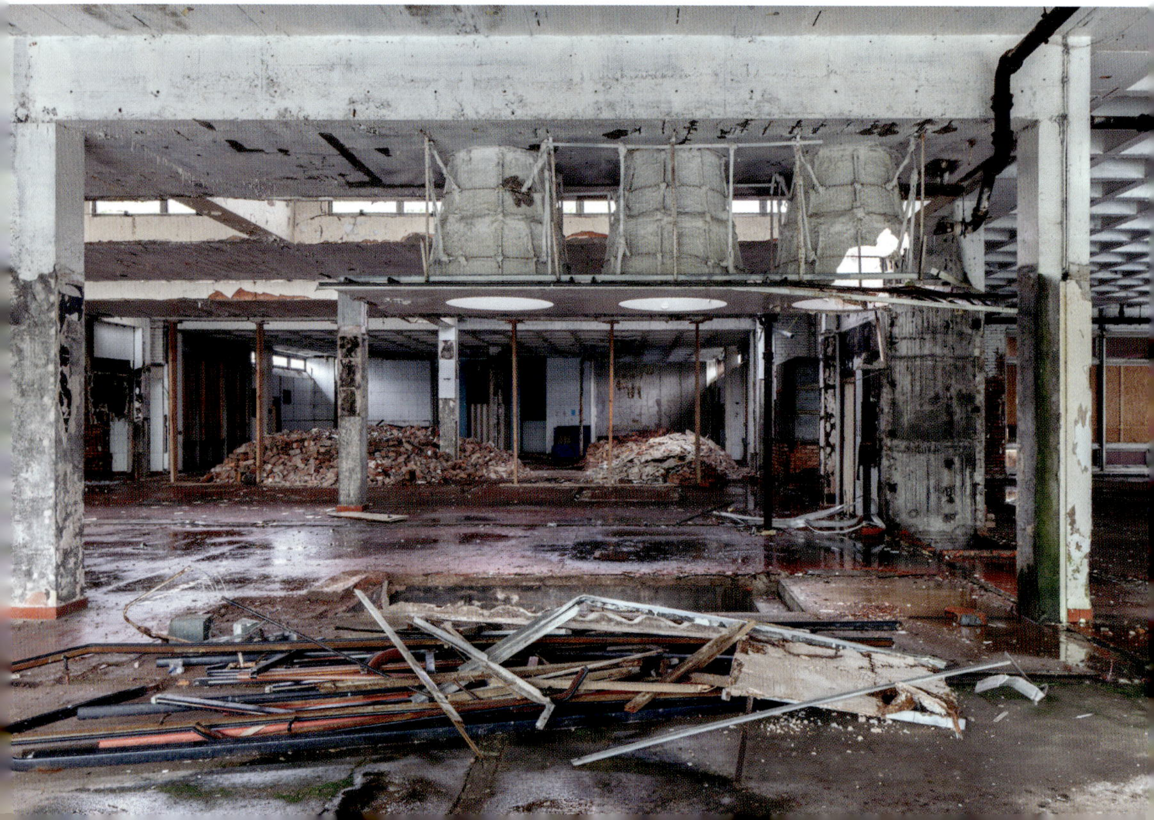

THE GRAND CASINO, SOUTHPORT

The building was originally erected as a car showroom and garage 100 years ago on Lord Street in the town of Southport. It was then converted into a luxury cinema in 1938 and used as such until 1966 when it closed. It reopened in 1966 as an independent bingo hall and used as a bingo hall under various different names up until its closure in 1999. Part of the building was still used after that time for a few years as a casino.

The Grand has in recent years had a fair bit of money spent on it and is now a fancy bar and restaurant retaining many of the building's features. (Images David Gooch)

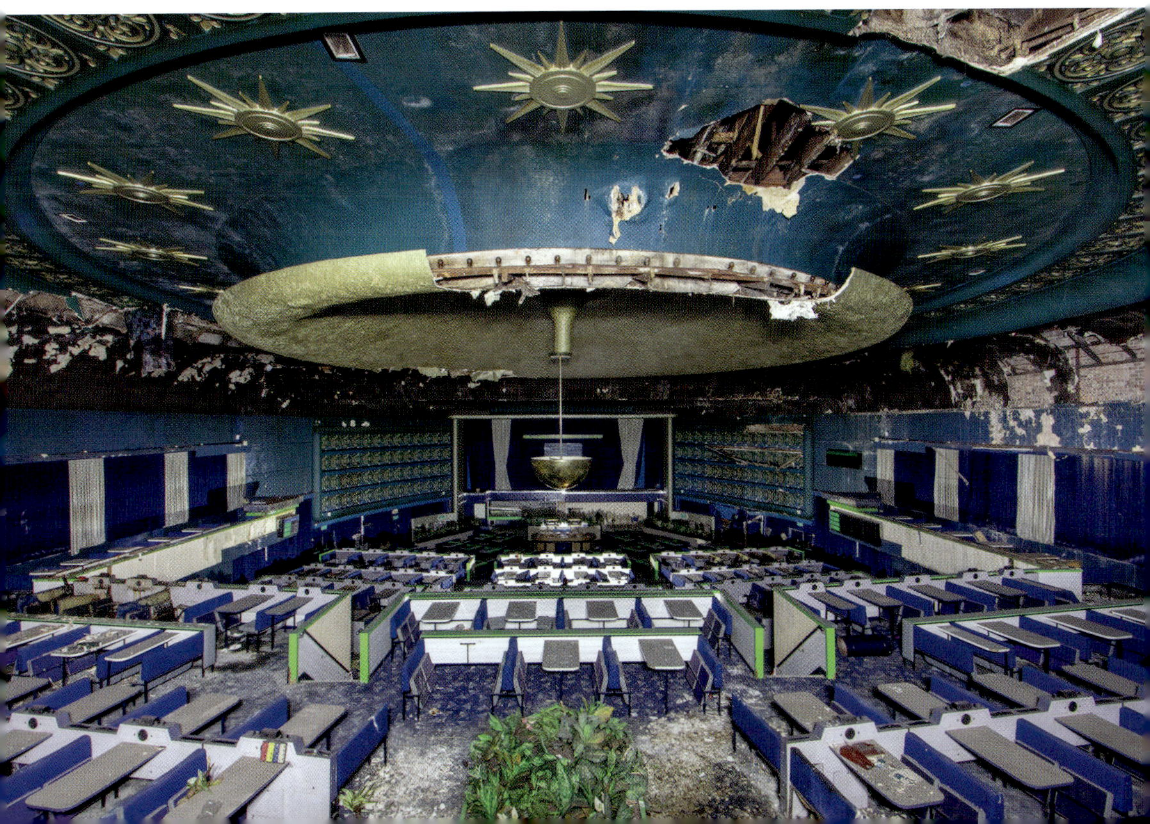

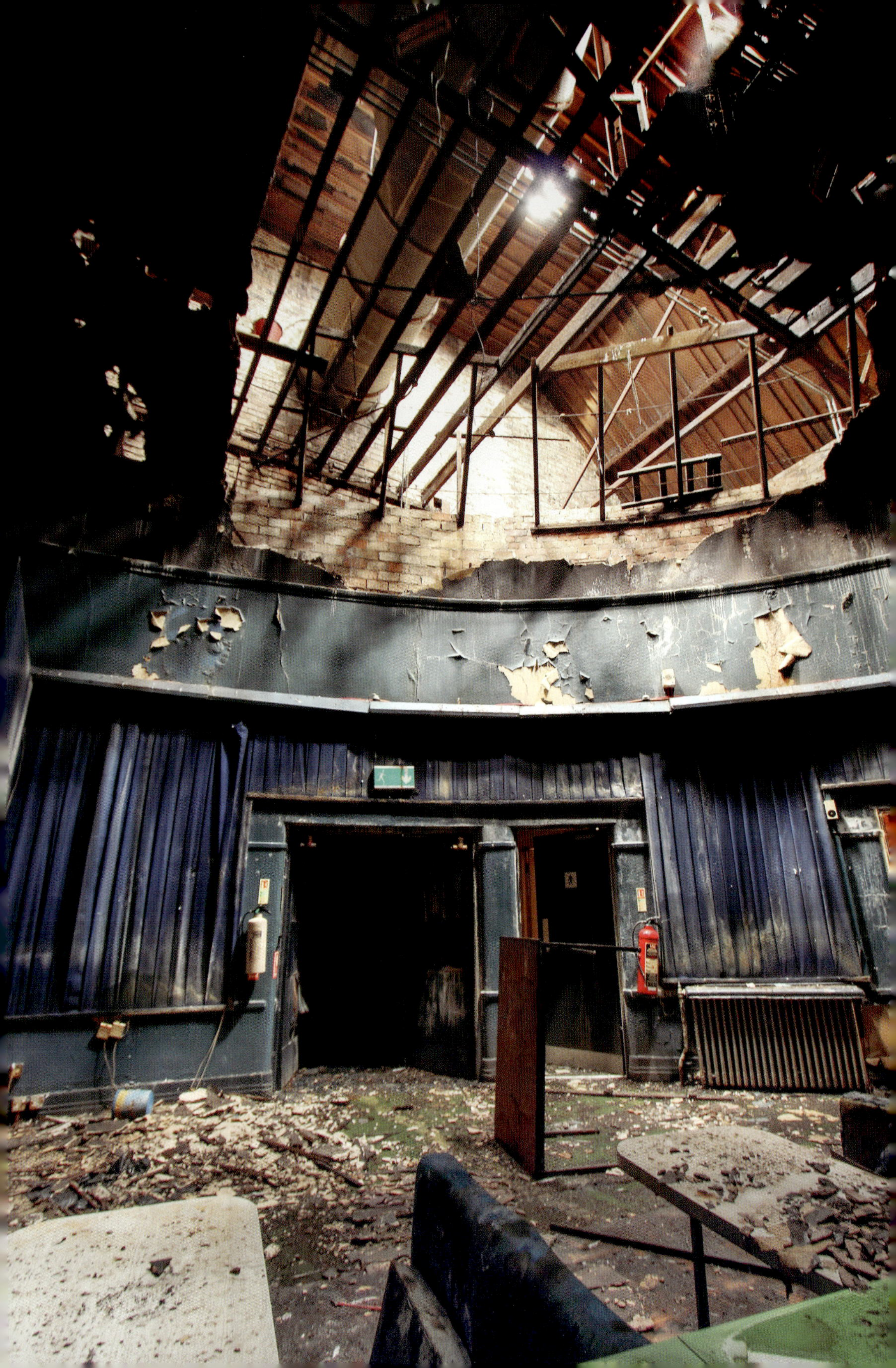

ST GABRIEL'S CONVENT

St Gabriel's Convent was constructed in 1828 and was known then as Knolle Park. The Grade II listed manor house later became St Gabriel's Convent and Knolle Park Children's Home.

The two-storey building was initially run by an order of Roman Catholic nuns as a children's home. At the outbreak of the First World War in 1914, the nuns returned to their country and were subsequently replaced by The Poor Servants of the Mother of God who took over duties at the site.

In the subsequent years after the war, many changes were made to the building, with many outbuildings being added as well as extensions to be used as a nursery and children's home.

In 2010, the building was closed for good and has been abandoned ever since, falling into a state of disrepair. In October 2022, a huge fire broke out at the site causing extensive damage to what was an already derelict building.

Since closing, the site has been subject to redevelopment plans as a care village and residential complex, but nothing has come of these plans. (Images James Lacey)

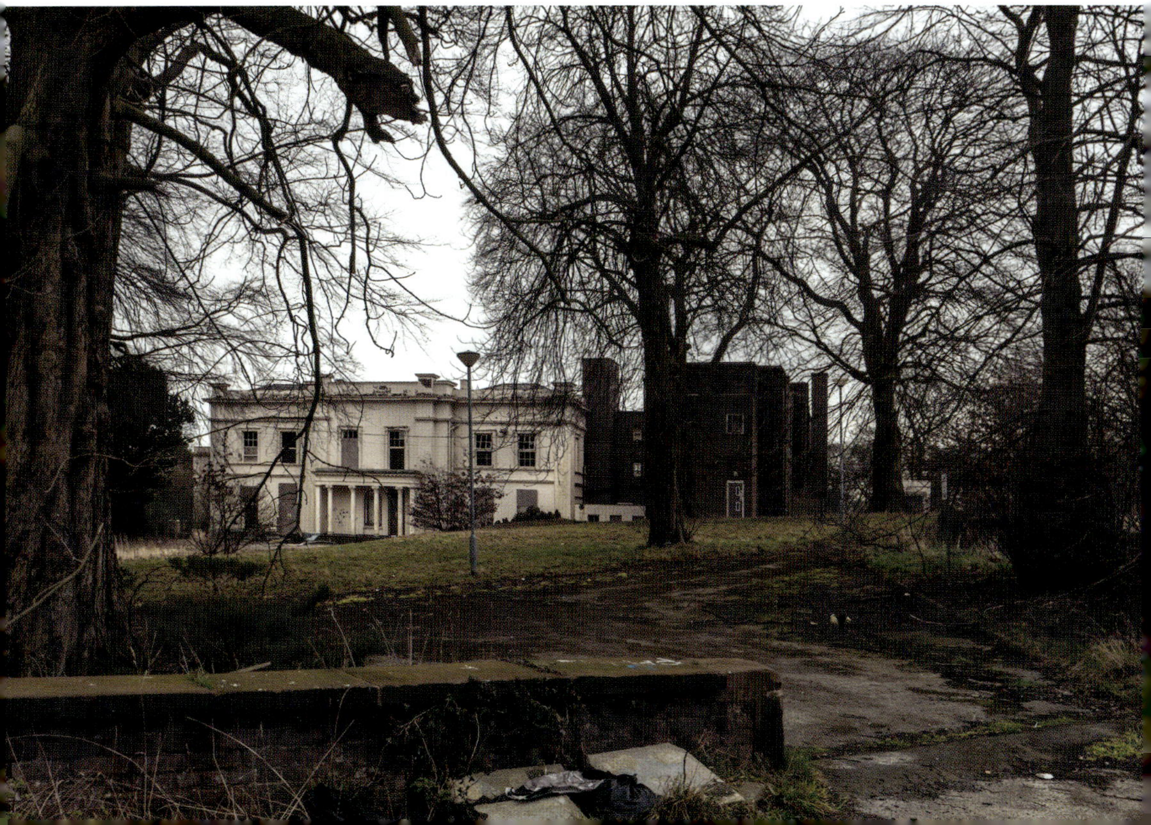

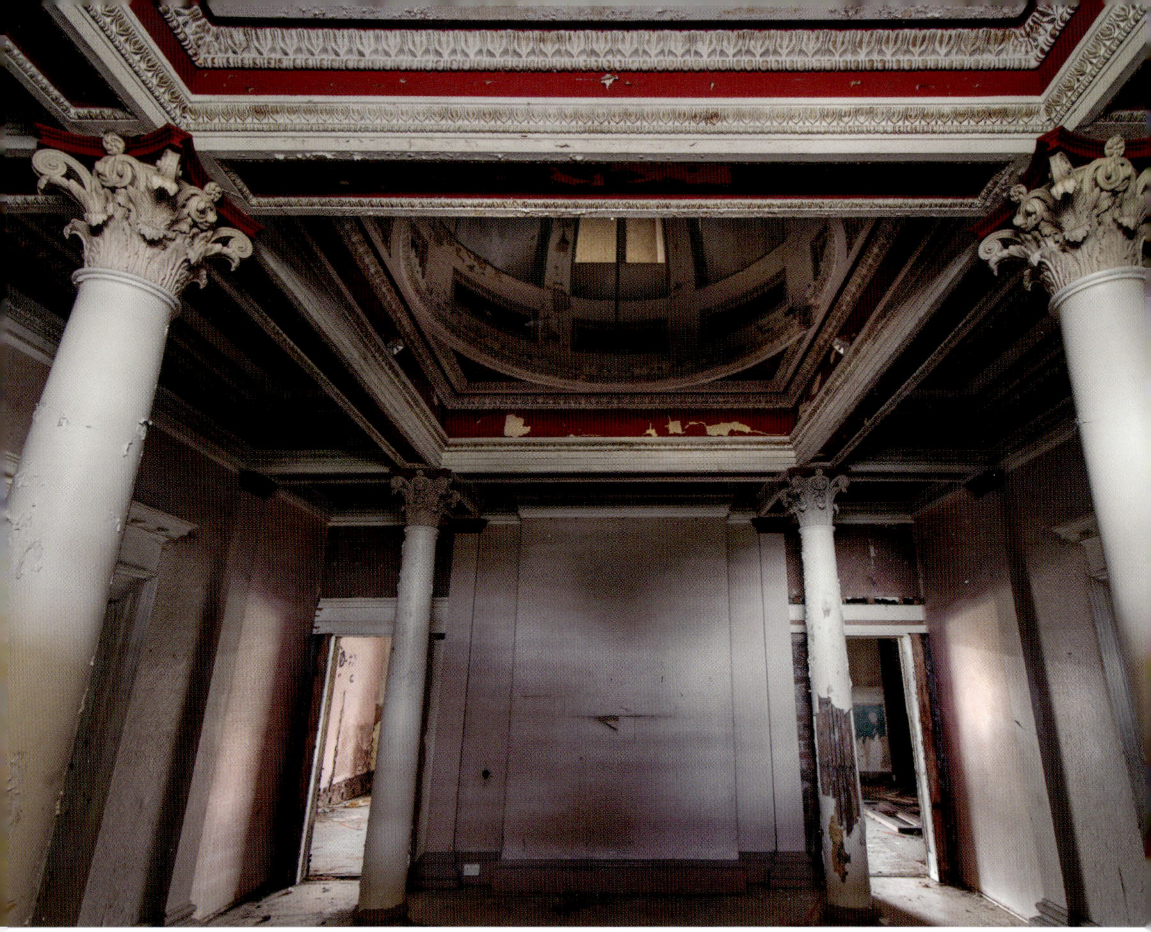

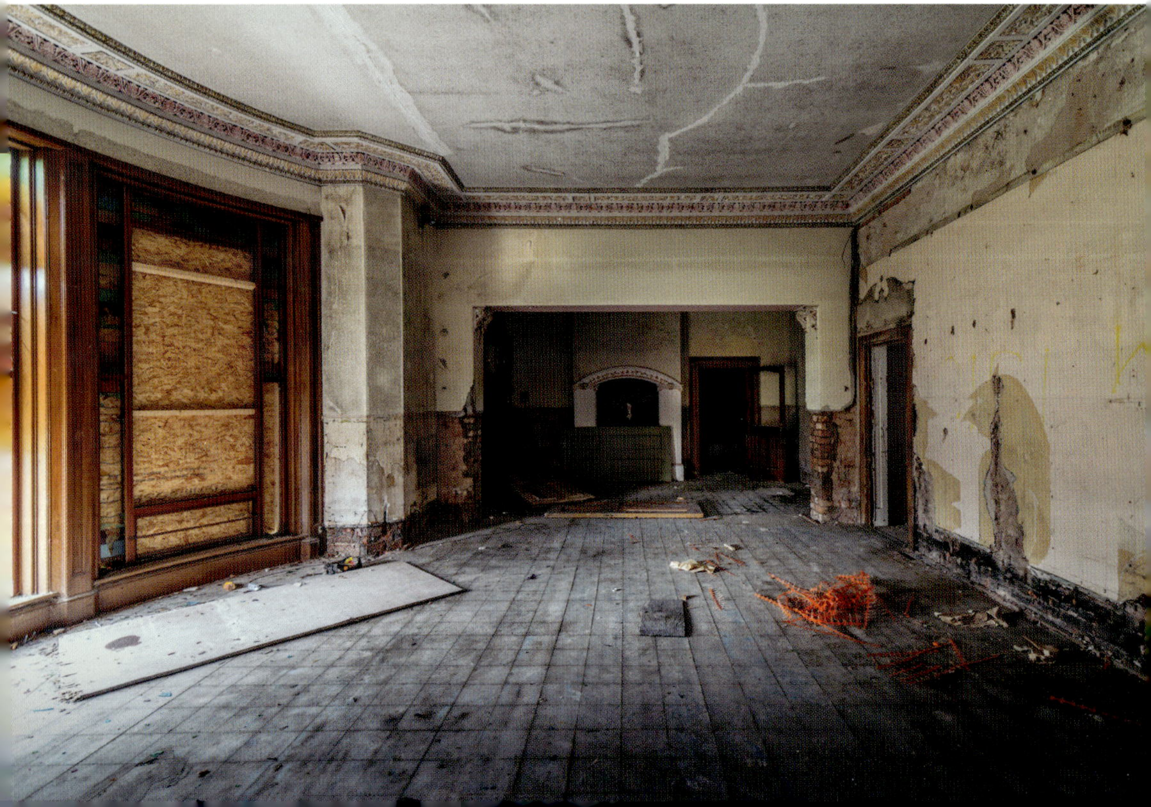

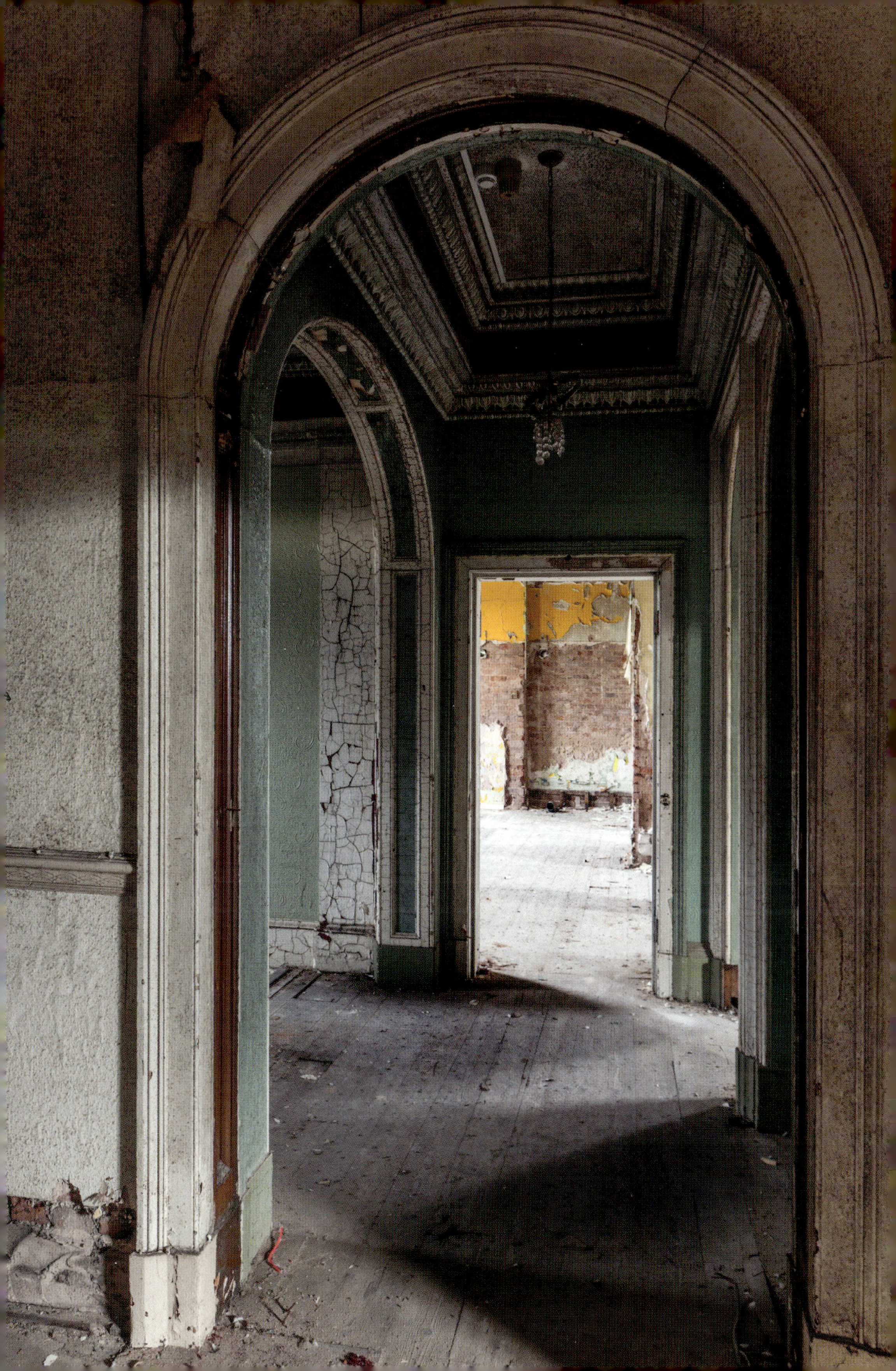

CAINS BREWERY

The iconic Liverpool brewery was established in 1858 by Robert Cain, who had started brewing his own beers in the city in 1848 at the age of twenty-four. The red-brick building you see today on Stanhope Street was part of the extension in 1901–02. The brewery ceased making its own beers in 2013 and the site closed, costing twenty-eight jobs. The site now boasts a hotel, bars, food hall and it has even started brewing its own beers again in 2022 using the original recipes. The site had planning permission approved to create an event space and bigger food hall in January 2023. (Images David Gooch)

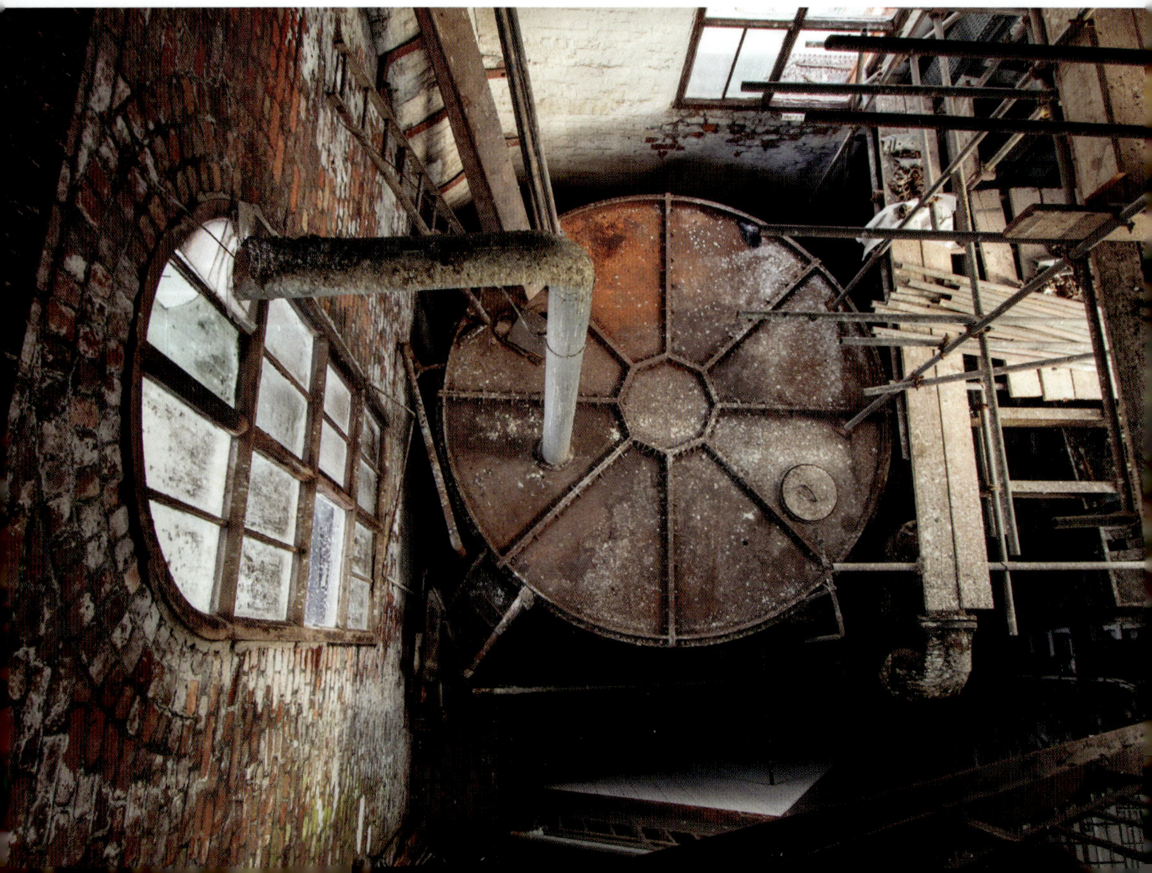

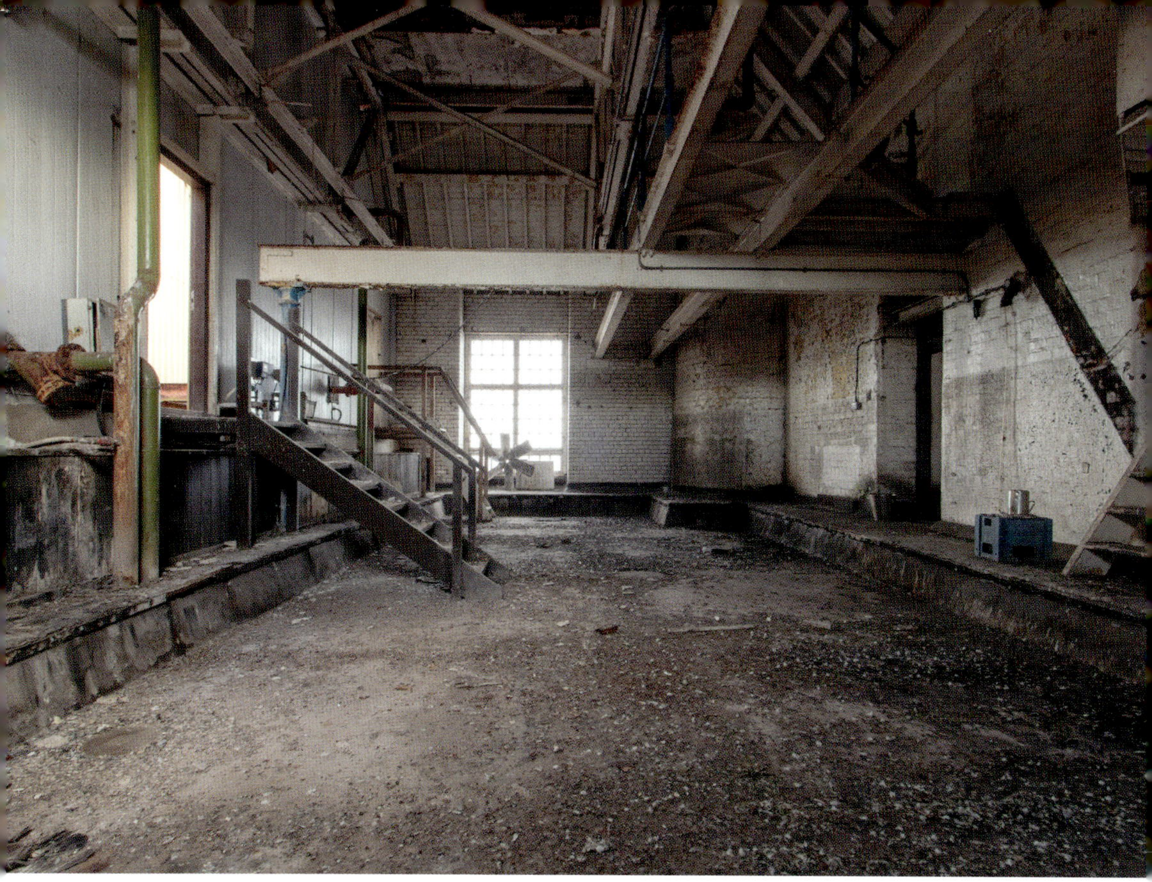

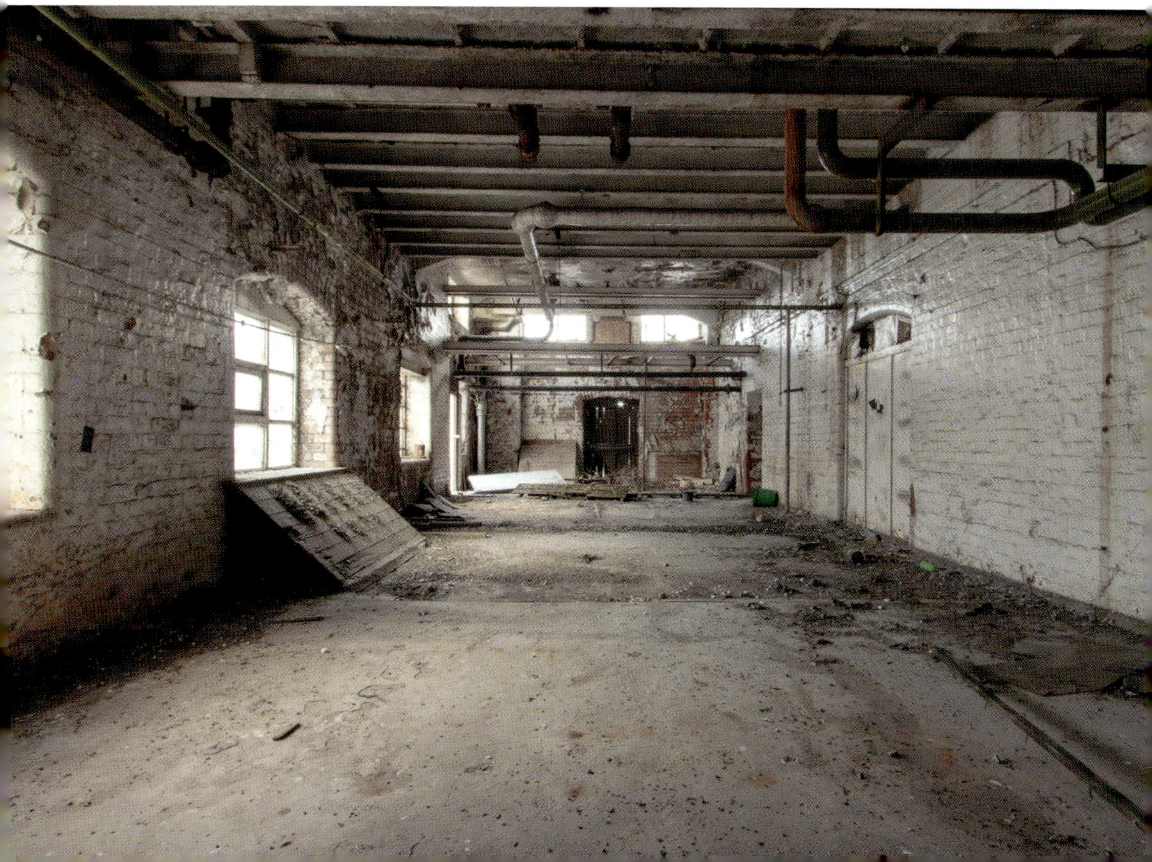

WOOLTON HALL

Built in 1704 and Grade I listed, this eighteenth-century manor house has had various uses including as an army hospital during the Second World War. Originally built for the Molyneux family, the hall has been home to distinguished figures like the Earl of Sefton as well as Liverpool shipowner Frederick Richard Leylands. Other owners of the hall were, from 1772, the Ashton family, then the Shand family and, from the 1870s, the Gaskells. In 1911 it was listed as a Hydropathic Hotel with the proprietor being Andrew McGuffie.

There was a Notre Dame convent at Woolton Hall by the end of the Second World War, where Sisters ran a private preparatory school at the convent for many years, as well as the High School.

This once grand house was purchased in 1982 by John Hibbert who ran it as a wedding venue. The current owners have plans to renovate, yet the hall stands empty and in a sad state of decay. Historic England declared the building at risk in 2021. (Images James Lacey)

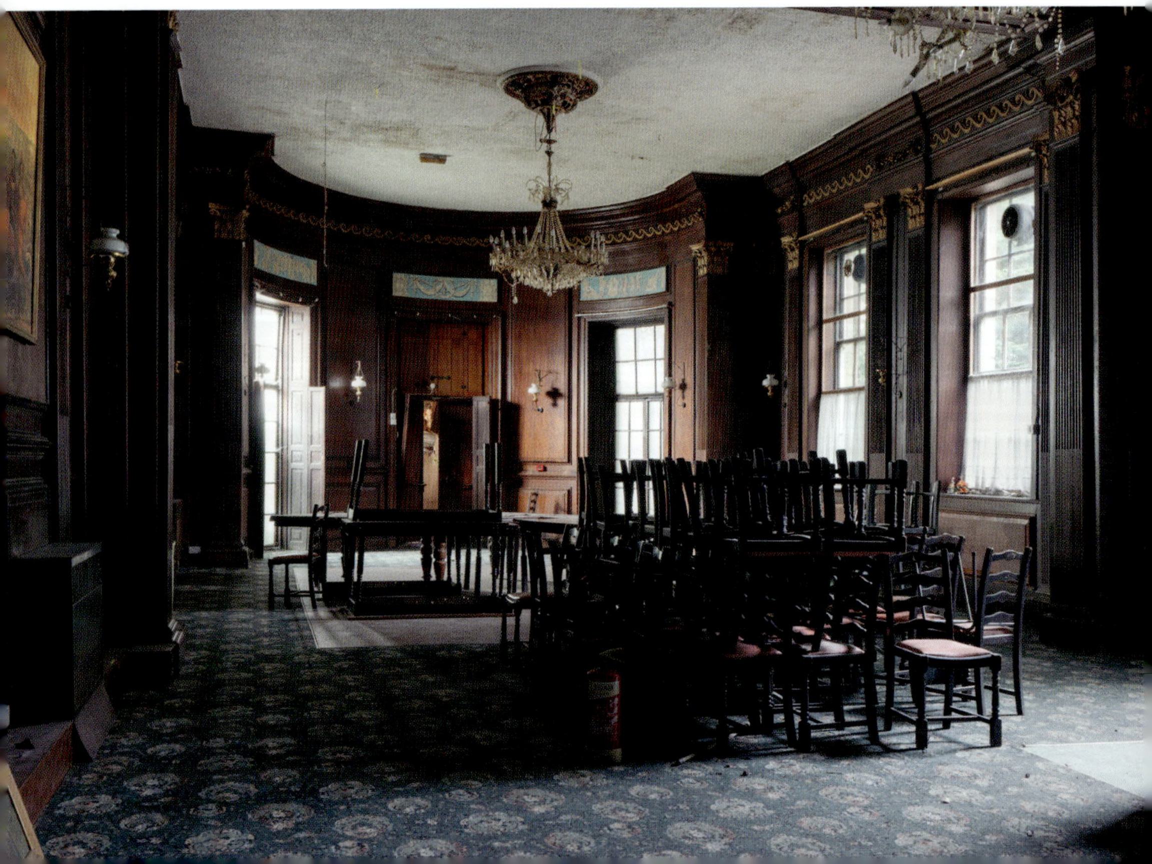

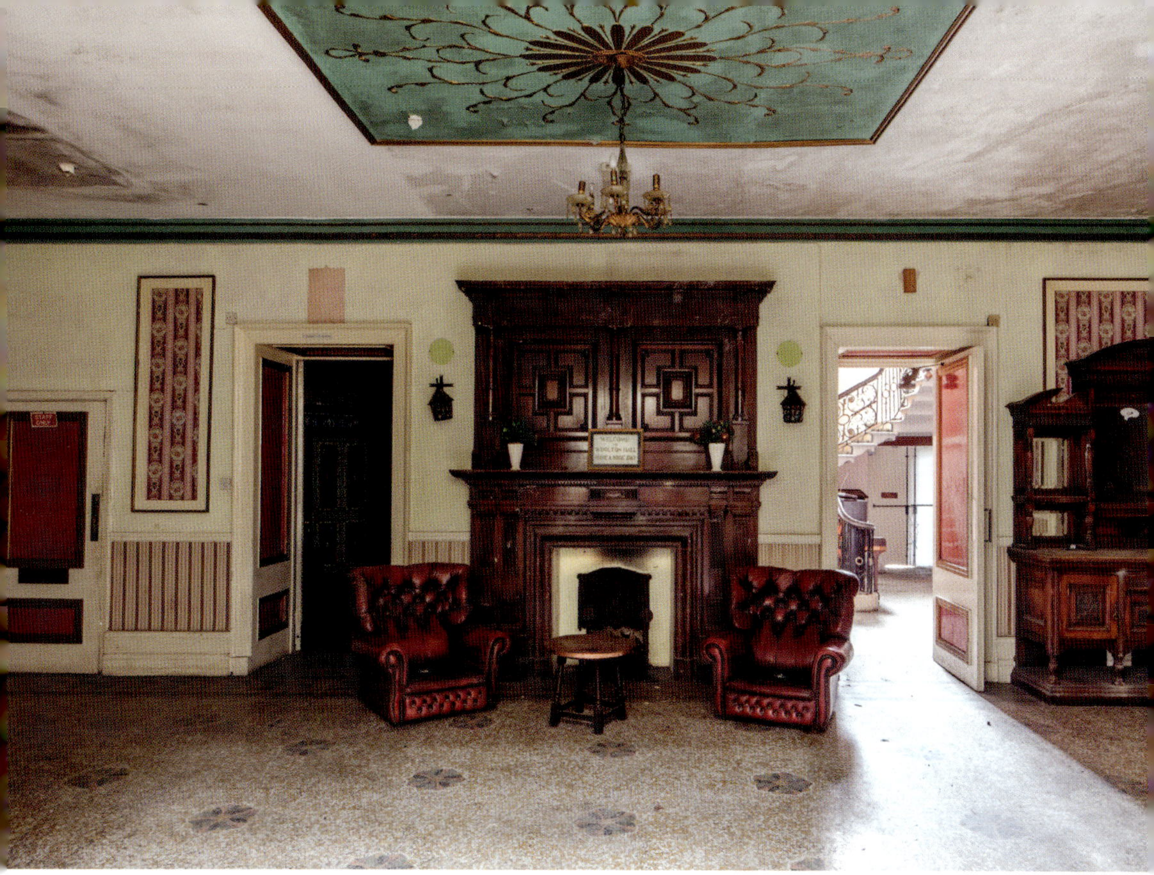

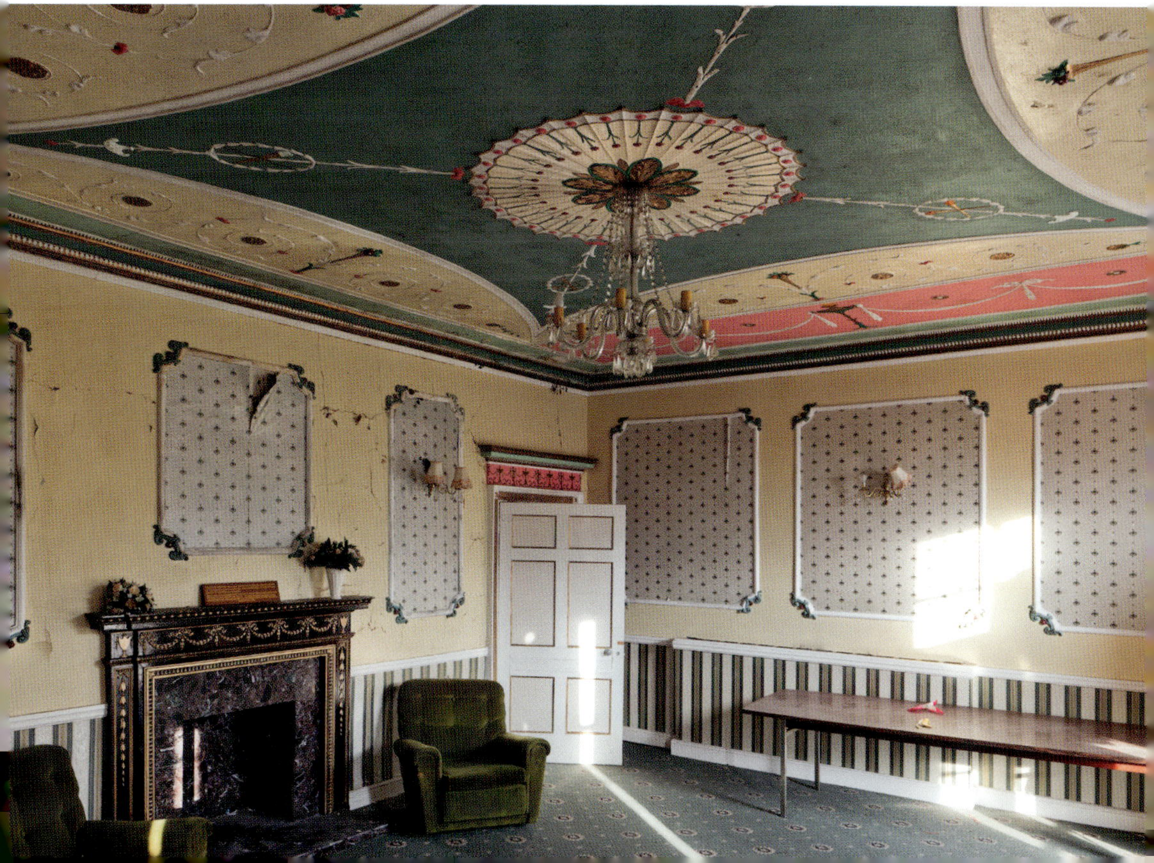

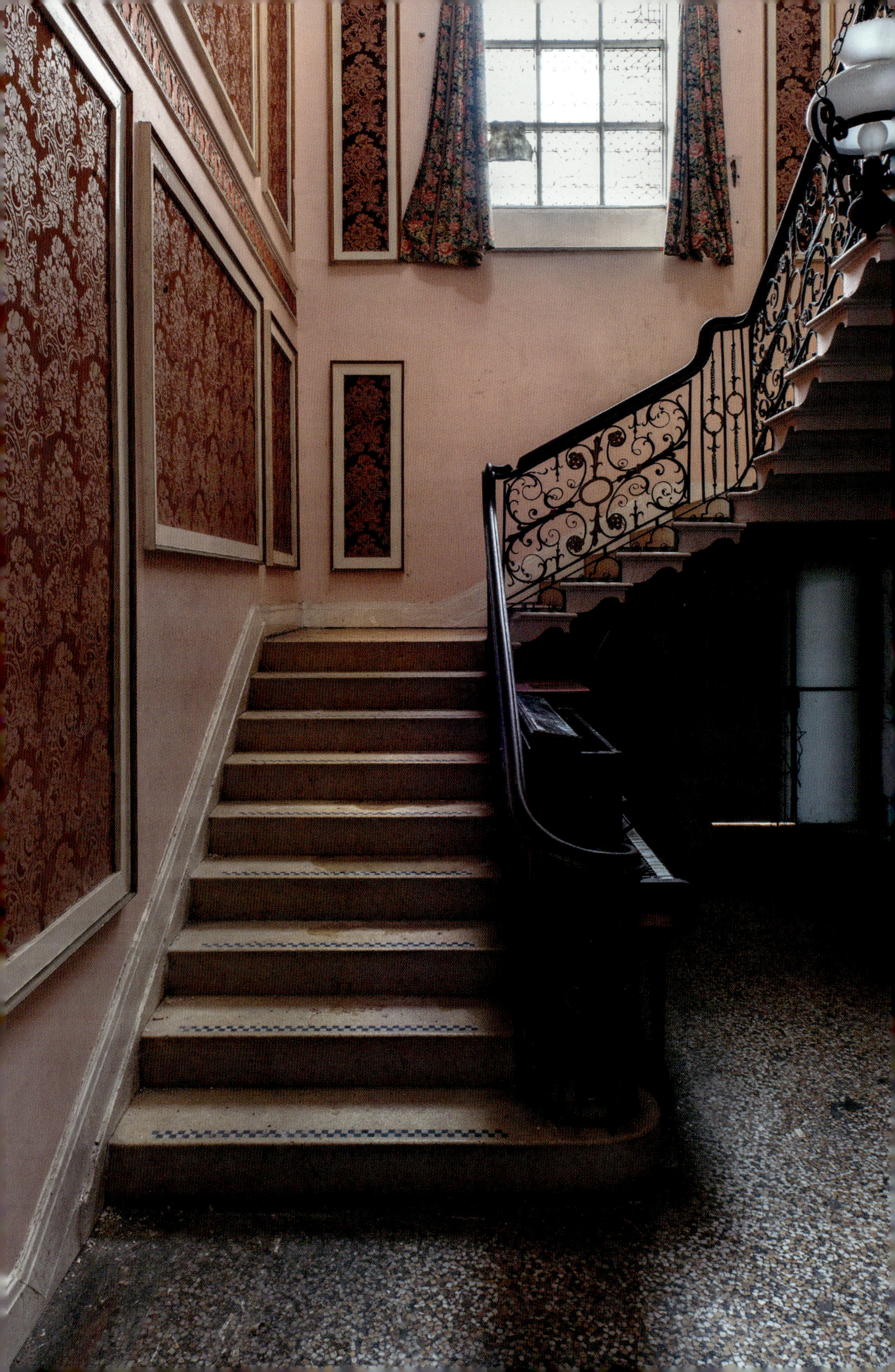

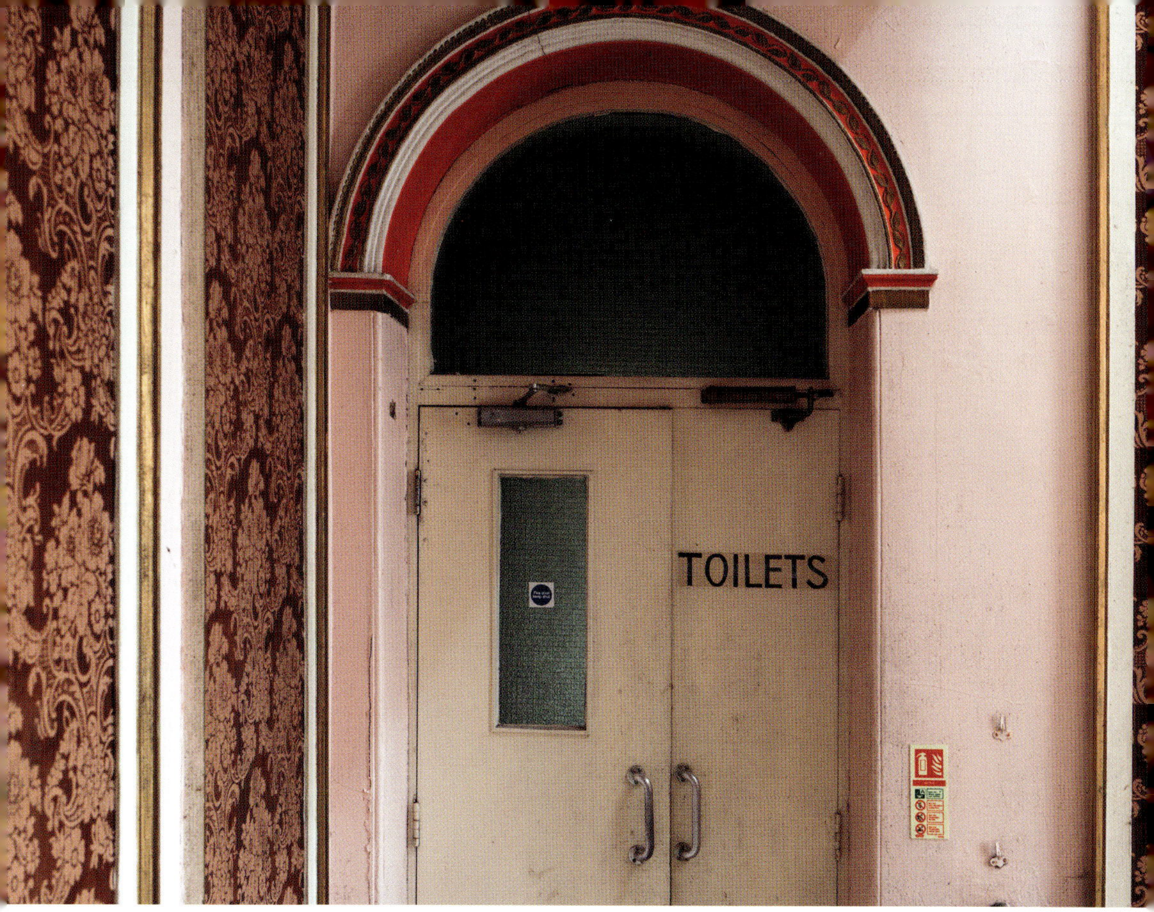
TOILETS

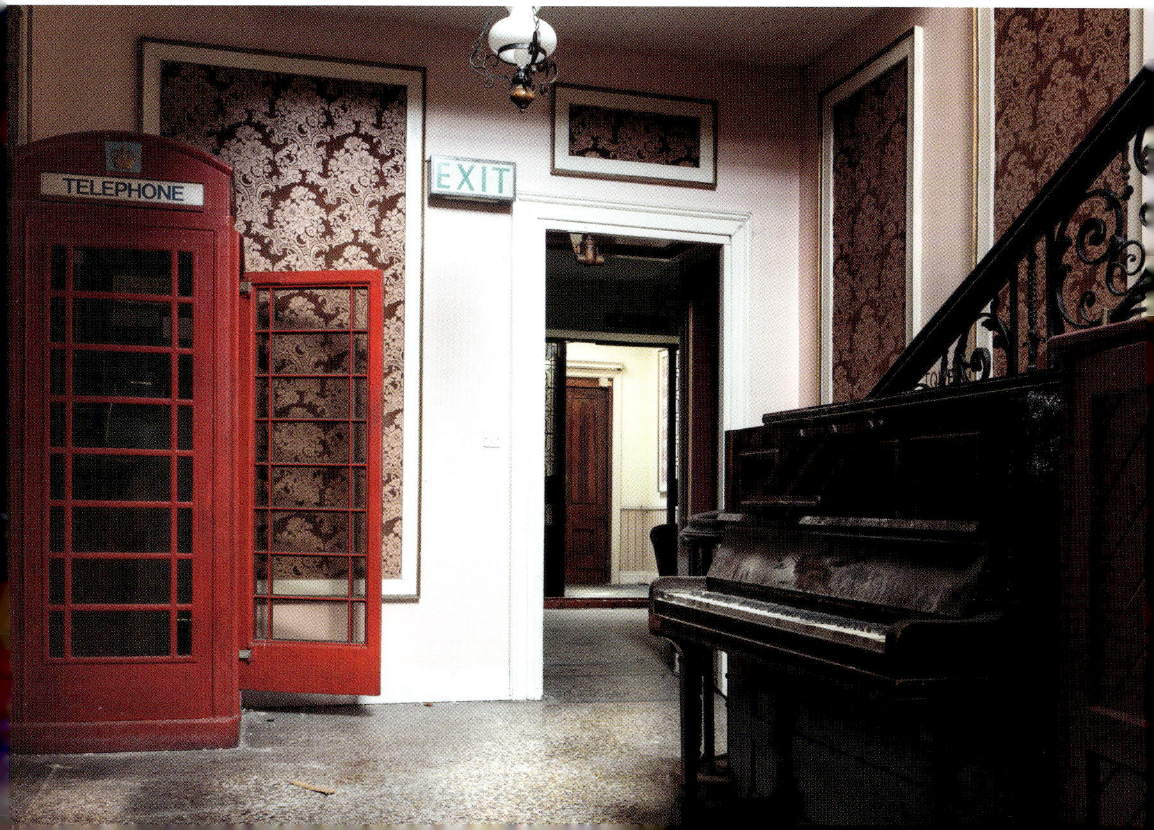
TELEPHONE
EXIT

UNITED MERSEY SUPPLY CO. LTD

Created in 1965 as a ship stores company, United Mersey provided food items, drinks and tobacco to docked ships. Back in those days when the docks at Liverpool were busy, all the crews needed large amounts of supplies to tide them over on their long voyages between ports. They traded with different agencies to provide wholesale stock of many kinds. The list of agencies was still up at reception before the building was demolished in the last few years. (Images David Gooch)

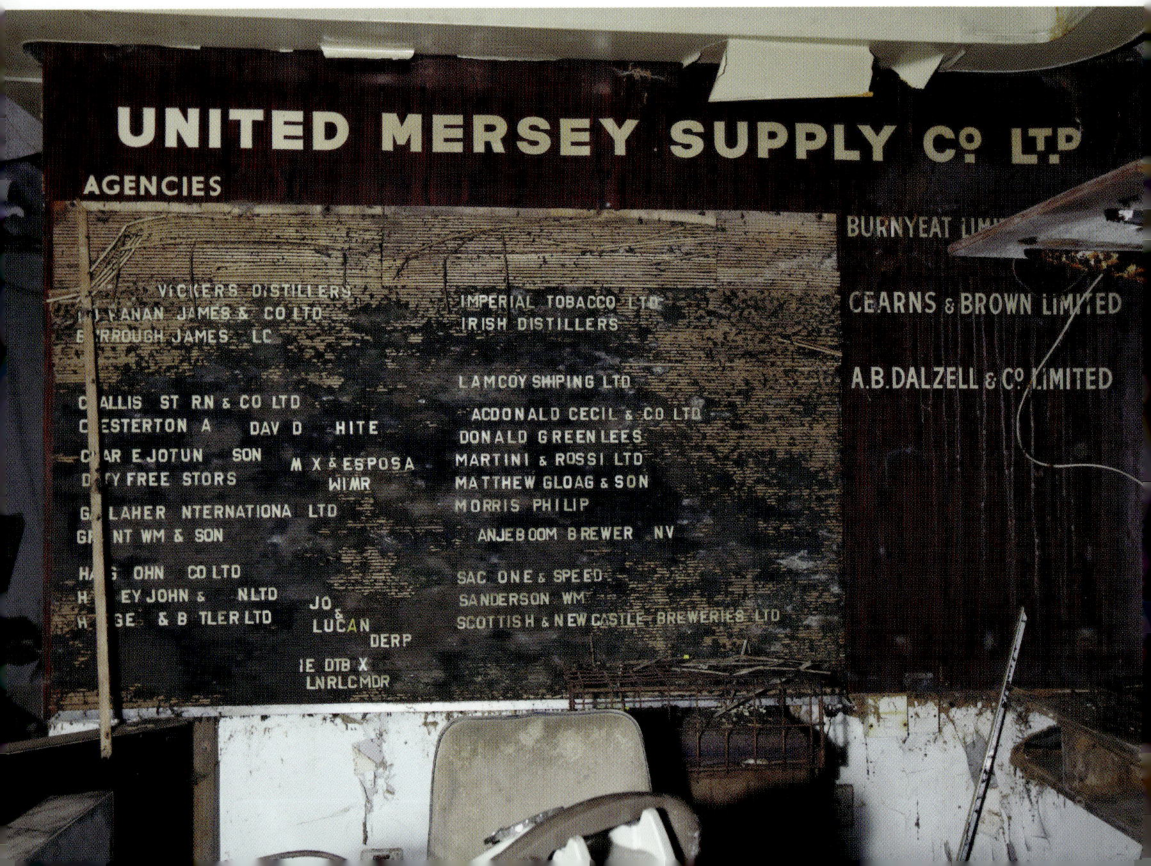

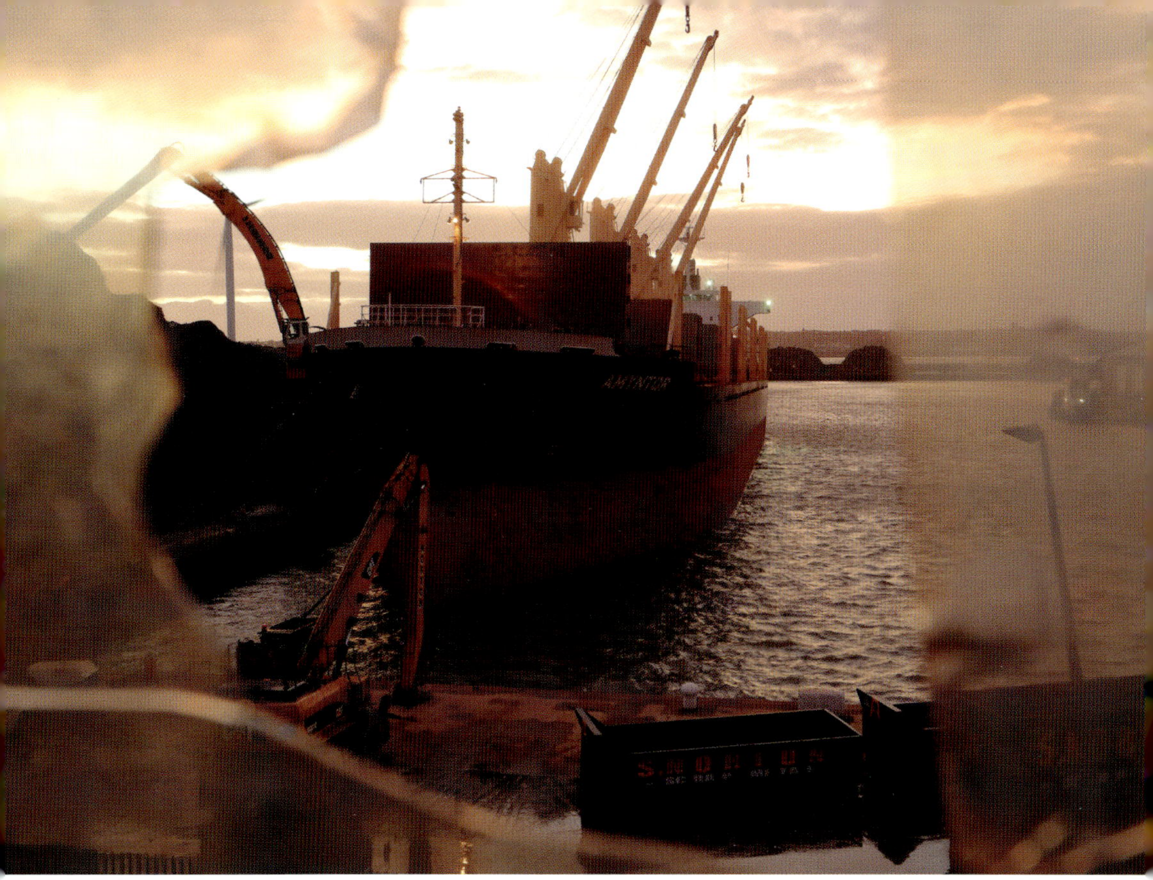

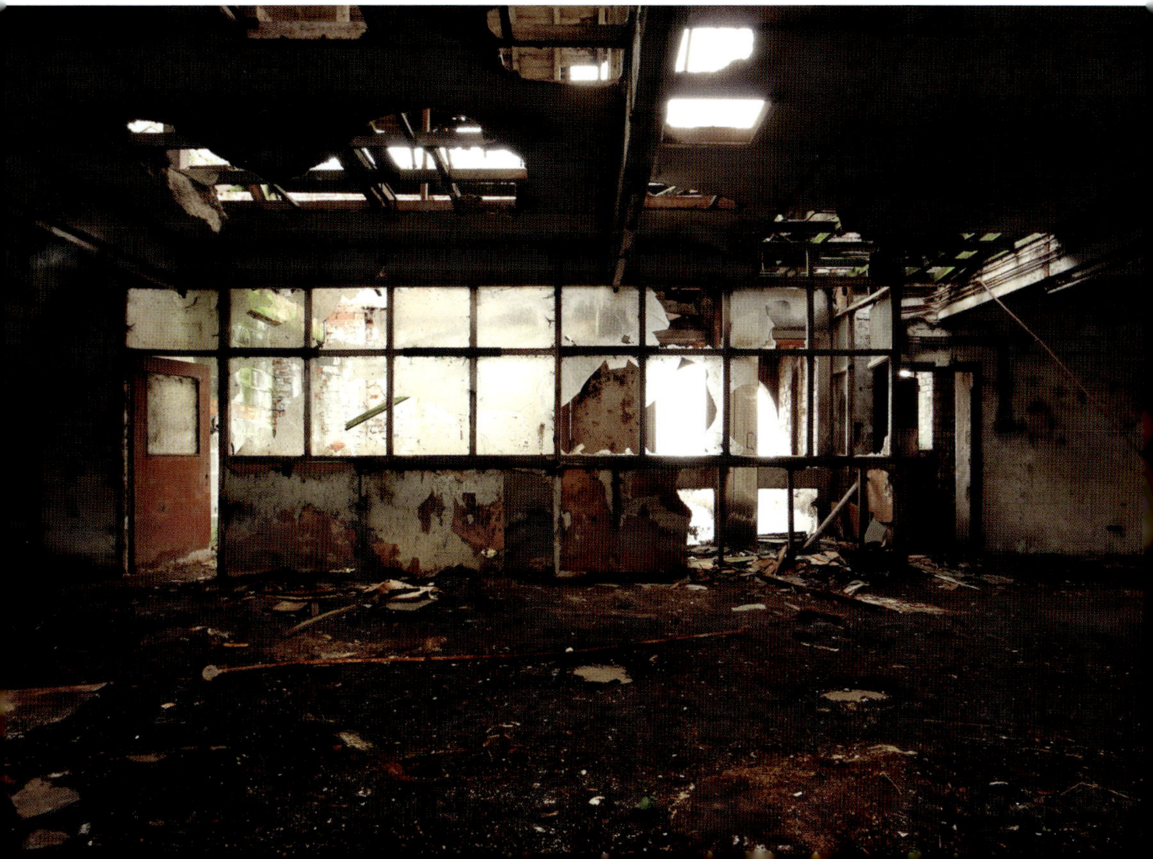

MOSSLEY MANOR CARE HOME

Built in the 1850s for the former mayor of Liverpool, Mossley Manor Care Home was originally called Elmswood House. In 1940 it became a maternity and women's home for the Salvation Army before being used as a children's home in 1970. Some years later it became a care home for the elderly until its closure in 2015.

The care home was forced to close after CQC inspectors uncovered a string of failures, with emergency powers used to close it for good deeming it an extreme risk to the residents' safety and welfare. Since its closure the building has suffered extensive decay and stands in a parlous state. (Image James Lacey)

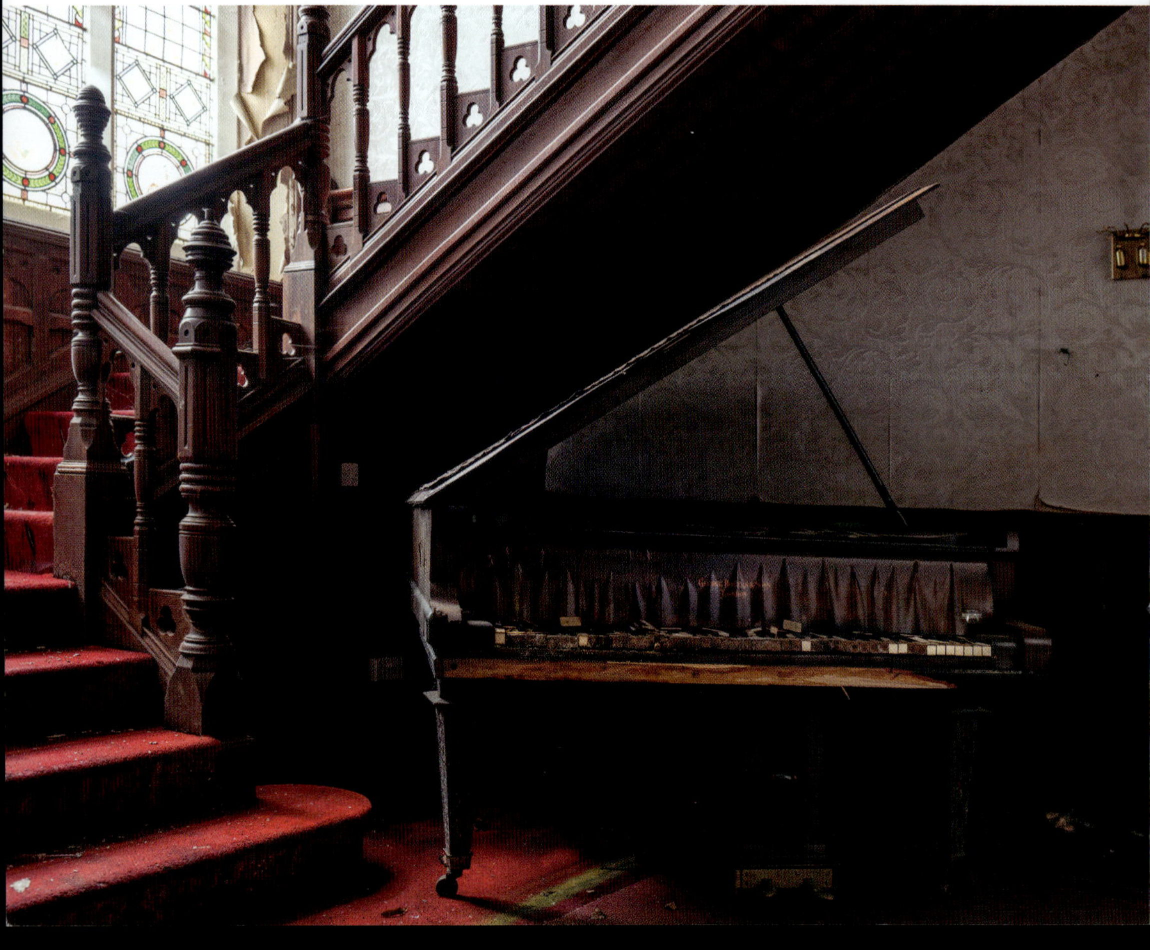

BROMBOROUGH POWER STATION

Bromborough Power Station was built in 1918 to provide electricity to the Port Sunlight manufacturing works and was owned by the Lever Brothers. It was positioned next to the River Mersey so that water could be used from the river for the condensing plant. Later, in 1929 electricity was installed to the houses of the village of Port Sunlight. The power station was only connected to the National Grid in the 1950s. In the 1970s it was partly decommissioned, and the rest shut off in 1998. All that survives of the site is the one control room. (Image David Gooch)

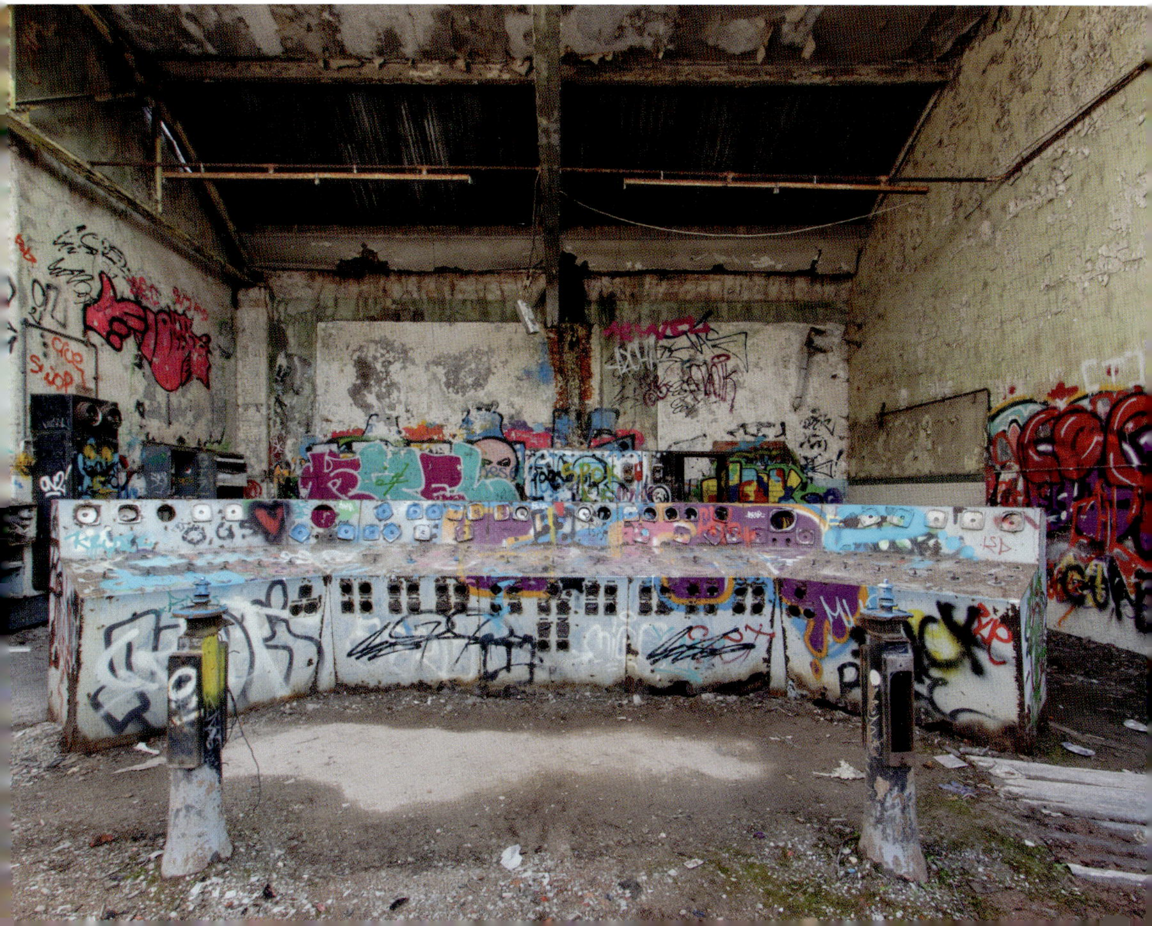

RUNCORN MANOR HOUSE

Manor Farm was commissioned by Lord Richard Brookes to supply stabling and farming supplies for his manor which was built on Norton Priory in the 1500s after Henry VIII's Dissolution of the Monasteries. In the early 1900s, the manor house and a large amount of land in the vicinity was given to the state and left to become derelict. Around 1926, the manor was demolished to show the remnants of the priory buried beneath. Manor Farm was later bought by a housing association and rented to tenants before being left empty for years. (Images James Lacey)

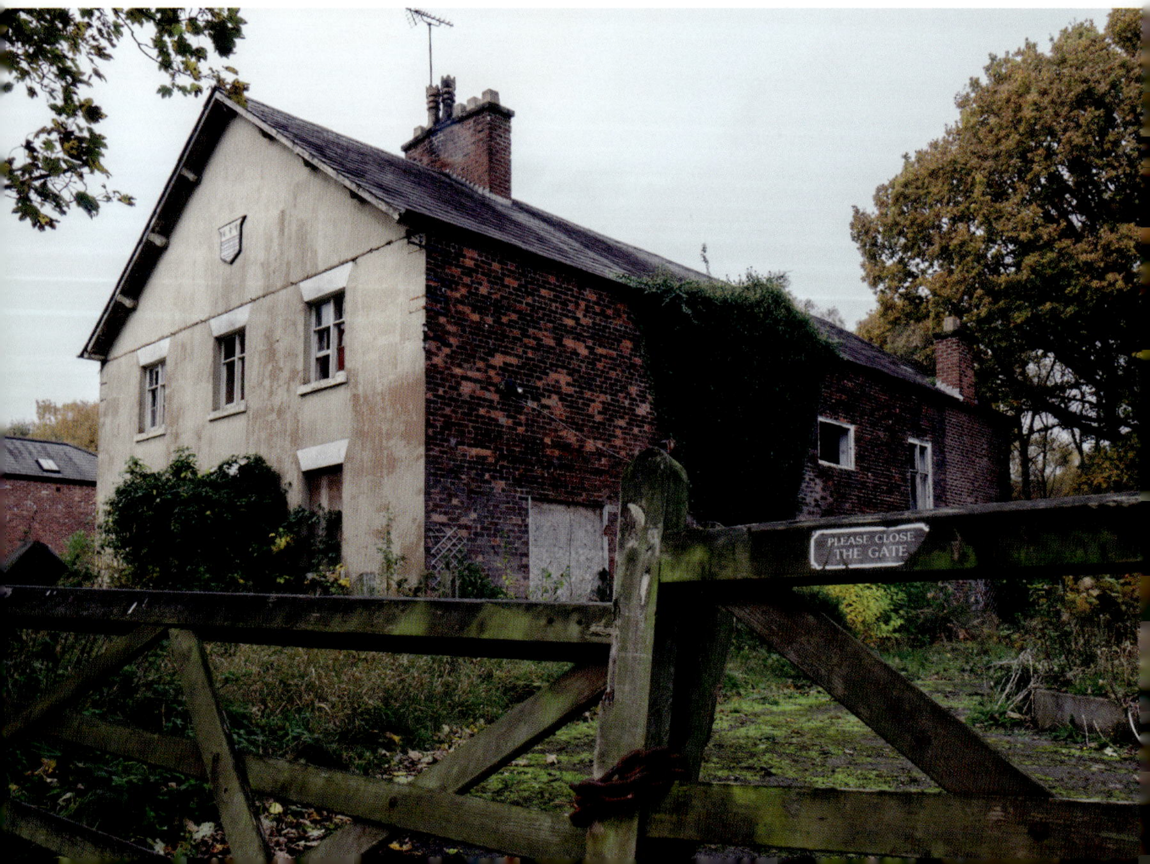

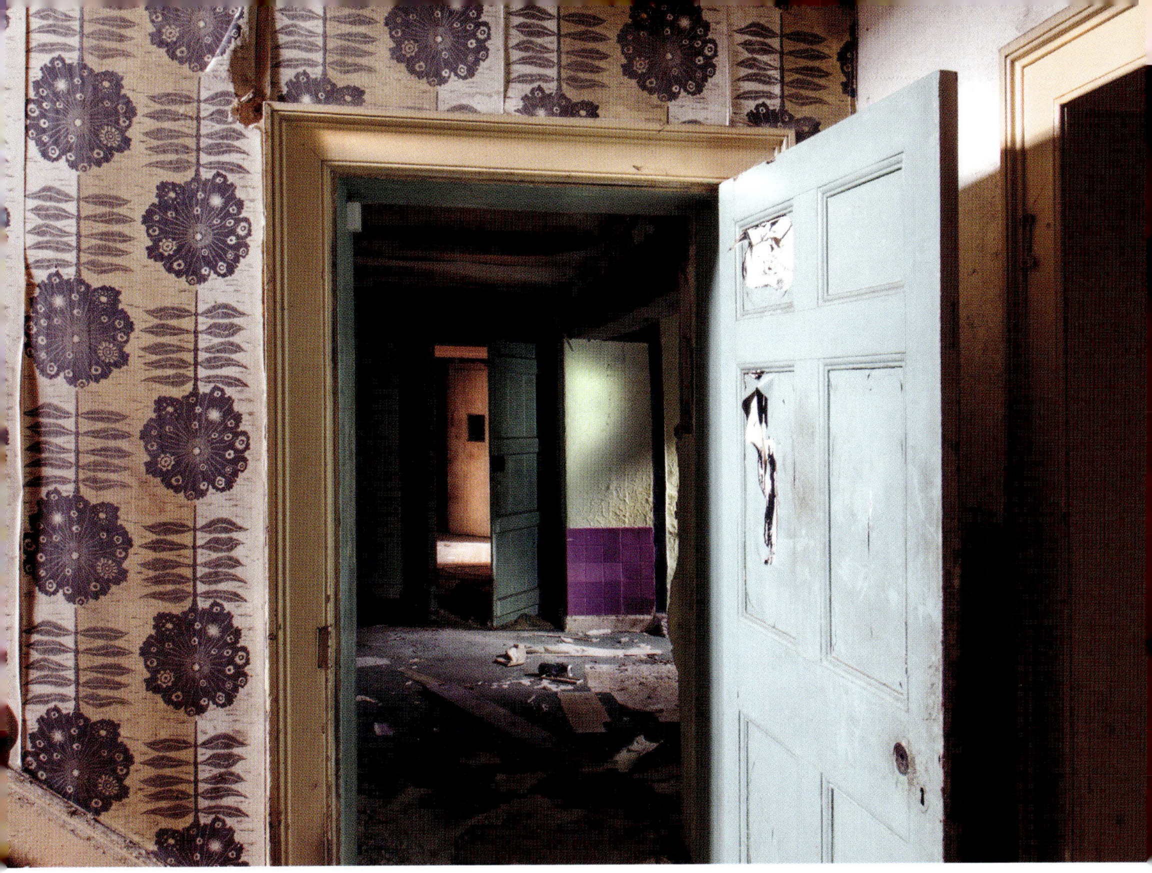

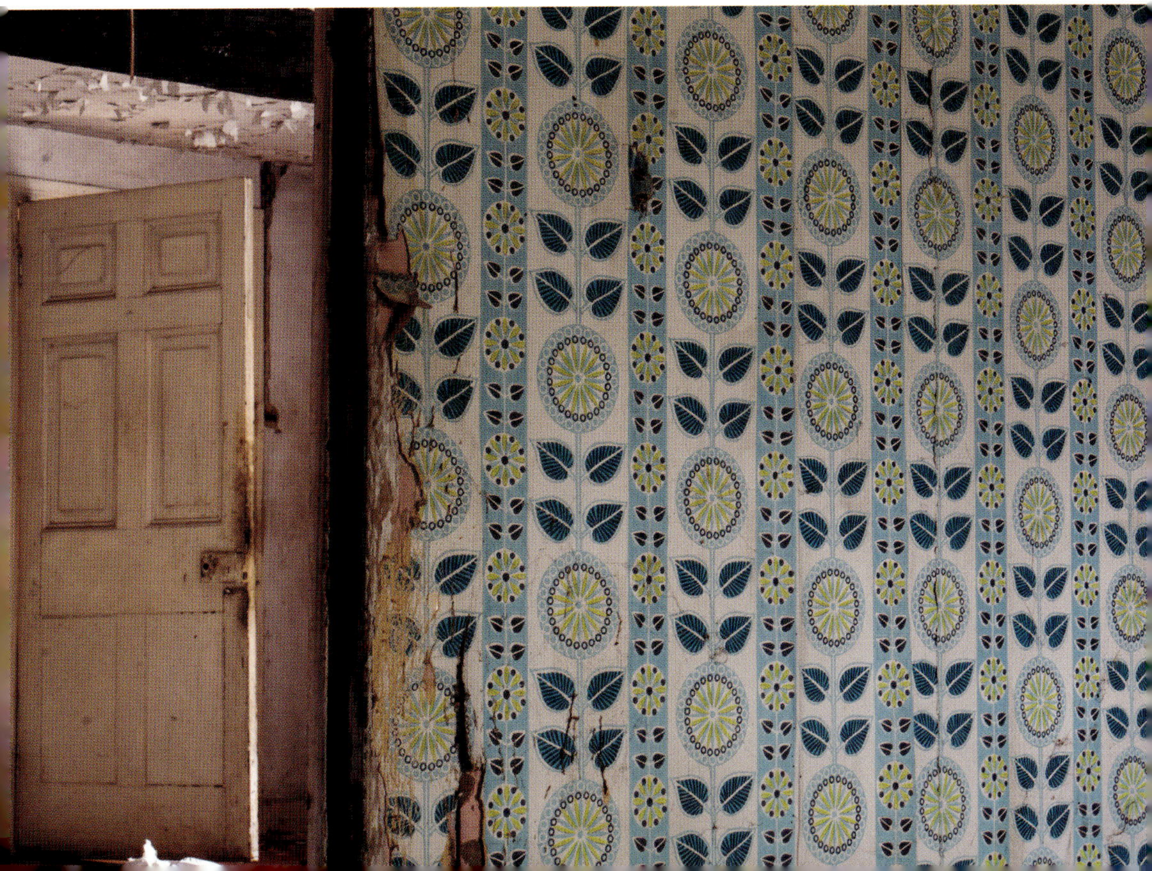

CARLTON CINEMA, TUEBROOK

The Carlton opened in 1932 in the Tuebrook area of Liverpool. At its time of opening it was Liverpool's largest purpose-built cinema, seating 1,948 in the stalls and circle. It then was taken over by the ABC cinema chain and named the ABC Tuebrook in 1935 until it closed in 1980. The day after it closed it reopened again under the name Carlton Cinema but unfortunately this didn't last, and it closed for good in 1982. The cinema then sat unused for thirty-three years until it was demolished in 2017 with no finalised plans for the site in place. (Image David Gooch)

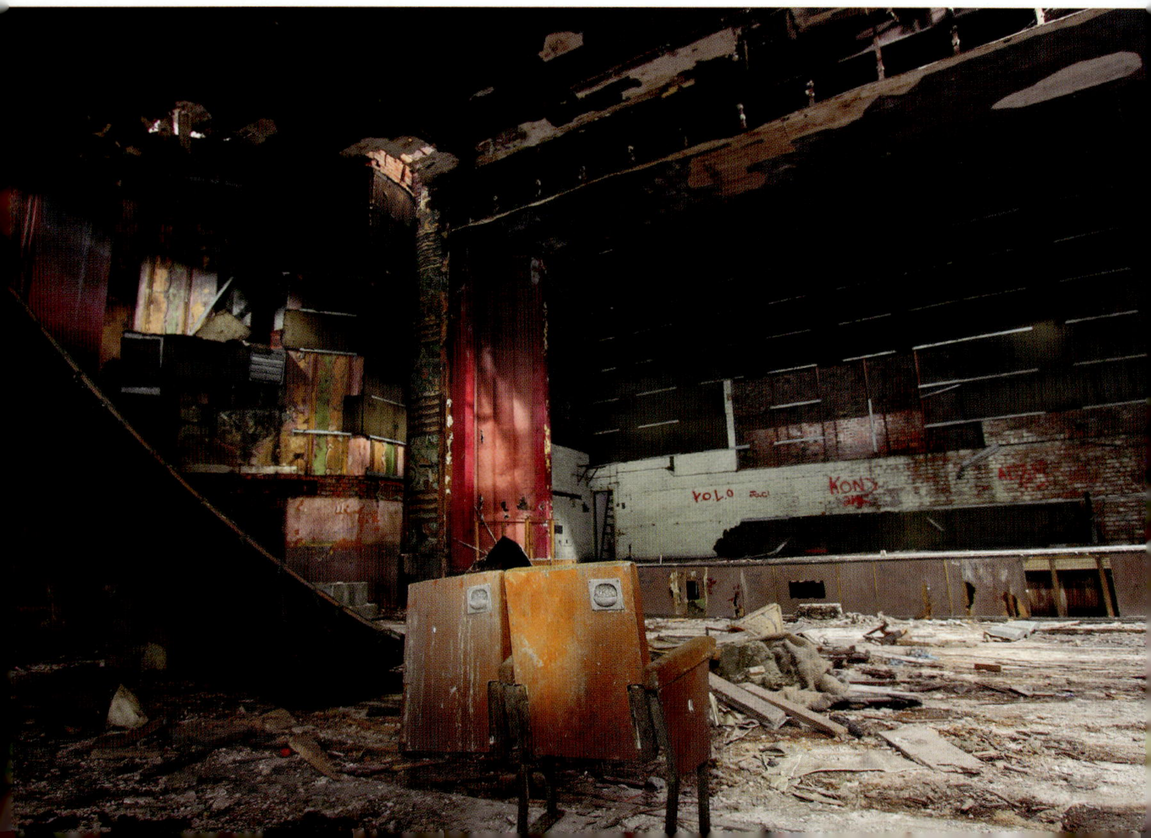

MERSEYSIDE FOOD PRODUCTS LTD

From the little history there is on this place it seems it made and packaged margarine in various different ways, from 250g paper wrapped up to 2kg blocks for sale to the catering industry. In addition, they had a line that tinned margarine for the MoD, and this was then sent out to the army overseas. The factory supplied margarine to all the major supermarkets during its time. In its day the site employed almost 250 people and also made pastry fat and fairy cake mix. The factory was made up of a production, packaging, warehouse, labs, chillers and a refinery. (Images David Gooch)

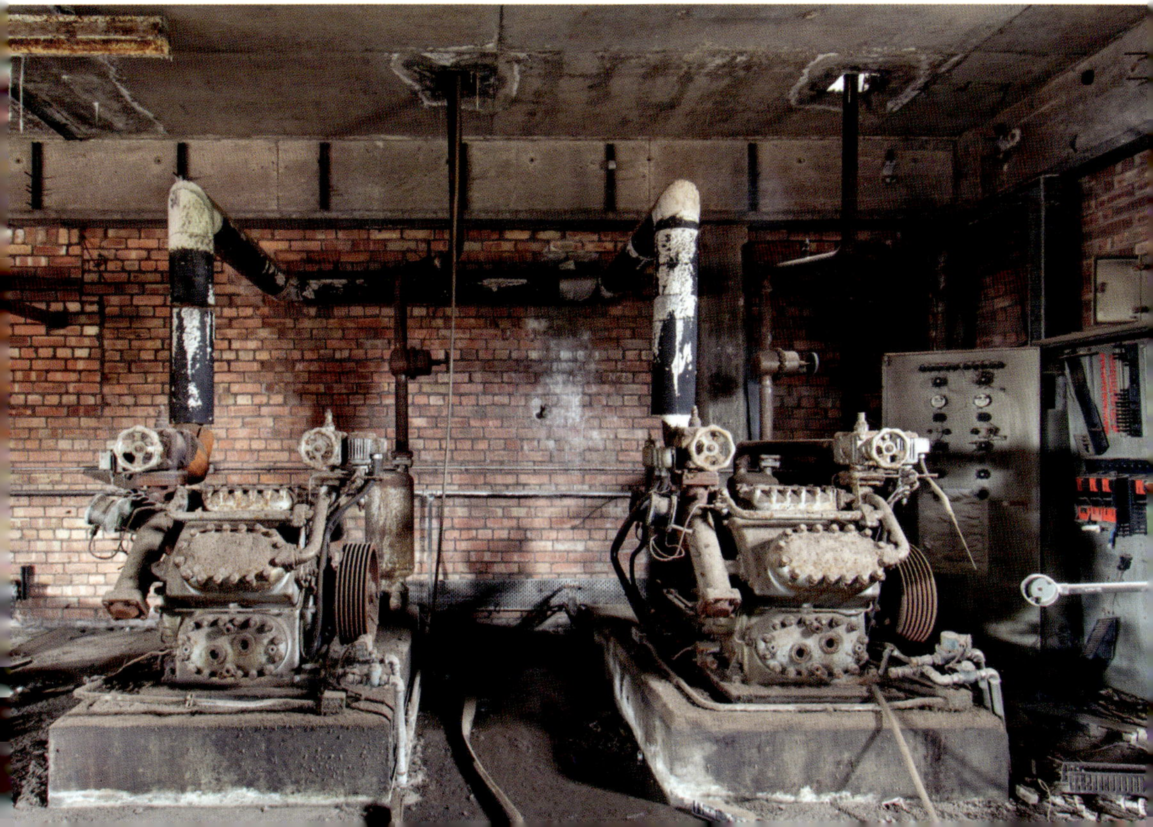

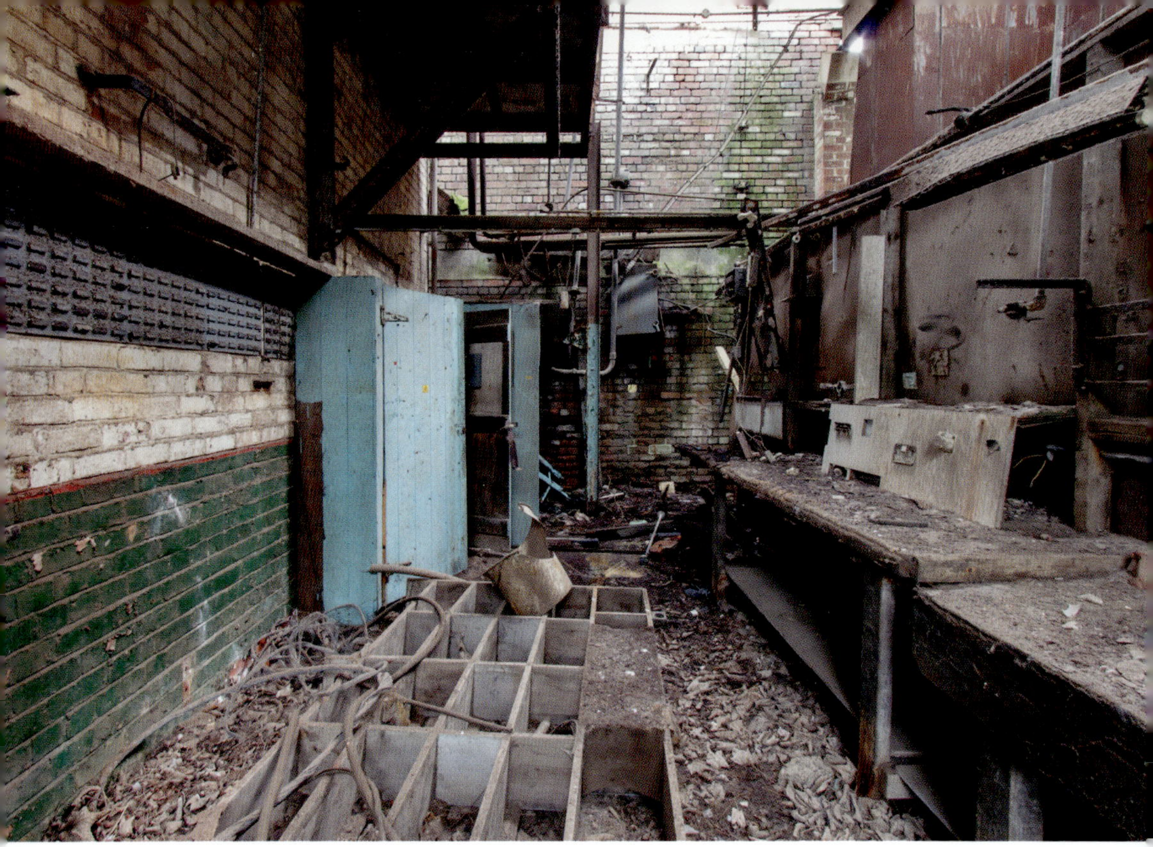

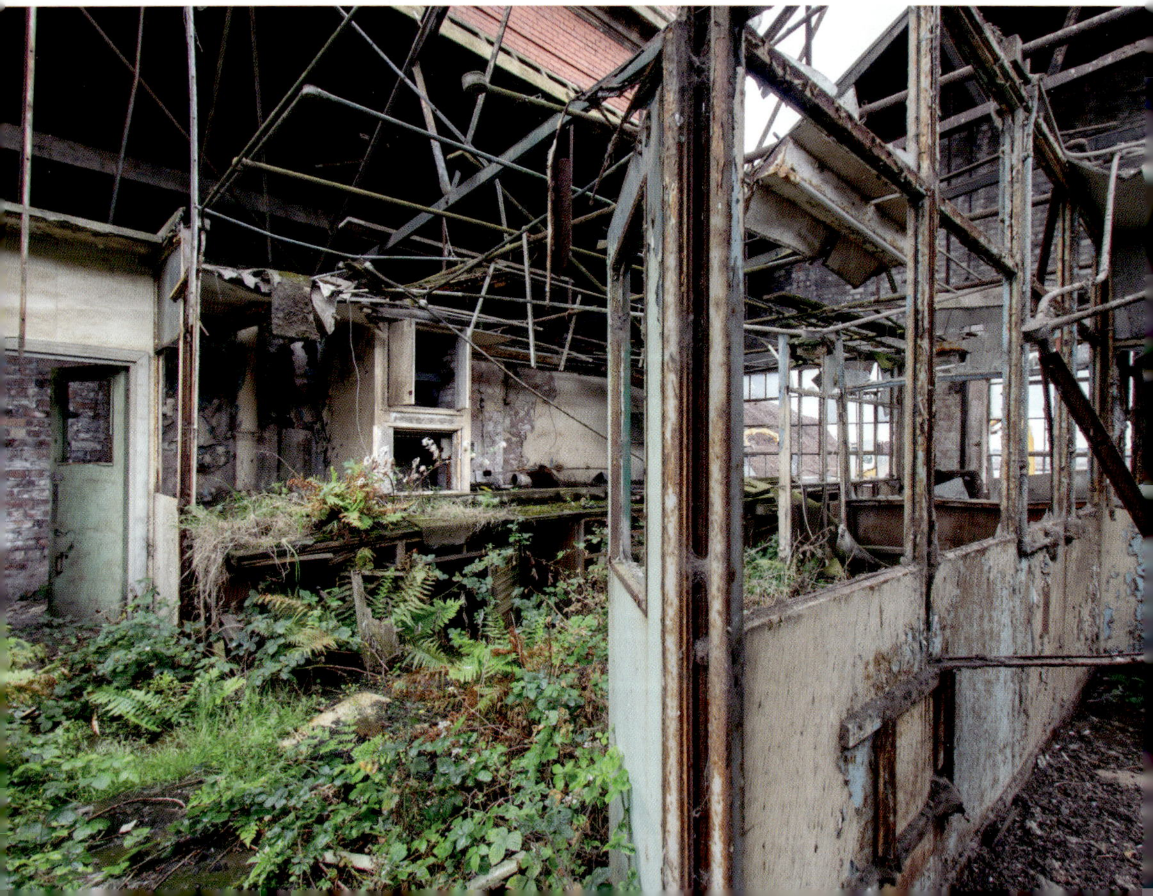

SHOREDITCH AND HOXTON IN 50 BUILDINGS

LUCY McMURDO

AMBERLEY

'I like this place. And willingly could waste my time in it'.
(William Shakespeare, *As You Like It*, act II, scene IV)

First published 2024

Amberley Publishing, The Hill, Stroud
Gloucestershire GL5 4EP

www.amberley-books.com

British Library Cataloguing in Publication Data.
A catalogue record for this book is available from the British Library.

ISBN 978 1 3981 1612 2 (print)
ISBN 978 1 3981 1613 9 (ebook)

Typesetting by SJmagic DESIGN SERVICES, India.
Printed in Great Britain.